STERN-
WHEELERS
UP COLUMBIA

BAILEY GATZERT
OF
PORTLAND

MAC MULLGN

STERN-WHEELERS UP COLUMBIA

A Century of Steamboating in the Oregon Country

BY
RANDALL V. MILLS

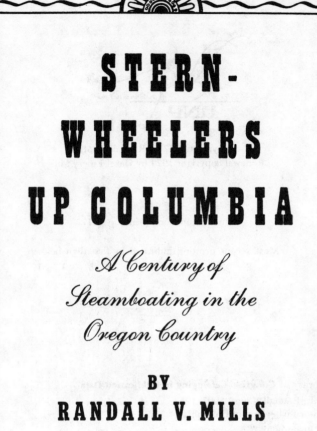

UNIVERSITY OF NEBRASKA PRESS
LINCOLN AND LONDON

Publishers on the Plains

UNP

Copyright 1947 by Randall V. Mill
Renewal copyright 1974 by Hazel Emery Mills

First Bison Book printing: 1977

Most recent printing indicated by first digit below:
1   2   3   4   5   6   7   8   9   10

Library of Congress Cataloging in Publication Data

Mills, Randall Vause, 1907–1952.
   Stern-wheelers up Columbia.
   "Bison book."
   Reprint of the ed. published by Pacific Books, Palo Alto, Calif.
   Bibliography: p. 206
   Includes index.
   1. Steam-navigation—Columbia River.   2. River steamers—Columbia
River.   I. Title.
VM625.C6M5   1977   386'.3'09797   77–7161
ISBN 0–8032–0937–1
ISBN 0–8032–5874–7 pbk.

Reprinted by arrangement with Hazel Emery Mills

Manufactured in the United States of America

PREFACE

A RIVER lives, assumes qualities of its own, and stamps these qualities upon the region through which it flows. Each steamboat, however small, takes on human characteristics until it achieves a personality of its own.

This is an account of the river boats themselves, a rapid tracing of what they were, where and when they went, what they did, and why they did it. Although the boats are the personalities involved, the book is dedicated to those who built and ran them and who deserve their own separate extended history.

Sometimes it seems as if all the elements of drama are present: the river and the boats as protagonists and antagonists in a struggle for mastery and control, with man merely the supernumerary, carrying a spear and boat hook. Captain W. P. Gray, a pilot on the Columbia and Snake rivers, sensed the drama when he wrote to George Himes:

Every change in the stage of water makes a change in the currents in and around boulders, bars, and reefs, and when the rapid comes in sight, every attribute of sight and brain is concentrated on the surface of the currents. The banks and cliffs are not noticed. The shimmer of the water on the bars, the exhaust of the engines of the boats, and the pressure of the water on the rudders were my guide.

In the conquest of the rivers, man conquered the region. Steamboating was part of the pattern that spread out and carried people and their goods farther and farther back from the ports and main bases. The Columbia River with its tributaries is a self-contained system in which the conquest can be seen clearly. Though the old Oregon Country included the Puget Sound area, a separate pattern developed there, and no attention to steamboating on the Puget Sound is here given.

Any history of steamboating in the region must depend heavily upon E. W. Wright's *Lewis and Dryden's Marine History of the Pacific Northwest,* a detailed account of events on the sea, Sound, and rivers up to 1895, and upon the work of Frank B. Gill, whose *Unfinished History of Transportation,* partly published as articles in *Pacific Semaphore* and partly in typescript, is a mine of information about ships, boats, stages and trains. Frank J. Smith's *Marine Record of Oregon* lists the steamboats to 1918 and adds information not otherwise available. General histories of the region, especially those by R. C. Clark and Fred Lockley, give some attention to steamboating. Descriptive accounts of the rivers abound in varying quality. A number of articles appearing in periodicals are of real value, such as those by Irene Poppleton, Dorothy Johansen, Judge Fred Wilson, and James Fitzsimmons. Also useful are the files of newspapers, particularly the *Oregon Spectator* and the Portland *Oregonian* which had recorded happenings of the region since steamboating began.

Many have aided me and I want to acknowledge their kindnesses and to thank them. Mr. L. Rex Gault of the Western Transportation Company, Captain Homer Shaver of the Shaver Transportation Company, and Mr. Lawrence Barber, Marine Editor of the *Oregonian,* answered questions and offered suggestions. Judge Fred Wilson of The Dalles opened his splendid collection of photographs to me. The interesting maritime collection of Mr. D. H. Bates of Portland supplied information on the pioneer steamboats. Mabel Eaton McClain, Research Associate in History in the University of Oregon, secured and made available much valuable material. Lancaster Pollard and Howard McKinley Corning of the Oregon Historical Society, and the staffs of the Bonneville Power Administration, the Port of Portland Commission, and the United States Army Engineers have all willingly provided information and aid. At the University of Oregon Library the entire staff has cooperated, especially Elizabeth Findly and Adeline Adams. Others who have furnished information or photographs are Mr. W. J. Gould of Seattle, Washington; Mr. Robert Parkinson of Berkeley, California; Mr. C. Bradford Mitchell of Washington, D.C.; Mr. W. Gibson Kennedy of Trail, B.C. Commander Jerry MacMullen, USNR, in addition to other aid drew the illustrations.

My wife, Hazel Emery Mills, herself an historian of Western steamboating, typed the manuscript and sharply criticized every word of it, thereby preparing me for any adverse comment.

This has been an interesting, amusing, lively excursion into the past. After all, a steamboat is a temperamental personality. To the steamboats I offer apologies for any omissions or errors.

RANDALL V. MILLS

October 1, 1947.

CONTENTS

ILLUSTRATIONS

MAPS

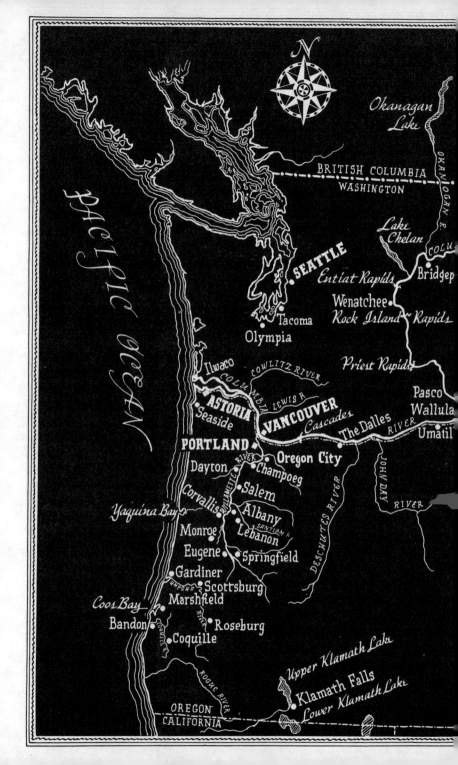

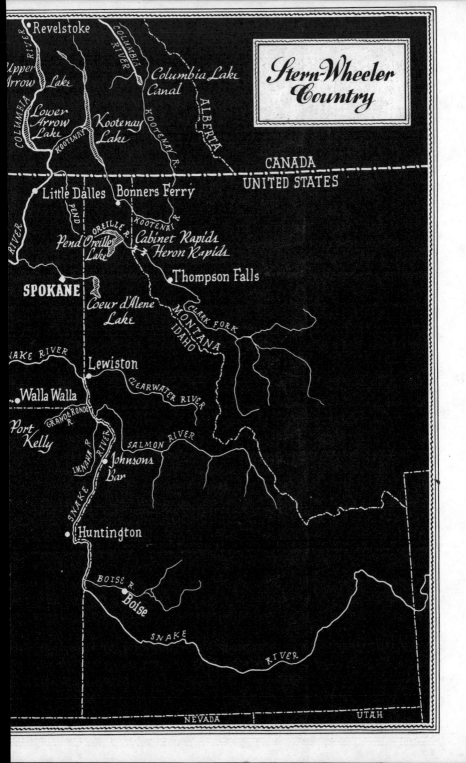

Chapter 1

O PIONEERS!

FINALLY the job was finished. Below decks, firemen threw long bolts of wood into the brick furnaces, the pitchy smoke belched from the tall iron stack; the safety valve lifted and a plume of steam shot up. In the tiny engine room the maze of pistons, cross-heads, and connecting rods came to life. Outside, water splashed against the hull as the paddle-wheels made their first turns. The *Beaver* was moving, and against the current. The time was mid-afternoon, the day May 17, 1836. The place was the Columbia River, at Fort Vancouver. A steamboat had come to the Oregon Country.

Dr. John McLoughlin, Chief Factor and general satrap of Vancouver and the Oregon Country, looked at the *Beaver,* the first steamship in the Pacific Northwest, with an unbecoming lack of enthusiasm. He had disagreed with plans to build her from the first word, and he doubted her virtues as an aid in handling the business of the Hudson's Bay Company in those parts.

Except for her importance as the Pacific's pioneer steamboat, the *Beaver* was not particularly impressive, even for 1836. Her tonnage was a modest 187 and when Lloyd's agent had measured her shortly after her launching, he had duly recorded her length as 100 feet

9 inches, her beam as 20 and her depth as 11; she drew a little over
8 feet. She was flush decked with a square stern, almost without
ornamentation except for the shield of the Hudson's Bay Company.
Her bow raked forward to a stubby bowsprit, and she had no figure-
head. Originally schooner-rigged with three masts, she was changed
to a brigantine when she made the long voyage out to the Northwest
Coast. Supported on sponsons and braces were paddle-boxes that
rose above the bulwarks; they were plain except for planking arranged as rays from a lunette. The hull was black and the bulwarks
and upperworks originally white—even to the stack, which on regular occasions was liberally doused with whitewash.

But she was staunchly built. A solid stick, a foot square, formed
the keel which was laid on the Thames, near London, in 1834. Good
English oak went into her frames, and her planking was of oak, too,
some English and some African. She was double planked—no doubt
with a view to resisting the hard knocks she would receive in navi-
gating that distant river—and she was copper fastened throughout.
Copper sheathing completed the structure of the hull.

To propel her, Boulton, Watt & Company built two engines,
side-lever action, with cylinders thirty-five and one-half inches in
diameter and a stroke of thirty-six inches. These engines turned the
shaft for her side wheels, which were mounted well forward, each
wheel thirteen feet in diameter with buckets six and one-half feet
long. To power the engine was an iron boiler, tested to provide
steam at two and one-half pounds to the square inch, a low pressure
favored by builders at the time. Below her boilers were brick furnaces which when properly stoked would develop enough steam to
turn the wheels thirty times a minute and send the ship through the
water at about nine miles an hour. Normally, such breathless haste
was unneeded, if not downright dangerous, and she plodded about
at a comfortable five or six miles an hour and satisfied everybody.

Lloyd's pronounced her A-1, just as her owners, the Hudson's Bay
Company, had determined she must be. On the Thames she ran
through final tests, had twenty tons of coal loaded in the coalboxes,
and was readied for the trip to her station, but before she set out,
her paddle wheels were carefully unshipped and stowed on deck.
There was no use overdoing a good thing by trying to use steam on
the run; besides, where would the fuel come from when the twenty
tons went up the stack? So, accompanied by the bark *Columbia* as
tender and nursemaid, the *Beaver* took aboard a pilot, cast off lines,

and drifted into the stream. On August 31, 1835, the pilot turned the ship over to her captain, clambered overside into a waiting boat, and the *Beaver* left Gravesend behind.

By mid-September the voyage was well under way, with the *Beaver* in sight of Madeira. Two months later she was at Cape Horn. Early in February, the *Beaver* crossed the long stretch of the Pacific and reached Honolulu, where she remained three weeks to overhaul and replenish supplies before starting on the final leg of the run. Finally in company with the *Columbia,* she headed for the mouth of the Columbia River, and sighted it in twenty-two days, having been one hundred and sixty-one days out from Gravesend. At the mouth she delayed a couple of days for her companion to come up, and then together they started up the river toward Vancouver, but what with bucking the Columbia's current and the contrary winds, it was two weeks more before the *Beaver* ended the long journey to her station. She had been launched without ceremony, had sailed without ceremony, and had arrived with only slight ceremony, for the signal gun that roared from Fort Vancouver greeted the *Columbia* and the mail she carried as much as it did the *Beaver*.

Fitting her for steam service did not take long. The wheels were swung overside and put in place, the engines cleaned and oiled, and the boiler filled. On the first run, her captain, David Home, took her a few miles down the river as a trial, and then she made a number of short jaunts to limber the machinery—to a sawmill, to a landing downstream where Indians reported that black stones would burn (and if they did, the fuel problem was settled), back to the sawmill, with the *Columbia* in tow, first of a long series of towing jobs that she and her successors were to handle.

Finally, there was an excursion, and that too was the first of many on the river. The *Beaver* took aboard all the dignitaries of the Fort, and their ladies, as the phrase elegantly put it, and some visitors; there were always itinerant mountain men, or scientists, or artists, or Yankee promoters, or missionaries hanging around Fort Vancouver. The captain ordered the lines cast off; the paddles turned, and the *Beaver* moved down the stream toward the mouth of the Willamette. It was during spring freshet, and the Columbia was backing the tributary over its banks, so that when the *Beaver* turned into the Willamette, it seemed as if she were in a wide, smooth bay. Up the smaller river she steamed, her passengers busying themselves at enjoying the outing; then she turned into a side slough, where they broke out lunch from the hampers. Everything else on that spring day fitted into the tradition. Along the slough went the *Beaver,* and aboard, her guests sang, although, as the Reverend Mr. Samuel Parker, one of the party, put it, "the gayety which prevailed was often suspended, while we conversed of coming days, when with civilized men, all the rapid improvements in the arts of life, should be introduced over this new world, and when cities and villages shall spring up on the west, as they are springing up on the east of the great mountains, and a new empire shall be added to the kingdoms of the earth."

Along the banks the Indians watched her, wondering at this new contraption of the white man that threshed the water so hard and had her sails furled. "Skookum ship" they described the *Beaver* in their jargon—"powerful" or, perhaps "strong demon." It was hard to predict the goings-on and antics of the white men anyway.

The Hudson's Bay Company had intended the *Beaver* as their trading vessel on the coast, but she drew too much water for convenient use on the Columbia, and moreover, there were no stations on the river for trading. Her main work would be from Nisqually, where she would be out of sight for Dr. McLoughlin. Once at Nisqually, she would give him no trouble and some satisfaction when each year he could report that she cost more to operate than she earned. It was a frugal Scotsman's way of getting even.

To fit her for the job at Puget Sound she took aboard an armament of small cannon, including a "long nine" from the *Columbia.* Around her rail was stretched boarding netting to fend off unwanted Indians. Her crew, a special one, for no ordinary group of sailors could handle her cranky engines, was drilled in discipline, and when she finally was ready to set out for the Sound, she was a ship of war. The crew had to be husky. There was coal in the country, but the *Beaver* never found it very suitable and burned wood instead. Sir George Simpson, riding on her from Nisqually to Sitka in 1841, marvelled at how much she could burn—forty cords a day, so that she made her trips in short, jerky runs, a day cutting and loading wood, a day burning it, another day stopping for more, and so on. At last the *Beaver* churned down the Columbia, over the bar, and up to the Straits to Nisqually. She came back occasionally, but the rest of her long life ran out on Puget Sound.

It was not an uneventful life. Every year in the spring she would head north toward the Russian settlement at Sitka (one year she had an overhaul there, for at Sitka the Russians soon had steamers themselves, built for them by a wandering Yankee shipwright). Then, her trade with the Russians finished, she would start down the broken coast, stopping at every isolated station of the Company and at Indian towns, taking aboard furs, trading for British goods, and slowly gathering a rich cargo for the *Columbia* to take back to the gentlemen adventurers in London. Eventually she became too small for the job (as she had been too large for it in 1836), and a bigger steamer took over the work. The *Beaver* then had cabins added and started carrying passengers between Victoria and the settlement at the mouth of the Fraser River. Frozen out from that, she did surveying work for the British government, and finally she was hauled out again, her upper works stripped down to an ugly cabin and small pilot house, and her masts removed, leaving her tall stack rising awkwardly amidship, and she went to work as a tug. Never a beauty, even in her prime, she became peculiarly unattractive in her newest dress, but no one noticed as she plodded about the Sound, busy towing freighters. At last, in 1888, she slammed onto a rock at the entrance to the harbor at Vancouver—a new Vancouver, on the Sound—and refused to be dislodged. Spitefully, a newer, larger boat swept by and the wash from the wheel rolled the old *Beaver* back onto the piercing ledge, and it was all over, though her hull was still solid and undecayed, and her copper bolts and fittings as strong as ever. Her builders had built well, half a century before, and she had outlasted her contemporaries, including her larger consort *Columbia,* and many later, more modern boats as well.

The *Beaver* was an episode on the Columbia River, but the *Columbia* was an annual event. Each year the *Columbia* sailed from London for Fort Vancouver, carrying supplies for the post, and letters, and trade-goods. She was the Fort's single dependable connection with the outside world. Of course, there were other vessels, stopping at the Columbia for trade, and fishing—the salmon could be packed in salt profitably—and refitting, but they rarely came up as far as Vancouver; and there were the American trappers, and the American missionaries, and the American visionaries (like the enthusiastic Wyeth). There were dignitaries: Sir George Simpson, chief of the whole far flung Hudson's Bay Company, and David Douglas, wandering botanizer. And occasionally there was one of Her Britannic Majesty's men-of-war, stationed on the Northwest Coast and keeping an eye on British interests.

So the arrival of the regular ship from home was the grand event of the year, for life at Fort Vancouver, in spite of alarms and excursions and visitors wanted and unwanted, was dull. There were the amenities to be maintained: the Chief Factor and his assistants and clerks were educated men who tried to maintain in the wilderness the trappings of civilization, and they conducted social affairs with scrupulous attention to the very best manners of society, but eventually everything boiled down to talk, talk, talk.

Fort Vancouver did not offer metropolitan entertainment; a typical frontier post, it was set back a couple of hundred yards from the riverbank, overlooking a long reach and the low rolling country across the river. The post itself was about three hundred feet square, walled with log palisades, with flanking log bastions at the corners and at the main gate. In the bastions were small brass cannon to repel Indian attacks and, their only real use, to signal the arrival of a ship or brigade of trappers. Within the walls were squared log buildings to house the residence quarters of the Chief Factor, the traders and clerks with their families, usually half-breeds, and other buildings housed trading goods and headquarters. Around the walls were shops of all sorts needed to maintain the station: tinners, blacksmiths, gunsmiths, a bakery, a powder mill. Beyond the walls were farms tended for the Company by superannuated trappers or by Canadian employees.

Vancouver had been an afterthought, established where it was because it centered the trade routes up the Columbia and along the Willamette and Cowlitz Rivers, and still afforded easy connection to the sea. The first post had been Fort George, taken over by the North West Company from the Pacific Fur Company during the War of 1812, and later by the Hudson's Bay Company after an informal war, fought on the Red River between irregular armies of both companies, had convinced the Northwesterns it did not pay to interfere with the operations of the Honourable Company. Fort George had been Astoria originally and became Astoria again, and its founding is known, so well was it told by Irving.

As the founding of Fort Vancouver had been the result of a series of accidents, so almost was the discovery of the river. The ubiquitous Spaniards, prowling the Pacific Coast, probably noticed the mouth and recorded it inaccurately on their maps, locating it within a degree or so of latitude, *poco más ó menos,* as was their wont and their skill in cartography and navigation. The Spanish had other business to attend to: their Manila galleons beating down the coast were kept lively clawing off the rocks, without stopping to explore, and Spain herself had a surplus of land to be settled and of Indians to be converted, without worrying about the alleged river. Nootka Sound was easier to reach and would do for the time being.

Then the English appeared, looking for a shorter trade route through a fabled Northwest Passage. One was Captain James Cook, whose ship ran along the coast out of sight of the headlands at the mouth. Cook went on to Nootka Sound and then to a group of islands that he first named the Sandwich Islands. Then Captain Mears, heading an expedition looking for a Strait, wandered down the coast in 1787, came close to finding the river, only not close enough. He sighted a headland that seemed to guard a bay, but when he turned toward it, he found breakers and shoal water of a bar. Without further effort, he turned seaward, named the headland Cape Disappointment and went his way. A few days later he spoke the ship *Columbia,* out of Boston, Captain Robert Gray, master, and swapped news. Captain Gray, intent on trade, eventually circumnavigated the globe, the first to do it with an American flag at the peak of his ship.

But Captain Gray came back. The Indians along the coast, as Gray and other Yankee seamen had found, were hunters and had plenty of furs they were eager to sell, furs that the Chinese were equally eager to trade for tea and silk and porcelain that the Americans in turn wanted. Trading vessels were beginning to cluster on the Northwest Coast and started the triangular trade: Boston, Northwest Coast, China, back to Boston. So, in 1792, Robert Gray came back in his *Columbia,* reaching the coast in late April. At the same time an English expedition was there, led by Captain George Vancouver, commanding H.M.S. *Discovery* and *Chatham,* sent to settle the simmering row going on between the British and the Spanish over who owned what at Nootka Sound. His ships sighted the coast at a point they named Orford after an English earl, the first of a whole series of names of British dignitaries Vancouver scattered along the region. Vancouver kept on, and during April 27 he came abreast a headland he identified as Mears' Cape Disappointment. The sea, he noticed, changed color, as if a large river were discharging into it, but he paid no serious attention and continued northward. Two days later, as an afterthought, he noted that the whole coast seemed inhospitable, with an unbroken line of breakers.

About a week later, Captain Gray in the *Columbia* reached Cape Disappointment, saw an opening in the same breakers and passed through into an estuary of a large river. Gray remained some time in the anchorage he discovered, finally naming the river Columbia after his ship. Then, the vessel needing repairs, he went north to Nootka Sound where he told Vancouver of his find. Promptly Vancouver, who had some idea of the eventual importance of Gray's discovery, sent his second in command, Broughton, in the *Chatham* to see what was what, and Broughton sailed up the river over a hundred miles, almost to the Cascades, strewing more English place names as he went. One of them was Hood, given to a mountain called W'East by the Indians. Hood was an English admiral, but he hardly deserved so grand a monument. Then Broughton returned to Nootka, and left the Columbia. After that, occasional trading vessels ran into the mouth to dicker for furs with the Indians, but for a long time nothing else happened.

What lay upstream beyond where Broughton turned back remained unknown until Lewis and Clark crossed the continent and followed the river from some of its tributary headwaters down to the flat, sandy plain at the mouth. Lewis and Clark wintered almost within sight of the sea before returning. Astor became interested and at the Columbia's mouth founded Astoria, which became a kind of casualty in the War of 1812 when the North West Company bought it—just ahead of the arrival of a British warship. Then in 1824 the Hudson's Bay Company took over the post, now Fort George, and Governor Simpson and Chief Factor McLoughlin, looking for a better site upstream, established Fort Vancouver.

The new fort was a headquarters post. Rather than conducting trade directly with the Indians, it served as a depot for supplies for the minor trading stations—at Okanagon, at Kettle Falls, at Walla Walla, at Nisqually on the Sound, and on the Umpqua. Each year the up-river posts would gather together their furs and ship them to Vancouver, down the Columbia, and at Vancouver would draw the trading goods, traps, powder, shot and necessaries for their own maintenance. The annual trips were made in brigades, a group of bateaux that went down the river in company. A bateau was a large framed boat, pointed at the prow, with a light draft for low water, but strong enough to take a battering from rocks and rapids. Packs of furs were stowed aboard until the boats sank low in the water; then Canadian boatmen, employed by the company, climbed aboard and went to work with sweeps and sometimes paddles to guide their craft down the river. One was the leader's boat, which carried less than half the normal load or only forty packs of furs. In it rode, in grandeur, the Factor; at the prow was the flag of the company, at the stern the Union Jack. The leader wore the outfit of the trapper, largely buckskin, similar to the outfits worn by the hunters and boatmen. But the boatmen had a taste for color and were gaudy in sashes and fringes of all the bright colors they could hang on themselves. Together they descended the river, working hard, singing, camping on the shore, eating salt pork when times were good and game when they were not. Through rapids they shot, and along placid reaches, and around rocks and over shoals, and when there were too many shoals or rocks, the boatmen unloaded the cargo and carried it—and the boats—around the portage to water deep enough below. At the end of the run would be the Fort and a regale, which meant about a pint of scouring joy juice, issued to help pass the night in noisy celebration.

Just above the Fort, the brigades put on their finery and formed a line of boats abreast across the river, the leader's slightly ahead. Then, with oars flashing, and with a whoop and hurrah, the little flotilla swept into sight, resplendent with flags and banners and all the fooforaw that the boatmen and trappers had found for decoration. As they came in sight, a cannon boomed at the Fort; the leader answered by firing his rifle. Promptly all the trappers aboard turned loose with their guns and filled the river with banging and shouting. Down to the bank rushed the people of Vancouver, Indians, laborers, everybody, pell mell to see the show. Behind them, and in befitting dignity came the clerks, and last of all, solemnly, Dr. McLoughlin in formal dark broadcloth to greet the leader. The boats ground their noses against the bank, the leader stepped ashore to pay his respects to the Chief Factor, and then the boatmen leaped overside, tossing the bales of furs onto the bank so the laborers could carry them to the warehouse for checking. After that, everybody could get down to the serious business of having a spree, whether it be a real carouse by the trappers and boatmen, or a dignified dinner—with brandy and wine—with Dr. McLoughlin and lady.

The coming of the ship from home was less colorful, but, to the men at the Fort, more interesting, for she carried mail, news, and books, in addition to regular supplies. Sometimes the ship would not make it but be lost on the way, even as close as the bar of the

Columbia. To cover such chances, the Fort always had in reserve a full cargo of supplies, enough to last for a year. It could not have a shipment of mail, though, and while business might go on, it would be a long dull time. So when a ship entered the river, and Indian runners brought word to Fort Vancouver, everyone went about his daily work with an eye cast downstream, and it was odd how many errands led the clerks to the riverbank. Finally the ship would come in sight, her tall masts and dark hull showing as she worked up the river, and then the gunner by the brass cannon waited for the signal. As soon as it came, he touched off the cannon, sending a ring of smoke across the plain, and a roar of welcome to the ship. From her side would come an answering puff, and then in a moment the rumble of her salute. As she edged to the wharf, again everyone would hurry down to see her. The Captain came ashore and exchanged solemn greetings with the Chief Factor, while the crowd on shore gaped at the tall sides of the ship, and the crew on board gaped at those on shore, especially at the Indian girls, whom they regarded speculatively. Then the work of unloading began. First came the letter pouch and the small packages entrusted to the Captain; next came the supplies, hoisted in crates and bundles from the hold and swung overside onto the dock. Slowly the ship rose in the water as her load lightened, and then slowly she sank as the bales of furs went aboard her. In time she would be loaded and gone, and another year would begin.

As the years went by the Chief Factor noticed more and more Americans around, clamoring for service, demanding aid, giving advice. He helped them out, gladly, and wondered at their number. Up the Willamette Valley he had established some farms, and by 1832, a water-powered sawmill at the falls of the Willamette; now there were Methodists with a chapel and high hopes, and around Walla Walla were other missionaries. There was talk by the Americans about "joint occupancy," and so on, but McLoughlin kept his troubles to himself.

The spring freshet of 1843 came and went. More American vessels were on the river. That fall not just brigades came down the Columbia to the Fort. No, there were crude flatboats, and rafts, and rickety canoes and bateaux, and they weren't carrying furs. They had household goods, and women, and even cows and such truck. What was Oregon coming to?

Chapter 2
STEAMBOATS ON THE RIVER

THE American settlers along the Willamette made 1843 their own year of decision. At Champoeg, meeting to settle a local problem, they went on and settled a national one: that Oregon was part of the United States. The Eastern politicians could decide whether the boundary would be Fifty-Four Forty—and fight over it—or Forty-Nine and compromise. Once the Oregonians, for that is what they had become, made up their minds, they set about doing what American frontiersmen always did: they made plans for more settlers. All along the lower Columbia and the Willamette hopeful townsites sprang into existence, each marked by stakes, ambitions, and a house or two.

By 1846, Oregon, at least that part south of the Columbia, was a going concern. Business was good; trade was brisk. Every fall new wagon trains came across the country to The Dalles and then on down the river or over the rough pass of the Cascades. At the falls of the Willamette, Oregon City began to put on metropolitan airs, living up to its ambitious name. Now there were a couple of mills, a whole main street of shops, and at least a hundred buildings. Down south, the Americans were still fighting the Californians; Fremont was showing off as usual trying to be a pathfinder; and Cooke's column of Mormons plodded painfully along the Gila. But in Oregon, all moved calmly, and the Oregonians established a newspaper, the *Oregon Spectator,* which, in true western journalistic spirit, began to demand internal improvements and to belabor its rivals—particularly the upstart sheet called the *Californian* that somebody started at Monterey. Especially did the *Oregon Spectator's* editor call for better transportation in the country, and in April he had the satisfaction of printing the advertisement for the "light draft and fast running boats, *Mogul* and *Ben Franklin*" that would run regularly between the Falls and Champoeg, about fifteen miles up-river, the landing distinguished not only for the meeting of 1843 but also for the amount of produce it wanted to ship and its convenience as a terminal for a short overland road to the Methodist settlement called Salem. The *Mogul* and *Ben Franklin* were keel-boats, rigged for sail and prepared to meet calms or contentious winds by having a crew of Indians that could pull sweeps. Each boat carried from fifteen to twenty passengers "abaft" and a fair tonnage of cargo. Passengers paid fifty cents in coin or a dollar "on the stores," the captains not having unlimited faith in unlimited currency, and fetched their own provisions and comforts for the voyage that took about seven hours. This was progress; this was opening the country. Already a small sailing packet had been running from Fort Vancouver to Astoria for a year, but it did not advertise.

Shortly the monopoly had competition. A new keelboat, the *Great Western,* went on the run, and two clinker built boats for the same service were launched above the Falls. At Fort Vancouver the lordly captain of H.M.S. *Modeste* did honors for the occasion and broke a bottle over the stem of a new schooner built by Mr. Scarth of the Hudson's Bay Company. This was *Callapooiah,* and as soon as she was rigged and fitted, she worked the route between the Fort and Oregon City. When the fall wheat crop began to be gathered at the landings, the *Mogul* and the *Ben Franklin* made two trips a week to Champoeg, going up on Mondays and Thursdays, and coming down on Wednesdays and Saturdays. The first feeder line got under way, too; these "new fixings for Oregon" were ox-drawn wagons that jogged from the "Tuality" plains to the river opposite Oregon City.

So the keelboats, schooners, and bateaux, interspersed by privately built flatboats, maintained the trade while the towns grew. Portland, named for a town in Maine, was a clearing on the river a dozen miles downstream from Oregon City; Milton was another clearing—but a flood finished the job and cleared it out. Down the Columbia, Plymouth, soon to become St. Helens, had hopes and some houses. Astoria struggled, but settlement seemed always to avoid the lower river. Salem, on the Willamette, had fine plans; so did a landing upstream called Albany, and another one beyond at Marysville, later Corvallis. On the Yamhill, Dayton was a convenient shipping point. Far up the Willamette, Eugene Skinner built a cabin near a hill, where the river could be ferried. Even there in time might be a town, he thought, as he laid out its site, platting narrow streets that crisscrossed the mud. Finally there was Milwaukie, at the foot of the rapids below Oregon City, where Lot Whitcomb was feverishly promoting all sorts of improvements. The country was growing, and a few of the old timers who had been there for five or six years complained about the crowds that were spoiling everything.

Then Yankee ingenuity appeared. To Oregon City came a man named Truesdale with a wondrous contraption. It was a vessel 82 feet long, driven by paddles operated by six horses on a treadmill, and rated at 80 tons. It should not have worked, but it did; Truesdale proved it by running down to Portland, coming back upstream in three hours, even crossing the rapids at the mouth of the Clackamas with hardly any trouble. Still, it was a makeshift, and the editor of the *Oregon Spectator* said so, adding with a flourish of optimism:

We are aware that some persons disagree with us, but we believe that a good steamboat, under charge of a careful business man, would defray its expenses, and pay for itself in three years upon these waters.

But the Editor was ahead of his time, although he must have felt a thrill when the Pacific Mail Steamship Company advertised for samples of local coal that might be suitable in the furnaces of its new steamers being built for the Isthmus mail route to Oregon.

In May, 1849, an American steamer did enter the Columbia, and under its own power. From Honolulu and the East Coast came the Army transport *Massachusetts,* bringing troops to aid in the Cayuse war east of the Cascades. The *Massachusetts* was doubly a pioneer. She was the first American steamer to reach Oregon and one of the earliest screw propelled, having been built at Boston in 1845. She headed from New York for Oregon in November, 1848, usually under sail, but occasionally, when the wind failed or the going was difficult, under steam. Without trouble, she crossed the bar at Astoria and moved up the river to Fort Vancouver where the brass cannon fired a welcome. She might be American, but Hudson's Bay would not neglect a salute, and Peter Skene Ogden, then in charge ("a rough old man" as an officer aboard wrote), entertained the new-comers. There she dropped the troops to form an encampment, and then ran up to Portland, before dropping down river to load lumber for Army bases in California.

In 1849, the Oregonians had more to think about than a steamer. There was gold in California, and the Oregonians with a whoop headed south by sea and by land to help gather it. Crops grew untended in the Willamette Valley. Cabins stood deserted. The able-bodied men and boys swarmed to get in on the rich placers, leaving Oregon to the weeds and the Indians. Then the Californians, in turn, headed north for provisions. The river saw a procession of coastal traders move upstream to Portland and Oregon City, after cargo. Slowly it dawned on the Oregonians that here was another way of getting gold—besides, they had pretty well cleaned out the best placers, anyway, and gold mining was degenerating into plain hard work. Why not, they asked themselves, let the Californians do the digging and then get the gold in exchange for Oregon produce? Let the Californians have the messy jobs, sell them lumber, wheat, potatoes, salmon, butter, and beef, and collect gold dust in return. The Oregon gold rush was on, and this time to the Columbia and the Willamette. And so it might be said that the gold rush that made steamboating on the Sacramento necessary, made steamboating on the Columbia and Willamette practicable. Before the gold rush, a steamboat in Oregon would have been sheer luxury; afterwards it was good business. Given the choice, the Oregonian will always take whatever is good business. That is the Yankee in him.

For a long time there had been talk that Oregon would be given mail service by steamer, and the Pacific Mail Steamship Company had been organized to operate the route. Oregon was to be the terminal, with a way station at Monterey, but the gold rush changed all that, too. Now, California commanded the interest, and Oregon found itself a remote outpost, beyond the profitable range of steamer service. When the first of the Pacific Mail steamers, the *California*, sailed from New York in 1848, she had the best intentions, for at the time California and Oregon were equally important; but when she rounded the Horn and reached Panama, her plans changed. There had been a hint of what was happening when she touched a South American port and fifty anxious passengers came aboard, but at

Panama there were seven hundred waiting frantically for her. The seven hundred had read Polk's message and Larkin's report and were rarin' to reach the banks of the Sacramento. What to do? There was room for two hundred and fifty aboard her, if the fifty South Americans were shoved into steerage, and into the space (for naturally the South Americans were shoved aside by the free born democrats of the United States) were packed over three hundred and sixty, about half of those waiting. Then the *California* went on to California where she turned back for another haul from Panama. Intention or no intention, agreement or no agreement, the Pacific Mail Steamship Company conveniently forgot Oregon as long as it could.

Finally, in May, 1850, the Pacific Mail steamer *Carolina* made the trip to the Columbia, immediately after arriving from her maiden voyage to the coast. Only half the size of the *California*, she was a wooden twin-screw, built by the Cramps in 1849. With the mail, some cargo and a few passengers, she stopped at Astoria, six days out from San Francisco, and then, taking two days for the trip, at Portland. This was the beginning of fairly regular monthly service from California, though sometimes a month seemed to have six or seven weeks in it. When, late in the year, an independent steamer, the *Gold Hunter,* arrived at Portland, Oregon had a real chance to reach a market and Portland a definite advantage over rival towns, like Milwaukie—providing Portland controlled the ship. Promptly the Portlanders kittied in enough to buy controlling shares in the *Gold Hunter,* gave her a cargo and sent her on her way, rejoicing. The *Gold Hunter* was about the size of the *Carolina,* but driven by side wheels and had been built for Sacramento River service. A handy size and a trim ship, she seemed ideally suited to the needs of Oregon, so that Portlanders burst with pride. Unfortunately, the pride did not last long. In San Francisco, the owners who had sold the controlling shares in her now quietly bought the officers' shares and had control again. Then they sent her into service on the Mexican coast, letting the Portlanders slowly discover, when she did not return, that they had been literally sold south. The citizenry of Milwaukie extended only the mildest sympathy.

Down the river at Astoria the *Carolina* had passed a jerry-built steamboat hull taking form on the bank. Captain Frost with some other men of the town had decided to speculate; they sent to San Francisco for a steam engine and put it together when the parts came to them finally aboard the brig *Grecian*. By July the job was finished, and the result was a steamboat named *Columbia* which slid into the river, the first of the kind in the Pacific Northwest. Built double-ended, something like a ferryboat, she was a side-wheeler 90 feet long, 16 feet in beam, and 4 feet deep in hold, and what might be called functional in design—that is, she was without ornament and jigsaw trim as were her more elegant successors. Nor was she very substantial, but when steam got into her cylinders, she would go, and that was what counted.

She was "not at all a harbor of comfort for her passengers," as one traveller said in tactful retrospect; she lacked sleeping accommodations and a galley, so that passengers toted their own provender for the trip. There were hardly enough Astorians to provide a good send-off for her maiden voyage on the morning of July 3, 1850—a memorable date in Oregon steamboating, but slowly she worked her way into the river, met the current and usually overcame it. Where the channel happened to be was anybody's guess, but a pair of young Indians who had been fishing on the river were hired to be expert guessers when others failed, and they guessed right. All day Captain Frost directed the *Columbia's* slow progress, and when night came he headed her toward the bank and tied her to a convenient tree. He had no intention to claw his way through the dark, and fifty miles were enough for the first day's run anyway. In the morning, Frost had the lines cast off and set out again. By three o'clock she came abreast Portland, where the collective citizenry, hearing her coughs and whistle, came down to the bank to whoop up a real welcome. It was the Fourth of July; they had plenty of noise lying around handy, and to spare. At four o'clock, the *Columbia* was above Clackamas Rapids and at the landing at Oregon City. The *Columbia* was a success, and the folks at Oregon City took up the celebration where the Portlanders left off.

After a second trip up the river to Oregon City, the *Columbia* began regular service, making two runs a month to connect with the steamer sent up from California by the Pacific Mail Steamship Company to Astoria. For passage either way, the *Columbia* charged only $25, the passengers to bring their own blankets and lunch baskets. Free deck space would be assigned at night. For freight, another $25 was charged for each ton. She was no floating palace, but until something else came along, she would do, and passengers flocked to her, ready to sit on her decks as she swept along at a brisk four miles an hour. Oregon began to feel the freedom that comes from easy travel. Now a trip up to Oregon City just to attend a party was simple, just a pleasant jaunt for a social evening. Yet consider the plight of one young lady from Astoria.

It was on the way back that the trouble started. To show his devotion to her, a young officer from the garrison at Fort Vancouver got leave of absence and accompanied her on the return trip. The boat was small and crowded, and the couple had no chance even to look at the moon without having a crowd of helpers, but all went along merry as the potential wedding bell, as probably the officer thought, until the *Columbia* came opposite Woody Island, about sixteen miles upstream from Astoria. There the *Columbia,* whose beam was generous as her length was not, met the tide and a nasty wind. Try as she might, she could make no headway, and the Captain ordered out an anchor. Stopped, the little steamer began a jerking, undulating roll, swerving and pitching in the chop of the river. Slowly the couple began to lose interest in each other; their eyes dulled, their cheeks paled, turned ashen, faintly green. In short, the river made them seasick.

There was a tiny cabin aft that had a narrow bench on each side, facing a table on which the passengers could spread their lunches. Into the cabin, the solicitous captain, anxious for the welfare of his passengers, led the limp and queasy couple. To each he assigned a bench, and a blanket, and laid them out, their heads close together where the cabin narrowed at the stern. Between them he placed a bucket for general convenience until the wind went down, and hung another blanket across their feet. And so he left them, but not to dream.

Between trips, usually not complicated by young love and head winds, the *Columbia* did towing and general steamboating between Oregon City and the Cascades, bringing down emigrant parties, towing barges, and generally competing with the small brigs, schooners and keelboats that had been carrying the traffic. For six months she had a monopoly on the river; no other boat could equal her regularity or her dependability. She charged high prices, but she got the business, skimming the cream while the chance was good. At Milwaukie, where *Columbia* passed, a hull slowly took form to give competition. Lot Whitcomb, an enterpriser with imagination, was hard at work with a crew of real shipwrights and engineers at building another steamboat. The *Columbia* was a makeshift; the

new boat, named for her builder, was not. The *Lot Whitcomb,*
building at Milwaukie, was going to be a first class steamboat.

And she was. From her keel that was a solid stick of Oregon fir, to
her pilot house, the *Lot Whitcomb* was a good boat. Measured at
six hundred tons, she was 160 feet long, 24 feet beam, and 5 feet
8 inches in depth of hold. Her side wheels were 18 feet in diameter.
Loaded, she would draw about three feet, and with a steam engine
of 140 horsepower, built in New Orleans and brought from San
Francisco, she would make twelve miles an hour on the river. Her
design followed the tradition of the Hudson River boats. From
twin boilers set forward on the guards lifted tall stacks; her wheels
were in housings that rose above her hurricane deck to the texas
and were set well back from center. She had a closed boiler deck, a
long cabin deck, a small texas and a plain pilot house set nearly
amidships, behind the chimneys, and altogether she was in appearance a hybrid of Mississippi and Eastern design. All her upper
works were painted white, without ornament; on each wheel-hous-
ing was her name in simple letters, and above the name a box carried
only a slatted fan radiating from a plain lunette. Simple, unosten-
tatious, but tasteful and elegant—that was the *Lot Whitcomb,* for
her cabins were carefully decorated and done in finest cabinet work
and paneling. She had plenty of cabin space, a ladies' cabin, and a
dining hall. On the boiler or freight deck a heavy cargo could be
loaded. Altogether, the new boat would be a credit to her builder
and the river, and everyone was impressed by her, even Portlanders,
who recognized that she would give the Milwaukie folks a real advantage in the race for supremacy as the big town on the river.

On Christmas Day, 1850, the boat was ready for launching. By act
of the Territorial Legislature, she would be the *Lot Whitcomb of
Oregon,* and to make it official, Governor Gaines came down to
make a speech and send her on her way. At the proper words spoken
by the Governor, the *Lot Whitcomb* slipped sideways off the cradle
and into the water. Then Mayor Kilborn presented a set of colors to
her, the gift of Oregon City; Mayor Kilborn made a speech, too, as
did others, and Lot Whitcomb himself responded to the plaudits,
speaking "in his usual and happy style"—the phrase of the Milwaukie
Western Star, Whitcomb's own newspaper. From Fort Vancouver
had come the brass band of the Army post, and between speeches it
played stirring and patriotic tunes "in most excellent taste." The
ceremonies over, the celebration began. Naturally cannons had to

be fired, and unfortunately from some cause the salute cannon blew up, killing a celebrant. Otherwise it was generally a festive occasion, and the whole affair ended in a grand ball, the music provided by the brass band, and the uniforms, sure to quicken the hearts of the ladies, by the officers from the Fort.

With the *Lot Whitcomb* ready to offer competition, the master of the *Columbia* in January reduced the fare from Astoria to Oregon City to $15, a rate the *Whitcomb* refused to meet, knowing that the advantages of elegance and speed were with the new boat. Instead the *Whitcomb* announced she would leave Milwaukie on Mondays and Thursdays at noon, touching at Portland, Ft. Vancouver, Milton, St. Helens, Cowlitz, and Cathlamet on the run to Astoria, and when the water was favorable, return from Pacific City (a hopeful promotion opposite Astoria) to Oregon City. For this trip, passengers would be charged $20 between Milwaukie, Portland, or Ft. Vancouver to Astoria, $2 between Milwaukie and Portland, and $5 between Milwaukie and Vancouver. It cost $2 more to go up to Oregon City from Milwaukie, and, significantly, the advertisement added: "Board not included in above rates."

Then the trouble started. Hardly had the *Lot Whitcomb* begun operations than she hung herself up on a reef at the mouth of the Clackamas River and perched there two weeks until coffers or weirs could be built to get enough water under her to float her off. It was just after she had been freed and was making her way to the boatyard, somewhat abashed and battered, that the editor of the *Oregon Spectator* saw her while he was travelling by whaleboat down to Portland to take a jaunt on the *Columbia*—at the invitation of the *Columbia's* captain. The editor merely mentioned the *Lot's* plight: the rapids at the Clackamas were not subjects for ridicule by denizens of Oregon City. Low water over the rapids meant no boats up to the Falls. Still, in the pilot house of the *Lot Whitcomb,* her captain felt chagrin.

The captain was not the sort to go around grounding steamboats carelessly; he was a man that could be depended upon in an emergency. This was J. C. Ainsworth, a Middlewesterner who had got his training as pilot on the treacherous upper Mississippi, on which he operated steamboats in packet service from St. Louis, past Hannibal to Keokuk, Dubuque and beyond. He was used to sandbars and shifting channels and swift rapids, and he could snatch a boat off a threatening riffle on the water and into safety when he had to. Ainsworth knew the tricks of steamboating: a captain had to on the upper Mississippi if he expected to keep a boat long. He knew other tricks, too: how to have pitch knots thrown into furnaces just before the boat came into a landing, to make billows of black smoke roll from the chimneys and a plume of steam spurt from the 'scape pipes, all to put on a good show and attract business. He had imagination and ability. Those who knew him well said that he was a young man who would make his mark in Oregon. They were right. When he took the *Lot Whitcomb* from Astoria to Oregon City in ten hours, they nodded sagely, and shortly later when he ran from Milwaukie up to Oregon City in less than an hour they were openly impressed. But there were dark mutterings about what the world and especially Oregon were coming to when he raced the *Willamette*.

Ainsworth had performed one of the first towing jobs of the *Lot Whitcomb* in March 1851, when he brought the iron-hulled propeller *Willamette* from Astoria. Built for the Pacific Mail Steamship Company on the East Coast and intended specifically for shuttle service between Astoria and Oregon City, the *Willamette* arrived at the Columbia under schooner rig, her engines disconnected; then, trailing the *Whitcomb* at the end of a hawser, she was taken to Portland for fitting and quickly put into service. By July she was doing her job, meeting the bi-monthly steamer at Astoria and bringing its passengers, mail and freight upriver. One day the *Lot Whitcomb* landed at Portland just before the *Willamette* cast loose, rang her bell, and set off down the river, "a splendid sight, a perfect streak," an onlooker described her, with her flag stretched out, a bone of foam at the stem, and the wake from her propellers at the stern. Quickly the *Lot Whitcomb* jangled her bell to call aboard the passengers, hauled in her landing stage and set off after the *Willamette*. She was quiet; the *Whitcomb* was not—her high pressure engines booming, and her side wheels threshing the water. At the mouth of the Willamette, the *Willamette* was still ahead, but the *Lot Whitcomb*, risking shallower water, cut between her rival and the bank. Slowly the side-wheeler pulled abreast, while the passengers on both boats lined the rails and yelled encouragement, privately hoping the boilers would hold. Delicately Ainsworth twirled the wheel, reading the face of the river and taking advantage of every current. A little angling wash or whip of froth swung out from the bank; Ainsworth spun the wheel, caught the current below, and swept a full length ahead. But it was neck and neck to

The old *Beaver* suns herself, drawn out on a marine
railway at Victoria, B. C.

A 49'er with a steeple-engine, all the way from Coney Island,
ties up by a fir-fringed shore

Elegance in the Eighties. The big *Wide West* of the O. S. N.

Every possible genteel luxury was in the Ladies' Cabin of
the *Wide West*—including brass gaboons.

The *Lot Whitcomb,* built in 1851 was a pioneer riverboat
on the Columbia

St. Helens, where the *Willamette* had to put a boat ashore, and that ended it, although the *Lot Whitcomb* had barely dropped an anchor off Astoria before the *Willamette* was rounding Tongue Point, close behind.

Oregonians had their taste sharpened for steamboating; the *Willamette* and the *Lot Whitcomb* were incentives. Promptly other steamboats appeared on the rivers. There were the tiny iron-hulled propellers *Eagle* and *Black Hawk,* each about 40 feet long with room for perhaps a dozen passengers or a ton of freight, that started daily service between Portland and Oregon City and did towing in their spare time. There was the equally tiny *Hoosier,* built out of a ship's longboat, somewhat lengthened, and powered by an uncertain engine from a pile driver. She tried her speed around Portland, then was portaged around the falls at Oregon City and became the first steamboat to work on the upper Willamette. In June, 1851, she was making three trips a week from Canemah (the landing a mile above the falls) to Dayton on the Yamhill. Even her owners must have recognized that the *Hoosier* suffered from mechanical limitations, but she was easy to patch and keep going. One day she snapped her shaft while trying to scramble over a shoal four miles below Salem, but the engineer was unworried. He unshipped the shaft and shouldering one piece of it and giving another piece to a deck hand (probably *the* deck hand) he started walking back to Salem to a blacksmith shop. There he had the pieces welded, shouldered it again, tramped back, put it in, and the *Hoosier* went its way. The *Hoosier* soon had real competition from the *Washington,* an iron propeller, and the *Canemah,* a light draft wooden side-wheeler built that year at Canemah, and both intended for upper Willamette service, perhaps as far as Marysville if the water were deep enough. It was not, for the *Washington,* and there was no freight for her either, so she was hauled around the Falls and was taken during the summer of 1853 around to the Umpqua River, thus becoming the pioneer steamboat of the coast region.

Before such signs of progress, the Oregonians stood amazed. From far corners came poetic praises for the new delights, for the Oregonians were inveterate writers of newspaper poetry, and seemed to have a continuous spontaneous overflow of powerful feelings. Thus, the mother of Edwin Markham (who in time would develop something of a reputation for his own verse) saw the *Lot Whitcomb* try to make its first ascent of the Clackamas Rapids, rushed home, and, taking her pen in hand, caught the emotion recollected in reasonable tranquillity. When the effusion was done, she sent it off to the *Oregon Spectator,* which in turn dutifully printed it.

> Lot Whitcomb is coming!
> Her banners are flying—
> She walks up the rapids with speed;
> She ploughs through the water,
> Her steps never falter—
> Oh! that's independence indeed.
> Old and young rush to meet her,
> Male and female to greet her,
> And waves lash the shore as they pass.
>
> Oh! she's welcome, thrice welcome
> To Oregon City;
> Lot Whitcomb is with us at last.
> Success to the Steamer,
> Her Captain and crew.
> She has our best wishes attained.
> Oh! that she may never
> While running this river
> Fall back on the sand bar again.

Elizabeth Markham had the poetic impulse, even if her poetic feet did stumble, just as she notes that the *Lot* itself had done on the sandbar. Then Mrs. Markham relaxed from frenzy to write poems like "The Voice of Intemperance," and let another sweet singer of Oregon take up the lyre, this time to strike chords to celebrate still another new steamer, the *Multnomah,* that had reached the mouth of the Yamhill on its maiden voyage. To tell the truth, Mrs. Markham had some edge on her anonymous rival in skill, but not in passion and movement. Hark, and attend!

> There comes the Multnomah! success to the steamer,
> Sweet sounding her music, high floating her streamer;
> The sound of her paddles the hills serenading,
> And her smoke high aloft into vapor is fading.
> There comes the Multnomah! shout fifty glad voices;
> Each heart beats with rapture, each bosom rejoices,
> Her structure so firm, yet buoyant and airy
> She skims o'er the wave like a sylph or a fairy.
> There comes the Multnomah! we greet her with pleasure,
> The choicest of welcomes to her is extended,
> Because with her welfare our interests are blended.

Then, having warmed to his work, the poet turned loose a genuine rash of regional rapture and continued without stopping for breath:

> Hallo! there, you farmers in this rich interior,
> That in all nature's kingdom admits no superior,
> Wake up to your interests, no longer lie yawning,
> The daylight of commerce upon you is dawning;
> Your uncertain markets continue no longer,
> Demand for your produce grows stronger and stronger,
> And old father Neptune your welfare espouses
> By sending his steamers "right jam" to your houses.

This last almost stopped the writer, but he took a long, deep breath of cool, fragrant Oregon air, and soared away into the infinite, letting his rhymes fall where they might:

> Success to Lot Whitcomb, to Ainsworth and Bissell,
> To Clark and to Frost, and each neat little vessel.
> May health and long life give unbounded enjoyment
> And fortune secure them lucrative employment.
> May Barlow and Hedges grow rich and be healthy,
> And Murray and White independent and wealthy,
> And long may their names bear a high reputation
> In Oregon commerce and steam navigation.

Thus, having given the boatmen of the day intimations of immortality, the poet signed himself "O.P.Q." and shipped off the verses to the *Oregon Spectator,* where, on August 19, 1851, they appeared to delight its critical readers.

What could have been this vessel that set the strings of the poetic lyre a-humming? This paragon, this *Multnomah?*

She was no beauty. Her hull, of iron and Jersey oak, was shipped from the East knocked down in numbered sections and assembled at Canemah (the first instance of pre-fabricated shipbuilding in Oregon) by fitting together the stave-like pieces by a kind of cooperage so that she was called, from her construction, the "barrel boat." When the parts were in proper places, the result was a vessel 108 feet long, 17 feet in beam, and only 18 inches in draft. On top of the hull, her guards and superstructure extended her width to 28 feet, including her small side wheels. The deck forward was open, and aft she had a closed, box-like cabin. Above the cabin were two small structures, one with windows serving as pilot house. Amidships rose a single stack, topped by a spark-arrester. The whole effect was bulky and rather ugly—she looked like a scow that had somehow sprouted paddle boxes in a hopeful ambition to be mistaken for a ferryboat. But in spite of her ungainly shape, she could travel. Her engines turned out 150 horsepower, and she could clip off fourteen miles an hour.

The *Multnomah* got up steam for the first time in June, 1851, at her launching place above the Falls. In August she made a trial run upriver as far as Cresman's Bar, twenty miles below Salem, where the water shoaled too much even to accommodate her scant 18 inch draft. "The river must be improved," stormed the *Oregon Spectator's* editor, telling of the trip, "and it must be done at the expense of the people to be benefitted by the improvement." By constructing wing dams, he suggested, the water level could be raised and a channel scoured not only at Cresman's Bar but at other places, including the troublesome Clackamas Rapids. The *Multnomah* worked at the bar and finally crossed it, leaving Cresman's behind, but at Matheny's, five miles farther, the bed of the river seemed to come to the surface and the boat turned back.

Salem took the hint and went to work on the channel so that in September a boat would find four feet of water all the way, and the *Multnomah* was able to land at the town and even go on a few miles farther to Cincinnati, at the mouth of the Rickreal. On the way back she made the trip from Cincinnati to Rock Island, a troublesome spot with a narrow, fast channel five miles above Canemah, in only five hours, which was good time. Shortly afterwards a stage line began advertising that it was now possible to go to Salem from Portland by daylight, using boats to Champoeg landing and stage coaches across country from there.

Times had changed in Oregon, and wonders seemed never to cease, although everyone had to admit they slowed down considerably during 1853. Down in California, the easy gold of the placers had been skimmed off and a surplus of miners clogged the cities and mining camps. Business in San Francisco slacked off, and orders for Oregon goods fell promptly. Prices declined and competition sharpened. Already the *Columbia* had given up the struggle. Too slow to keep up with the newer boats, she had lagged behind, and in January of 1853 her engines had been removed and put in a new vessel called the *Fashion. Columbia's* hull still nosed against the bank, but the spring freshet caught that, too, and swept it past Astoria and onto the sands at the mouth of the river. Then, in August, 1854, the *Lot Whitcomb* left the river, sold to a California firm for use on the Sacramento River. Renamed the *Annie Aber-nethy*, she sedately followed the steamer *Peytonia* on a tow line down the coast. In San Francisco Bay she ran the Napa Creek and the Sacramento routes for the California Steam Navigation Company.

Though 1853 was a bad year for steamboat business, steamboat builders remained busy launching new vessels. One was the *Wallamet*, a big side-wheeler built after the fashion of the Mississippi River packets. Unhappily, Mississippi fashions were not suitable to the Oregon rivers, and the *Wallamet* made no money so regularly that after a year's trial on first the upper Willamette and then the Portland-Astoria run, she was sold south and was towed down to California to try her luck there. She did not last long there, either. The *Belle of Oregon City*, another boat built in 1853, was a real development in Oregon steamboat building, for she was iron, fabricated and assembled in the iron works at Oregon City by Thomas V. Smith, who had come out from Baltimore and established himself as a foundryman and builder of machinery. From the iron sheets that formed her hull to her engines she was an Oregon product; Smith built it all, even the boiler and engines, in his own shops. The *Belle*—her qualifying *of Oregon City* usually was forgotten by those who spoke of her—had a hull 90 feet long with a 16 foot beam on which a deck formed wide guards so that she had an overall length of 96 feet and a beam of 26 feet, with ample room for her side wheels. When she was finished, her owner put her on the run between Portland and Oregon City on which she maintained a fast schedule. She left the warehouse at the base of the falls at 7:30 in the morning, Oregon City at 8, Milwaukie at 8:30, and arrived at Portland at 9:30. Then she started back at 2:00 and was home at 4:00 every afternoon. Fare between the terminals was $2. The *Belle* was, with the exception of the little *Eagle* that had come out in 1851 and kept running for twenty years, the longest lived of the pioneer boats, her iron hull, like that of the *Eagle's*, giving her a stamina the others of her age lacked. The *Belle* knocked about a good bit: she did her stint on the Cascades route and helped carry reinforcements to the Cascades when the Indians attacked; she ran to the Cowlitz and to Vancouver in her day; she became part of the fleet of the Oregon Steam Navigation Company and watched newer boats wear themselves out; and finally in 1869 she went to the scrapper, her iron sent to China and her engines, still faithfully turning over, to power a sawmill. A lot prettier boats had come and gone in the meantime, but few hardier ones than the *Belle of Oregon City*, the first iron steamboat built wholly on the Pacific Coast.

The *Lot Whitcomb* in leaving left a gap to be filled by a successor that had her qualities of elegance and speed. Certainly the *Belle* did not qualify, nor the other contemporaries, but the new *Jennie Clark* did, when she came from the hand of the master builder Jacob Kamm at Milwaukie and passed to her master Captain Ainsworth, who ran her for the Abernethy and Clark Company. Her construction went on under difficulties and called for about as much letter writing as boat building, for her engines were ordered especially from a manufacturer in Baltimore, and plans and details had to make the long, slow trips back and forth by steamer on the Isthmus route. Meanwhile her hull was taking shape at Milwaukie, and it was necessary that the two fit when they came together. Finally, the ship *Golden Racer* came up the river, all the way from the East Coast, and unloaded the pieces after Kamm and the company paid $1030.02 for the freight—almost as much as for the whole engine which cost at Baltimore $1663.16.

The *Jennie Clark* was different from other boats on the river because she had her wheel at the stern, Ainsworth and Kamm having decided from experience that the stern-wheeler was the best type for the waters of the Pacific Northwest. All others had been either small propellers or side-wheelers, but practice showed them to have disadvantages. The propellers fouled in shallow water, bent their blades, and snapped their shafts, and the side-wheelers were hard to manage in swift currents and winding channels. The *Jennie Clark*, being a stern-wheeler with her rudders close to the wheel, could be maneuvered easily. She had two engines, so connected that one man could handle them, each with cylinders having a 4 foot stroke with a 16 foot connecting rod turning the single wheel which was 15 feet in diameter. She was 115 feet long and 18½ feet in beam, with a 4 foot hold; on her hull was a single cabin, in which the boiler was centered, with the engines aft to reach the wheel. Forward of the boiler, where Kamm did not want it, was the passenger cabin. On the roof a tall stack rose from the boiler, and before it was the pilot house in which was a touch of ostentatious display—a mahogany wheel, ordered by Kamm to be "neat and plain finish and not costly." And so the *Jennie Clark* set the pattern for a long line of successors—all neat and plain finish, but some costly.

When the *Jennie Clark* took to the water and went into service in February, 1855, Captain Ainsworth found he had a good boat under him. She responded to the helm at a touch, her stern wheel bit into the water firmly to give her speed when she needed it, and delicacy in tricky water when landing. That decided the builders. After she started her run, carrying the mail daily between Portland and Oregon City, there were fewer side-wheelers built on the Columbia or the Willamette. She could show her heels to other boats when she had to, and without racing to prove it soon got a reputation as a fast, comfortable boat. Her predecessor, the *Lot Whitcomb,* had liked a race, although there had been few chances, except for the *Willamette* and once the *Goliah,* on one of her peripatetic trips along the coast. That time the *Goliah,* still in her prime, accepted the challenge and, quite characteristically for the *Goliah,* lost. The *Lot Whitcomb* ran away from her. Now the *Lot* was in California, but the *Jennie* would carry on the tradition.

Half a decade had passed since the *Columbia* labored upstream against the current, and steamboating had arrived to stay. There were steamers between Astoria and Portland, and between Portland and Oregon City. Above the Falls, more steamboats ran to Dayton and Corvallis. Still others worked up the Columbia to the Cascades, and beyond there, back in the wilderness, two or three were running. They carried passengers and freight, mail and express. They moved the people and the business. And they had made Portland outstrip its rivals. Milwaukie's ambitions were withering, and St. Helens was losing out. The Clackamas Rapids handicapped Oregon City by blocking the river below her, and the Falls blocked it above. Oregon City would have its water power for milling.and would retain transfer business but was slipping back in the race. It would be Portland, all the way.

Still the emigrants were coming, working their way across the plains to the Columbia, and moving down the Columbia to the Cascades, and they had to be brought through. The Army was busy as well, protecting the trail, establishing posts and forts for garrisons, mapping and exploring. At The Dalles a detachment of troops established a fort, and there were other forts up the river beyond. The Columbia above Vancouver had traffic, but most of it moved in scows and superannuated old brigs like the *Henry.*

Above the Cascades business developed, and D. F. Bradford, who was located at the portage, with Captain Van Bergen, determined in

1851 to bring progress to the middle stretch of the Columbia. They hauled in an engine and began putting together a hull that amazed the newly arrived emigrants who passed it. Finally the job was done and the boat ready, a side-wheeler 60 feet long with a beam of 12 feet, not a floating palace by any means, but glorying in the name *James P. Flint*. She made steam and ran a few trips, back and forth from the Cascades to The Dalles, carrying emigrants and their plunder and stock on the down trips, and a few army supplies and troops on the upriver runs. Still, it was obvious that a steamboat was a luxury, and as soon as the fall rush of the overlanders was over, business disappeared. The business, Bradford and Van Bergen recognized, was a bit slow in reaching so far into the hinterlands, and if it would not come to their boat, they would take the boat to the business. To do it, they had to haul her up on the bank, put skids under her, and drag her around the worst of the rapids until she would find quiet water again. Once below the Cascades, she went back into service during 1852, but not for long. In September she bashed against a rock near Cape Horn on the river bank and sank, leaving her upper works above water.

Sinking a steamboat was to become more or less a commonplace event on the Oregon rivers, and the *Flint* set the pattern. In January she was pumped out, patched, and taken cautiously down to Vancouver where the shipwrights went to work on her. What happened then again set a custom. Her hull and cabin were refurbished, but her engine had never been very much to brag about; on the other hand, the pioneer *Columbia's* hull and cabin had been unwieldy and shoddy, but her engine was all right, given a decent boat to move. So into the hull of the *Flint* went the engines of the *Columbia* and the result was the *Fashion*. It was a happy combination; the new boat ran to the Cowlitz River, to the Cascades, to any place her owner demanded, and did it without complaining until 1861 when, having reached a respectable age for a steamboat, she was robbed of her fittings and junked. What became of the old *Columbia's* engines then became anybody's guess. Perhaps they went to China— some engines did; perhaps they went into a sawmill, for a great many eventually found themselves sawing wood.

The *Flint* had been much too early, but it was a good try. Soon there would be need of steamboats above the Cascades and above the Dalles as well. Those were troublesome waters beyond Cascades; they would lead a few to fortune and others to real grief.

Chapter 3

TROUBLES AT CASCADES

ABOVE Vancouver the hills on either side of the Columbia begin to close in and grow taller and taller until the clear river is flowing through a slot in the mountains, a slot sawed by the running water. At one place the sawing is not finished, and there the river fights through broken rock and reefs and churns itself into angry froth. There, according to Indian legends that have been told, retold and improved, once existed a natural arch, the Bridge of the Gods, under which the Columbia tranquilly flowed; but the mountains fought like men, the bridge fell, and the river has since been tortured in its passing. Geologists tell a different story, to them as romantic and more satisfying. Boatmen, coming to the place, merely swore to relieve their feelings, because they had to climb out, tote everything around the cascades by a portage, reload and go on. It was a bad portage, too; the mountains closed in the river so tightly that hardly space for a footpath remained. Whoever controlled that portage controlled the upper river; it was strategic, militarily and economically, and both helped to make the Cascades an important place.

So far Indian wars in the Oregon Country had been remote, or at worst, informal scraps between belligerent tribes. When, in October 1854 a fight broke out at Oregon City the paper treated it casually:

[29]

On Tuesday last, quite an Indian warfare took place near the lower end of this city, between the Klamath and Clackamas tribes. Five were killed and several others wounded. But little attention was paid to their proceedings by the whites.

At the same time, down in the Rogue River Valley, the whites very definitely began to pay attention, because there the whites were quite intimately concerned—the Indians were after them. There the whites had been contemptuous of the natives and had killed them off as if they regarded the extermination of the Indian as the whole duty of man. In time the Indian began to take occasional pot shots at the whites in return, and the whites promptly yelled for military protection. General Wool, commander of the military district, investigated, sent in troops, and made unkind if uncomfortably accurate reports about the doings of the whites, and the shootings went on. By the next year, the fighting had broken out all through the Pacific Northwest from Puget Sound to the Klamath River and east to the Walla Walla country, and the whole region had a real Indian war on its hands.

Governor Curry of Oregon called for volunteers, eight companies of them; Governor Mason of Washington asked for two companies. The men gathered, signed the rolls, and marched off, heading for The Dalles, where the concentration of forces was being made. Then followed a two-way campaign: the Army and the Volunteers against the Indians, and the Army and the Territory of Oregon against each other. General Wool was adamant; Curry was equally adamant. The Army brass and the civilian butter-nut refused to agree on certain matters of who ought to belong to what. With deep suspicion the two groups set out to chase Indians, and considering their somewhat spectacular lack of co-operation, did a reasonably effective job. Whether the Volunteers were ethically sound in accepting the flag of truce offered by the Indian Peo-peo-mox-mox and then caging him as a prisoner and shooting him can still be debated; whether they should have cut off his ears and scalped the redundant Indian and then pickled the souvenirs in alcohol for the delectation and edification of the home folk was probably a matter of frontier taste. Anyway, Lieutenant George Derby, doing a job of surveying in Oregon at the time, got off some of his best witticisms at the expense of the Volunteers, referring to them as those heroes who, never peppered in battle, were mustered out. Lieutenant Derby did not, thereby, endear himself to the Oregonians.

Suddenly the Cascades roared into prominence. The steamer *James P. Flint* had been too soon on the upper river; now there was plenty of business for steamboats above the Cascades, carrying Army supplies for the troops taking part in the Indian war, carrying emigrants, carrying miners who were prowling after gold they had heard about at Colville, far up the Columbia. To handle the business, a group which had established itself at the upper end of the Cascades began work on a wooden tramway to replace an earlier hopeful venture built in 1851; then, at the mouth of Mill Creek where they had a sawmill for getting out timbers to use on the railroad, they put together a small side-wheeler they called *Mary,* and began running her from the landing to The Dalles. By July of 1855 a regular line was in operation, the *Belle* making three trips a week between Portland and Lower Cascades to connect with the portage road and the steamer *Mary* above the rapids. A month later, the *Wasco,* another small side-wheeler, started running above the Cascades connecting at the portage with the *Fashion.* Costs on them were high, the charge for freight between Portland and The Dalles being $30 per ton. And still they could not handle the business.

Orders had come to Fort Vancouver to transfer headquarters to The Dalles and so be closer to the seat of hostilities, and piles of army freight began to be dumped at the portage, waiting transit across it. A rather bad pack trail was hacked through the brush on the Oregon side of the river, and on the Washington side, the Bradfords, who owned the portage facilities, pushed their tramway slowly, mile by mile, from the upper to lower landing, about six miles. The Army, recognizing the importance of the place, built a blockhouse at the middle landing and garrisoned it with a squad under a sergeant; at Upper Cascades, where the Bradfords had a large store, warehouses, sawmill, and wharf, and where a group of settlers had built cabins, a small town grew in the cove at the mouth of Mill Creek, and to defend it, the Army sent thirty men commanded by a lieutenant. It would be best to prepare for any emergency.

When January of 1856 came, the snows fell and the cold winds swept howling through the gorge. Ice in the river tangled shipping, and soon the ice spread from bank to bank, far down the gorge and beyond the mouth of the Willamette. For three weeks, the river was locked, no vessels moving even from Astoria. But when the ice broke up, the *Fashion* and the *Belle* started again bringing load after load of supplies and army baggage to relieve the troops gathered at The Dalles. Ox-drawn wagons ground slowly through the mud from lower landing to the end of the railroad; there the goods were piled onto the small flat cars, a mule was hitched between thills, and the train rattled off to the upper landing. There the *Mary* waited at a flatboat moored by the bank and serving as a wharf. Three times a week, on Mondays, Wednesdays, and Fridays, she took on cargo, loaded wood, and made her way up to The Dalles. The *Wasco* was busy, too, often picking up loads from the pack mules that came up the Oregon portage path. So far, the Indians had caused no trouble, except in the far reaches, and Colonel Wright, commander at The Dalles, was preparing to march his troops east along the river to begin a spring campaign. In order to reinforce him, General Wool ordered the detachment at Upper Cascades removed, and on Monday, March 24, they boarded the *Mary* and went up to The Dalles, just in time to join Wright, who was ready to start his march on the 26th. The Cascades were left without guards except for the squad at the blockhouse.

When the detachment left, people at the Cascades wondered, and the *Oregonian,* at Portland, complained bitterly. As the *Oregonian* was certain to complain at anything the Army or the Democratic Territorial government did, that could be disregarded, but there were uncomfortable signs and portents. During the first week of March, the *Wasco* making a regular trip up to The Dalles was passing the mouth of Dog River when a band of Indians on the bank let out a whoop and without further ado sent a shower of bullets at the passing steamboat. Not being equipped to take part in naval activities and being no *Decatur* or *Massachusetts,* which took part in the Indian War on Puget Sound, the *Wasco* merely went away from there as fast as a tied-down safety valve and a busy fireman could make her. Promptly, Major Haller and a small force of troops came down the river by steamer and went beating about the brush after the Indians to round them up or at least to keep them from crossing to the Oregon side of the river. At about the same time, another steamer had a hail from the shore and put in to answer. At first, the captain could see no one, but finally he spotted a settler, roosting in a tree and wildly waving with one free arm. Indians, it seemed, had suddenly chased him from the cabin, and he had hidden in the tree to wait for help. If the Yakimas and Klickitats moved south toward the river, there would be real trouble, and apparently some of them were on the way. The Cascade Indians were tame and peaceful salmon eaters, but it would be good to keep an eye on them, too.

On Tuesday, March 25, the *Mary* and *Wasco* came down the river from The Dalles, running light, to pick up loads. The *Mary* tied up at the landing by Bradford's store and put ashore what cargo she had, while the *Wasco* crossed the river to pick up what might be waiting at the end of the pack trail. Work of loading the freight onto the waiting cars was easy, but the job of putting aboard all the stuff collected at Bradford's from below would take most of the next morning. Captain Baughman of the *Mary* had the fires in her boiler killed and tied up the boat for the night, leaving part of the crew aboard, letting others go ashore. It was just another routine trip. In the morning, he would load freight, take on wood, and run up the river; below, the *Belle* had left her freight and had started back to Vancouver.

The morning of Wednesday was bright, a nice spring day, and the little town of Cascades came to life early. Smoke curled up from the cabins, and at eight o'clock, the men were gaping and stretching, ready to begin the day's work. Slowly the crews set out for the bridge being built to connect the bank with a small island facing the settlement; other crews headed off down the portage railroad, herding the mule cars that carried timbers and tools. Captain Baughman with an aide was beyond the creek above the *Mary,* which was drowsing by the bank, her boilers cold, her wood racks empty. On board the boat, the negro cook cleared away the remains of breakfast and the steward's boy toted dishes. Beyond was the river, green from the reflected hillsides, and by the far bank was the *Wasco,* white against the dark shore.

Suddenly a bullet snapped, and from the brush came flame and shots. With a yell the Indians began closing in toward the settlement. A family, caught in its cabin, was shot down, scalped, dragged to the river and dumped in. Men at the sawmill had no warning, and at the shooting made a break for the store—all but one, and he was dead. Captain Baughman looked about him, sorted out his chances, and with his companion sprinted for the woods. Three members of the crew, running through cross-fire, got to the boat and sprang aboard, the Indians hard after them. On the boat, the crew grabbed whatever arms it could find, and sallied out. Buckminster, the engineer, had a revolver; the steward's helper, John Chance, grabbed an old dragoon pistol; the cook, Dick Turpin, crazed with fear, seized the only useful gun aboard, a rifle, and jumped into the flatboat alongside. But the Indians were at the gangplank, and already the fireman had been hit in the shoulder. In the flatboat, Turpin took a bullet, screamed, and leaped into the river, drowning and carrying the rifle with him. Johnny Chance scrambled to the hurricane deck, had a ball go through his leg, but succeeded in making a pot shot at an Indian trying to come on board and tumbled the enthusiastic native into the water. Below deck, when the Indians rolled back and turned their attention to Bradford's store, the crew got a fire going and just as soon as the pressure began to mount, Hardin Chenoweth, the pilot, made a run for it across the hurricane deck and into the pilot house. Promptly from the shore, the Indians peppered the place, but Chenoweth dropped flat on the floor and held the wheel. Quickly the lines were chopped free, and someone began valving the engine. Once the side wheels bit into the water, watchers shouted directions up to Chenoweth who, still on his back, turned the wheel and guided the boat into the stream. There was a chance that she would be caught in the current and swept into the rapids, but the wheels held and slowly she moved out of range.

Ashore, those at the store had watched the black smoke rise from the boat, but, cut off from sight of her by the trees and bank, they had thought the Indians were burning her. When she finally got into the stream, and Chenoweth dared to stand up, the people in Bradford's saw that there was a chance for help. Chenoweth yanked the whistle cord defiantly, and the hoarse yell of the big brass whistle jeered at the Indians. Still, chances were not good. The *Mary* had only fuel enough aboard to raise steam, and not enough to keep her moving very far. There were wounded aboard, too, who required attention. Chenoweth guided the boat in a wide turn and then angled her back to the bank around the bend above the settlement. There a deserted clearing seemed free of Indians, and he nosed the boat to a landing. Desperately hurrying, the men rushed for what wood they could find—rails from a handy snake fence—and toted them down to the bank and threw them onto the deck as rapidly as they could. Loading a boat is a slow job, and from beyond the bend they heard shots and saw the rising clouds of smoke as building after building at the settlement was set ablaze.

While the *Mary* was wooding up, the *Wasco*, caught also without steam, built her fires and began gathering settlers who crossed to her in canoes. By then it was noon or later, and the fighting still kept up at the store, now under close siege. At last, in early afternoon, the *Mary,* followed by the *Wasco,* headed toward The Dalles and help.

Downstream hell had broken loose at the same time as it did at the upper landing. Indians surrounded the blockhouse and began shooting; inside, Sergeant Kelly hauled out the cannon and let fly. The Indians were out of range, but it discouraged them with enough emphasis so that they took to the brush and gave time for a soldier or two and some settlers to take refuge within the fort. Farther down at the lower landing, men at work at the wharf boat heard the cannon and firing at Middle Cascades at about the same time that a friendly Indian brought word of the attack above. Hastily everyone rushed to the river, many of the settlers getting into small keel boats and catboats along the bank. The crews of the portage promptly built a barricade of freight on the wharf and prepared to defend it. Then they realized they had not a weapon among them. Soon the Indians arrived, shot wildly, but did not rush. All day long the men waited, and then at evening cast off the wharf boat and in company with the settlers' vessels floated quietly down the river toward Vancouver.

So the night came, with the Indians still close. At Bradford's store, any chance to escape in flatboats disappeared when the Indians set fire to a warehouse and lighted the landing. Then, to pass the time they would sneak to the brow of the hill and heave hot irons or blazing pitch knots onto the roof of the store, trying to burn out those within. The fires, the defenders found, could be put out by cutting holes in the roof and splashing the burning shingles with pickle brine from a barrel in the store's stock. By morning, they hoped, the *Mary* would be back with help, unless Colonel Wright had moved beyond Celilo. Reassuringly through the day and night came the ponderous boom from the blockhouse's cannon; at least the Indians had not taken it.

Word of the attack travelled slowly. A friendly Indian messenger paddled down the river in a canoe and by early evening was at Fort Vancouver with the bare outline of the attack. That was enough for Lieutenant Philip Sheridan to call up his company of dragoons and prepare them to move. From Vancouver to Portland the word travelled faster, and late in the evening of March 26, the same day as the attack, Portland broke out in a sweat of apprehension, and a public meeting to discuss ways and means promptly went into session. Quickly a company of volunteers formed, but, on demand, was refused Territorial equipment. Without arms, the company was useless, but it scurried around town and dug up twenty rifles. Twenty men to use them were selected, yet it was not until the morning of the 28th that the Portland volunteers boarded the *Fashion* and headed for the Cascades. They would arrive too late for a fight, but not as late as it would seem.

Sheridan and his dragoons, together with a handful of volunteers, started upstream early in the morning of the 27th aboard the *Belle*. Midway the boat met the sad flotilla of refugees who brought the Lieutenant the story of the previous day. Itchy for a fight, the men on the wharf boat volunteered to return with Sheridan, who swore them in as troops, and the *Belle* went on up the river.

What, in the meantime had happened at The Dalles? The *Mary* and *Wasco* came in late on the evening of the 26th to hear that Colonel Wright's forces had marched out of the post that day. Promptly a courier set out in pursuit and came on the troops camped at Five Mile Creek. Wright's men had not broken the march until late, and rather than have them pick their way back in the dark, he held them in camp until just before dawn when the force turned back to The Dalles. Once there, Wright loaded his troops onto the *Mary* and the *Wasco* until their guards skimmed the water. For the baggage, and for horses to mount a platoon of dragoons intended to pursue stray Indians, Wright commandeered a flatboat, put aboard his impedimenta (and the word suddenly took on a vivid meaning), ran a line to the *Wasco,* and the fleet got under way down river. He did not make fast time. First, the towed flatboat was hard to manage, and the *Wasco* had hardly enough power, even helped by the current, to stay ahead of the barge and keep it headed in the right direction. And second, a new fireman on the *Mary* kept having trouble by clogging flues and deadening his fire, so that by the night of the 27th, Wright's forces had covered less than half the fifty-two miles to the Cascades when the *Wasco* and *Mary* had to tie up at the bank. Boats did not try night running yet, not with belligerent Indians lurking along the shore.

The *Belle,* with Sheridan, had better luck and reached the lower Cascades by afternoon, where the dragoons went ashore to find everything destroyed by the Indians. Cautiously Sheridan advanced, but meeting ambushed hostiles, he fell back toward the landing, his retreat covered by a light cannon on the *Belle* which stood by. He

The *Harvest Queen* tied up, handy to the Umatilla House
and Columbia Hotel at The Dalles.

To keep from setting afire the
fields by the riverbanks, some
wood-burners had spark arresters
on their stacks.

Below. Deck hands, cook, and
pilot help the *City of Salem* pose
for its picture.

The Cascades Railroad with its engines lined up for display.

The *Mary Moody* takes aboard a pack train on the shore
of Lake Pend Oreille.

Rough water on the Columbia near Wenatchee.

arranged his defences for the night, and the steamboat dropped down the river for more ammunition to bring up to the troops. That night, the second for the besieged at Bradford's, passed the way the night before had passed: the Indians burning buildings to keep the whites from reaching the river either for escape or water.

Morning broke the siege. Sheridan crossed his men to the Oregon bank, reconnoitered, and recrossed toward Middle Cascades, where the Yakimas were feasting on stolen beef. The *Belle,* he knew would return shortly. At Bradford's, too, the morning was still early when the *Mary* and *Wasco* came in sight, puffing and panting, their guards lined with blue uniformed troops spoiling for a fight. Hardly had the two boats closed to the bank before Colonel Wright's dragoons were ashore and running, and Colonel Steptoe's men forming to march down the river.

There was no battle. At the sight of the troops, the Indians promptly went away from there and disappeared into the hills, leaving the store free. Steptoe's men began moving cautiously down toward the blockhouse, not knowing what to expect. Below, Sheridan, having no word of what was happening at the upper settlement, moved toward the hostile camp. Close to the shore was an island onto which the friendly Cascades Indians had adjourned at the first shot, keeping well away from the trouble, but as they had been crossing and recrossing the river freely and becoming mixed with the Yakimas—and who could tell a Yakima or a Klickitat from a Cascade in a fuss?—Sheridan was not sure about them. On one bank he had the Cascades; on the other were probably a hundred Yakimas, hunkered down over fires and stuffing themselves with chunks of meat. Sheridan shoved the bateau into the chute and prayed, his men at ready. Then, to his delight, he saw, coming down the river, Steptoe's command. With Steptoe behind them and Sheridan in front, the hostiles were cut off and could be captured or destroyed at will. Sheridan made ready for the kill.

Poor Steptoe! Later he would lose a whole command in the Inland Empire by bad luck and bad management, and here his troubles started. Suddenly, from his command, into the clear morning air rose the brassy blare of a bugle. Now, when silence and surprise were worth forty dollars an ounce, Steptoe followed the military handbook and sounded calls for commands. The troops heard it and obeyed; the Indians, being sensitive about noises, also heard it. When Steptoe came up to Sheridan, not an Indian remained—except for an old crippled, tame one who had not tried to get away in the first place. Sheridan's chance was gone, but so were the Indians, and if he had not distinguished himself, he had at least done his job competently. So, ironically, had Steptoe. The Cascades were clear of Indians. The Columbia ran once more unvexed to the sea.

Now, while the casualties were being counted and tended, and the damage assessed, an oversupply of help began to pour in. To Lower Cascades returned the *Belle* with more men and ammunition, and close behind her came the panting *Fashion* with the Portland volunteers. They were too late for the fight, but they were willing, and they piled ashore and went into camp. By the next day, still another volunteer company arrived in the *Jennie Clark,* to be received by jeers from the hardened veterans of the *Fashion's* company. So the *Jennie Clark* turned around and took them home. Portland would have need of them, because Portland that day, had held a second public meeting, a noisy one, to plan for the defence of the town. Where might the Indians be? Perhaps across the Willamette. Or in the hills behind the place? Who could know? Portland would go down fighting. The brave would sign as volunteers.

In the morning, the *Oregonian* would appear with all the news, including a last minute flash that the *Jennie Clark* had returned with the volunteers. Somehow, the defence of Portland seemed, now, on the 29th to be a kind of embarrassing memory. Quietly everyone set about forgetting.

At the Cascades, they would not forget. There, eleven civilians and three soldiers were dead, and two more were mortally wounded. Twelve others had wounds, too, and all around was desolation: cabins burned, warehouses burned, freight burned. The Indians had vanished, however, not to return, and the *Belle* and *Fashion* began again their trips to lower landing; the *Mary* and *Wasco* picked up the freight at Upper Cascades; the mule railroad clattered along. And there was still the river, battering its way through the reefs and rocks. But there would be shortly a new, large blockhouse on the bluff above the landing, and there would be some troops as long as the war went on in the Oregon Country.

Chapter 4

O. S. N.

ONCE the Indian troubles were over, business picked up on the Columbia. More steamboats came to the river, too many, to tell the truth, and although their rates were high, they still were sharply competing. Now Captain Ainsworth stepped in and by 1860 he had worked out a series of agreements to form a kind of monopoly calling itself the Union Transportation Line. From Portland to the Cascades the steamers *Carrie Ladd* and *Mountain Buck* ran three times a week, connecting at Bradford's portage railway with Capt. Baughman's steamer *Hassaloe* for The Dalles. An independent group ran the *Independence* on three other days to connect with the *Wasco,* but the arrangement lasted only a month or two. Freight from Portland to The Dalles travelled at $20 a ton; passengers paid $6 apiece, the same rate charged for horses and cattle. Above The Dalles, the traveller paid plenty for the privilege of having himself and his plunder hauled by wagon over Humason's portage road to the landing where he could go aboard one of the bateaux run by L. W. Coe and R. R. Thompson. Their accommodations were not elegant, for actually they were rough barges shoved along by square sails when the wind was right, but they charged $100 a ton for freight to Fort Walla Walla. Business was good at the price, and the owners soon built a small stern-wheeler, the *Colonel Wright,* above Celilo and cut the freight rate to a mere $80 a ton— or an even hundred from Portland. There were on the middle and lower Columbia other boats: the *Mary* and *Belle,* and the *Fashion,* and the stern-wheeler *Julia,* and above Celilo Thompson was at work on a new boat, the *Tenino,* for the upper river.

The Union Transportation Line could not last. The agreement was too loose, and the steamboatmen were at the mercy, usually not tender, of the owners of the portage. Following the old steamboat-men's principle that if you can't lick 'em, join 'em, the men of the Union Transportation Line did just that, and in 1860 they incorporated in Washington Territory (State laws in Oregon made it at the moment impossible) a new organization, the famous, debated, and very powerful Oregon Steam Navigation Company. The name is reminiscent of the California Steam Navigation Company, the outfit that had been running steamboats high, wide, handsome, and profitably, on the Sacramento in California. Moreover, Ainsworth's good friend, Ralston, was involved in the California concern and may have given the hint. Whatever the source, the idea flourished in the Oregon climate. Among the incorporators of 1860 (and the re-incorporators of 1862 in Oregon) some were to emerge as dominant figures in the company and in Pacific Northwest steamboating: men like Ainsworth, Thompson, and Coe, and S. G. Reed, Thomas Myrick, and Jacob Kamm. Into the single company went a pool of a dozen steamboats: on the lower river below the Cascades were the old *Fashion,* the *Senorita,* the *Mountain Buck,* the *Julia,* the *Belle,* and the *Carrie Ladd;* above the Cascades on the middle river were the *Mary,* the *Wasco,* the *Hassaloe,* and the *Idaho,* while above Celilo on the upper river were the pioneer *Colonel Wright* and the *Tenino.* And it included within company control both Bradford's and Ruckle's portage roads at the Cascades and Humason's at The Dalles. As soon as the organization was completed, the Company announced itself ready for business. The *Julia,* soon to be converted to a cattle boat, and the *Carrie Ladd* did the work on the lower river, connecting with the new side-wheeler *Idaho* at Cascades, and then with the *Colonel Wright* above Celilo for Fort Walla Walla and Priest Rapids. A new steamer between Priest Rapids and the Okanogan and Kettle Falls was promised also to attract business for that district. Freight and passenger charges changed both up and down, the fare to The Dalles becoming $8, but freight to Fort

Walla Walla, or Wallula as it came to be known, dropping first to $75 a ton and finally to $42.

The Oregon Steam Navigation Company started out to give good service, and it did, always; its white boats were known for their speed, good accommodations, and regularity. At the beginning, most of the fleet was nondescript with the exception of the *Carrie Ladd* and she set the pattern for later boats to follow. A stern-wheeler, she had a freight deck and cabin, a single tall stack centered, and a pilot house; inside, her cabins opened onto a parlor that could be used as a dining room. At one end, forward, was a "Ladies' Saloon," to which the delicate might retire to be away from tobacco and general male contamination. Boats became longer, and broader, and grander and faster, but they still turned back to the *Carrie Ladd* for their design.

Hardly had the O.S.N. (for by its initials it was known) been organized before a windfall dropped into its corporate lap. There was gold in Idaho, plenty of it, and the best way to get to it was by way of the Columbia River. Moreover, for those hardy travellers who had to reach the East, the fastest route was by boat to Wallula or Umatilla, by stage to Utah and there to connect with the Overland stages east. Freight, all kinds of it, crowded the docks and wharf boats, and passengers swarmed aboard. Times were good. Money was plentiful. And the rates were high. By 1862, the O.S.N. had boats running up the Snake River to Lewiston and was charging $120 a ton from Portland. Occasionally there would be a flurry of competition. At times like that, the O.S.N. merely cut its rates until it froze out the opposition. When the Merchants' Line entered the river, the O.S.N. promptly dropped the rate to $12 a ton to The Dalles, and the fare to $4, with a dollar extra for meals, and when the rival kept up the struggle the freight rate fell as low as $5 a ton. Then, as soon as the Merchants' Line had retired, the Company hiked its rate to $25 a ton. Soon the People's Transportation entered, and the rate went down to $10, with the rate to Wallula a mere $15. The People's Transportation Company recognized the inevitable, and agreed to stay on the Willamette, leaving the Columbia to the O.S.N.

Yet the O.S.N. did not always depend on competition to lower rates, and passed on lowered costs of operation to the customers. Nor were the rates particularly outrageous for either the times or the conditions; the Civil War was forcing a paper inflation, and travel conditions through the Inland Empire were difficult and expensive. A shipper might pay his own fare of $18 from Portland to Wallula, a distance of 240 miles by river, and carry with him a ton of goods, on which he paid $90; but if he went on to Walla Walla, 30 miles inland from the river, he paid $5 more for a ride in a slow stage coach, and $20 more for his freight. The interruptions in the river caused many necessary handlings of the freight, too; first, manufactured goods might come cheaply to Portland by sailing vessel around the Horn, but at Portland they were unloaded onto a dock, moved to the steamboat dock, and loaded on the first steamboat. Unloaded to the railroad at the Cascades, they were carried to the upper landing, reloaded onto a second steamboat, unloaded at The Dalles, freighted by wagon to Celilo, loaded again to a third steamboat, unloaded at Wallula, loaded onto freight wagons, hauled to Walla Walla and finally unloaded for the consignee. All that took time and labor.

The O.S.N., following the usual procedures of shipping companies, charged by the measured and not weighed ton. That is, forty cubic feet of freight regardless of the weight of the material constituted a ton for shipping costs. A good many legends persist about the quaint ways of measuring freight—the cubic content of a farm wagon was taken by measuring its extreme breadth, its extreme length with tongue extended, and its extreme height with tongue turned upward, and then it was rolled aboard with the tongue beneath the wagon box. It is a picturesque story, but probably a product of folklore. Still, the O.S.N. did charge high prices and did make a profit.

On the other hand, the Company gave good service. Ainsworth looked out for the interests not only of his stockholders but of his employees and his shippers. A purser, for example, received $150 a month, a high salary at the time, and had to make a good many decisions about policy and practices on the spot. No passenger was denied travel if he honestly was unable to pay for a necessary journey; and no shipper, particularly a settler, was refused his freight if he could not meet his bill. Ainsworth would wait; in addition to the good will built up for the company, the country would be aided in its development. A good many of the ideas of Jim Hill, the builder of the railroad empire, about developing a region so that it would provide business, were hardly new; Captain J. C. Ainsworth had been following the system since he assumed control of the O.S.N.

As long as the Idaho boom lasted, the Company had trouble providing enough boats to carry the traffic. In 1861, the first full year of operations, it carried 10,500 passengers between Portland and The Dalles, and 6,290 tons of freight; but in 1864, when the gold rush was at its height, 36,000 rode the boats to The Dalles, and 21,834 tons of freight moved. Profits were good, running from $591,838 in 1862 to $783,339 in 1864. To keep up with the business, new boats were built and large ones purchased. By 1866, the *New World, Cascade,* and *Wilson G. Hunt* were making daily runs to Cascades from Portland, and beyond there the *Idaho* and *Oneonta* continued on the short run to The Dalles. From Celilo a daily boat went to Wallula, and others continued up to White Bluffs, Palouse, and Lewiston as the traffic demanded. On the upper river, the *Yakima, Webfoot, Tenino, Nez Perce Chief, Spray,* and *Okanagon* did the work, and from Olds Ferry on the upper Snake the *Shoshone* carried miners toward the Boise diggings. In addition to these, the passenger and freight boats, the old *Julia* and the *Iris* carried cattle from lower river points to The Dalles. Also, on the lower river, the passenger boat *John H. Couch* made two runs a week between Portland and Astoria, and the *Rescue* three runs to Monticello, near the mouth of the Cowlitz River, where the stage line to Puget Sound ports connected.

The boats were good, but the passengers had to get up early to ride them. Those heading up the Columbia from Portland loaded all night; lines of drays strung out along Front Street for blocks waiting their turn to drive out on the big two-level company dock at Ash Street. By 4:30 in the morning the passengers began to arrive, and at a little before 5:00 the last freight was stowed, and the pilot climbed into the pilot house. The wheel was lazily turning, but now black smoke began to roll from the tall stack. Late passengers rushed up the landing stage, and the lines were cast off. The big wheel threshed the water, moving the prow of the boat away from the dock, and a pillar of steam shot from the tall escape pipe. Then with a flurry of white foam the long white vessel turned into the current, pointed downstream and slipped past the town. It was five o'clock in the morning. One hour later the downstream boat for Kalama and Astoria would pull away, and then the dock would be quiet until eleven, when the boat from the Cascades came in.

Usually passengers took breakfast from tables in the main saloon, and paid for the privilege, at first two bits, but later the price went up. Then, after the boat ran out of the Willamette into the Columbia and touched at the landing at Vancouver, they would begin to gather on deck, for already the spectacular scenery of the gorge had become widely advertised. Slowly the fir-covered hills moved higher and closer to the river, and tall basalt outcrops and columns rose like flanking portals with many falls veiling down the face of the rocks. By then the sun was out, and the ladies strolled the deck while the gentlemen retreated to the bar. The O.S.N. usually was engaged in a company battle about the bars; at first, Captain Ainsworth had been dead set against them, but after a few months the bars were installed and rented out, at a good stiff price, to concessionaires whose barkeepers also ranked the honorary title of "Captain."

At eleven o'clock the boat docked at Lower Cascades, where a train of the portage railway waited, and the passengers went ashore. There was no need to hurry; all the fast freight had to be trundled by handcart out onto the wharf boat and into the stubby freight cars, and the job usually took an hour. If there was a great deal of freight, that which did not have prepaid premium simply waited for another boat, usually a smaller one that worked only in the freight run. Then the small locomotive whistled and the train moved up the line, the passengers housed in elegant, light colored coaches.

At Upper Cascades, everything had to be unloaded from the train and put into the second boat, and the passengers had another wait. Some spent it looking at the churning rapids and the scenery; some took lunch at the hotel that stood by the landing. Some idly visited the blockhouse built after the attack of 1856. And some, no doubt, of the gentlemen went aboard the second boat to seek solace forward at another bar. Whatever they did, they had an hour or two to kill before the journey was resumed. By the time everything was ready, it was early afternoon, and it would be evening before the boat pulled up to the landing at The Dalles. The town was on a bench above the river, the large shops of the O.S.N. dominating the foreground along with the incline of the portage railway. Then rose the wooden business blocks and the town below the bluff. But the passengers by then had been sated by scenery and were anxious to get ashore and find a place to spend the night.

They had a choice: the Cosmopolitan Hotel or the Umatilla House, the former being somewhat smaller and less gaudy, but still popular, having seventy-five rooms together with such touches of luxury as a billiard room and a ladies' parlor, with piano. The

Umatilla House was said to be the best outside of Portland, in spite of its notoriously friendly fleas and occasionally chummy bedbugs and lice. Its fittings were elegant—the only word that seemed to be appropriate to describe them. When the passenger entered the lobby he was confronted by "the handsomest counter and most elegant key-rack in the state," and there he signed the register. Of course, he would get no single room—if he were lucky he only shared the room with three strangers; if he were unlucky, he tried the Cosmopolitan, and if misfortune still dogged him, he would try some small flea-trap down the street. But he hoped for the Umatilla, which had 123 rooms and a couple of baths, with a lavatory in the basement. Its dining room was large, and a corps of cooks and waiters could serve the mobs of patrons that moved through the hotel every day.

Yet the passenger had to take much of this luxury on faith. He had to be up early in the morning; passengers leaving downriver were called at four, and that woke up the others who left on the train that stood in front of the hotel. It would pull out at about five and, if the wind had not blown sand across the tracks, would be at Celilo, above the Tumwater Falls, in about an hour and a half. There he finally boarded an upriver boat that would get him to Umatilla by afternoon and to Wallula a couple of hours later. At Umatilla he could take the stage for Boise, for Salt Lake, for the East. At Wallula he would stay over night at a second hotel, an hostlery that by comparison gave the Umatilla House much of its reputation for luxury. After a night at Wallula, a traveller would believe any other place was luxurious. In the morning he would ride Baker's narrow gauge railway to Walla Walla.

If the hotels were not perfect by all standards, the O.S.N. prided itself on its fine vessels and established a tradition that Columbia boats would be fast, safe, comfortable, even luxurious. Altogether, the Company during its life owned about seventy steamers, most of them small and sometimes inconsequential, but among them were some real floating palaces, as the favorite description put it.

In the beginnings, the boats were not particularly fine. The *Fashion*, for instance, was a kind of hand-me-down. After having been in the Cascades affair of 1856, she rammed herself onto a reef that later bore her name, and sank, but she was raised, pumped out, patched, and lasted until 1861 when she was robbed of her engine and allowed to rot. The *Senorita* was another patchwork, a reincarnation of *Gazelle*. Probably the best of the early boats was the stern-wheeler *Carrie Ladd,* built by Ainsworth and Jacob Kamm in 1858. For one thing, she looked like a steamboat, although her hurricane and texas cabins were curiously combined under one roof. When her engines got down to their job, she could travel, running from Portland to Vancouver in an hour and a half and on up to the Cascades in five hours and forty minutes. On her way back, she did the whole trip in four and a half hours. The *Carrie* was fairly small, only 126 feet long, but her engines had cylinders 16 inches in diameter and 66 inches in stroke.

The Company's first fine boat was the *Oneonta,* built at the Cascades in 1863 for the run to The Dalles. She was built in close approximation of the Mississippi River type, with two tall stacks forward, pilot house behind them and side wheels set well back from center. Her housed-in freight deck extended over the guards as did her cabin deck which stretched from stem to stern. And she was big for her day, 182 feet long. She had outside escape for exhaust steam and made a noise that any good steamboat should, so that her chuffing set up echoes in the gorge. But she was expensive to operate, and though a fine boat to look at and a comfortable one to ride, she made so little money that in 1870 Captain Ainsworth himself mounted to her pilot house and steered her through the roiling Cascades to use her on the more heavily travelled run to Portland. Finally, in 1877, the O.S.N. gave up and made her into a barge. *Sic transit gloria mundi.*

Sometimes the Company picked up boats where they could find them, boats like the *Wilson G. Hunt* and the *New World,* each of which reached the Columbia the long way around, by the Cape and California. The *New World* by the time she arrived at Portland had settled down to a sedate middle age, but she had had her moments. A side-wheeler, she was 220 feet long, driven by a walking-beam engine, familiar enough on some later boats, but never common on the Columbia. She was a staunch, fast boat, and she had to be, because probably no other vessel on the coast had got under way with such a burst of dramatic fireworks as she did. First, she had set a precedent by having been launched ready for sailing. But she had not sailed, for her owner was in financial trouble, and the *New World* was tied up to a New York pier, with sheriff's officers aboard while the captain, Edgar Wakeman, became unusually amiable. That should have given them a hint. Captain Wakeman had a fine, explosive temper, and a sign that the fuse was burning was obsequi-ousness. Normally Captain Wakeman didn't give a damn for any-body, and when he let on that he did, then it was best to go ashore. The officers thought nothing of it when, just before dinner Captain Wakeman asked whether it would be all right if he had the engines turned over slowly, just to keep them lubricated and in shape. Go ahead, the officers told him.

It was odd that the sheriff's men failed to notice that the vibra-tions from the engines increased and that the slap of the tide gave way to a slow steady roll, but when they came on deck, they saw New York dead astern and a whole lot of water between them and it.

Captain Wakeman rose to the occasion, as he could always rise to the occasion. They objected, did they? If they did not like it, there was a dinghy and they could row ashore. They did. Captain Wake-man was off to the land of gold, to the banks of the Sacramento, and no cussed pair of shyster's heelers could tell him what to do. Maybe he did not have full bunkers of coal. Maybe he lacked clearance papers. Maybe he would have a hard time explaining who he was, what he was doing, and where he was going, and maybe, too, any prowling cruiser could bring him in as lawful prize. So what?

He made it, though there were some tight squeezes at Pernam-buco, at Rio de Janeiro (a British frigate chased him into that port), and at Panama where by popular demand, literally, he staved off seizure, and brought two hundred and fifty gold seekers into San Francisco, getting there at the height of the rush in the summer of 1850. Then Ned Wakeman went on to other seas, collecting adven-tures and stories that he later wrote up in a book and that Mark Twain heard him tell. According to one of Ned's stories, in a dream he visited heaven. It must have been a dream; he would probably not have made it otherwise.

At San Francisco the *New World* entered the Sacramento River run for the California Steam Navigation Company and kept at it until the O.S.N. got her and put her to work on the Columbia in 1864. From the Cascades on one trip she carried a ton of gold, and made the round trip between Portland and Cascades in six hours and fifty-seven minutes, which was good, fast time for any steamboat and particularly one that had been around as much as she had.

Her companion on the run was another East Coast boat, the *Wilson G. Hunt*. Built also in 1849 at New York, she had been des-tined to carry excursionists to the fashionable seaside resort, then developing, at Coney Island, but the gold fever caught her, and she, too, came to the Pacific Coast during the rush. After serving time on the Sacramento, she went to Puget Sound waters in 1858 to run between Victoria and New Westminster, carrying miners heading up the Fraser River. Then in 1862 the O.S.N. bought her for the Cascades run to help meet the rush of business for the Idaho mines. Sometimes she carried as many as 300 passengers, a hundred head of stock, and freight cargo besides. For seven years she worked the route. The *Wilson G. Hunt* was a side-wheeler, too, with a pilot house on the cabin deck, separate from the cabin, but her oddity was her engine—steeple type. Between the wheels and rising high above the cabin was a tall steeple-like frame in which the piston rod rose and fell in guides and moved a pair of connecting rods or pitmans that turned the wheel. Such engines had been common on the Hudson but were becoming rare when the *Hunt* was built. Normally left exposed, on the *Hunt* the engine was housed, so that the boat seemed to be carrying a tall wooden wedge amidships, thereby not improving the appearance of an otherwise graceful steamer.

But the prizes of the O.S.N. fleet came later. The pride of the Company was the *Wide West,* built in Portland in 1877 and intended to be the very last word in steamboat excellence and elegance for passengers between Portland and the Cascades; above there, the *R. R. Thompson,* built at the same time as a near-sister, would take them in almost equal grandeur to The Dalles. The *Wide West* represented the very latest refinements in steamboat design, and John Gates, who was the consulting engineer for all of the O.S.N. operations, had a right to be proud of her. She measured 236 feet from the stem to the waterfall, or housing, of her stern wheel. Her hull, practically unsinkable, was divided into eighty water-tight compartments, and was braced and cross-braced with heavy timbers. It had to be; she was intended to carry 550 tons on her cargo deck, besides all her superstructure and passenger load, without having her guards awash.

Fortunately for Columbia steamboats, the problem of boiler-flushing was minor; Columbia water carried practically no silt or sediment and boilers required only a weekly washing. The *Wide West* had a single, sectional boiler that supplied steam for her two horizontal high-pressure engines, each with a cylinder 28 inches in diameter and 96 inches in stroke, and built at Wilmington, Delaware, especially for her. They could drive her through the water, fully loaded, as fast as any other boat on the river, and were later, placed in another hull, to make the *T. J. Potter* break all records.

In addition to the main engines, a whole series of minor ones did various chores; a donkey pump played water on the cinder pit to douse sparks (that cut down the amount of trash the chimneys dropped on the white upper works and saved painting); another pump supplied water for the lavatories; still others worked the hydraulic steering gear.

Above the engine room and freight house on the boiler deck, real grandeur set in. There was the main cabin with offices for the purser and freight clerk, and a number of small "bachelor cabins." All opened into a central hall, done tastefully "in a delicate tint of lilac, and the floors . . . covered with mosaic oil cloth." Here, too, was the dining room, filled with small tables for four, and opening from it twenty-two cabins, each fitted not with bunks but with bedsteads, with a single berth above, commodious and comfortable, which, in the delighted words of a local editor, "contrast favorably with the cramped up little dens called staterooms on eastern steamboats." Forward was the ladies' saloon, done in pale lemon, with gold beading on the door, and carpeted with Brussels.

It smelled nice, too, for the lavatories, provided in both the main saloon and the ladies' cabin, had constant jets of water playing in the facilities while the boat was in motion, "so that no offensive effluvia taints these sumptuous cabins,"—the editor's words again. The long main saloon was lighted by day from panes in a clerestory that extended its length and formed its ceiling; some panes were clear, others tinted, so that the sunlight threw bars of colors on the woodwork and carpets. At night, stewards lit fancy nickel lamps that hung from a rod down the middle of the saloon. Above, on the hurricane deck or roof was a long texas, with staterooms for the officers, and the pilot house rising above it where the tall wheel was operated both by hydraulic gear and, when necessary, steel tiller rope controls. Her decks were neatly railed, with cornices of geegawed scrollwork. The *Wide West* brought luxury and Eastlake architecture to the Columbia. For ten years she plied the river, and then, metamorphosed, she emerged as the *T. J. Potter.*

When the *Wide West* took to the river, new times were in the air. Ben Holladay, who had made his fortune by selling out the Overland Stage at the proper moment, had gone into steamship operations and railroading on the Pacific Coast and already was in control of

the Willamette River boats. Soon he would be supplanted by Henry
Villard, the German journalist who had such a knack for high
finance that he was able to build the Northern Pacific. Ainsworth
and the other owners of the O.S.N. read the future; they could build
their own railroad, or they could sell out to Villard. They sold out
to Villard who promptly organized the Oregon Railway and Navigation Company. Villard had great plans, saw visions, made vast
decisions; sometimes he lost, but usually he won. For a time at least,
he won steadily. Part of his winnings was a railroad that paralleled
the Columbia from the Snake to Portland, and the railroad ended
the great day of steamboating on the upper river. The O.S.N. had
served its purpose; it had done its job well, if a bit expensively, and,
it must be admitted, profitably. Yet long after it had gone, those who
cursed the memory of its monopoly reminisced of the white boats
that rode the river, the meals in the dining room, the feel of the
wind that made the hurricane deck well named, the surge and thrust
of the wheel, the hoarse whistles at the landings.

Chapter 5

BEAUTIFUL WILLAMETTE

STANDING at a point where he commanded the reach of the river at Albany, Sam Simpson caught the mood and infinite variety of the Willamette for his poem. It is a river that crowds into its length the spirit and strength of many streams, combines them into its own, yet retains a little of each. At a cold, winter dawn it is a gray river, reaching slowly out to join the Columbia. In early sunlight at Portland it is bluish and glassy, with its banks lined by wharves and vessels that take on unreal, brittle colors of the morning. When the sun comes above the basalt cliffs at the Falls, the water is white, a living force rimming the U-shaped pool below. It is brightly green, reflecting the banks up beyond Rock Island, and as it turns up the reach toward Wilsonville it is calm and quiet, tame and gentle. In the high noon it is lazy as it twists and bends through the flatlands of the valley, the edges of its oxbows fringed with brush and trees, the banks low, the water pale in the shallows. At late afternoon it is somnolent and darkening under the high banks at Albany and Peoria. It reflects the sunset as it glides west past Eugene, and above, as evening comes, the water whitens at the forks where the mountain cold rushes down. And at night, divided into small, hurrying channels, it is silver, flecked with tinsel, and the covered bridges that span it are calm and white in the moonlight. From the mountains to its mouth it is many rivers, many in one.

On either side is the valley, now wide and flat, now narrowed by hills, but always tamed by farms and busy with towns. It is a valley for people to enjoy, a valley of lush crops where there hardly seems need to hurry. Only the weeds hasten, and the river. And the river was the highway, on which boats could travel rapidly downstream, and slowly upstream, over the bars and reefs, shallows and rapids. Steamboats came early to the Willamette, for on its banks were crops to be moved and along its length goods to be carried. The pioneer *Hoosier,* sloshing along with its pile driver engine working frantically, broke the stillness of the stream in more ways than one. When her successor of the same name got under way, her engine was as busy as a cheap clock with the balance broken; she could be heard for miles, her rods clanking, and her gears, through which the power wandered uncertainly, grinding protestingly. Ordinarily the first hint of a coming steamboat was a cloud of smoke beyond a bend and a faint mourn from her whistle and then the rhythmic whoosh of the escape pipes and wheel—but not the *Hoosier*. A farmer hearing the racket could drive his team to the barn, hitch up the wagon, and trundle casually down to the landing in serene confidence that he would be there before the steamboat made it.

The *Hoosier* brought to the river a spirit of informality that continued. The *Canemah* was the mail boat, and on her the first postmaster for the Territory set up his office where he leisurely sorted the mail and distributed it while the steamboat went up and down the river. It was convenient but now and then embarrassing to its captain, especially when he was in a hurry. On one trip Captain Cole had as passenger Governor Joseph Lane, on his way to the capital at Salem. The *Canemah,* forced to wait at Canemah for the boat up from Portland, tried to make up time and was furiously belaboring the river, her wheel setting up a strong wave that lashed the banks. Suddenly from the shore came a hail—a woman waving wildly at the steamer. Ordinarily, with the Governor aboard, Captain Cole would stop for nothing short of a delegate to the Legislature, but his gallantry got the best of him and he ordered the pilot to make the landing. On the bank the woman held out a letter— would the Captain take it to Salem for her? The mate, wrathy, started to haul in the plank. "Mate," ordered Captain Cole with studied calm, "take the lady's letter."

"Thank you, Captain," the unabashed lady shouted. "I know you are a gentleman." Cole swept off his hat, bowed, and felt his ears turn red at the laugh that came from the passengers, but Lane saved him. It was the most gallant act he had ever witnessed, Lane said, saluting Cole. But it was a good thing that a lady had stopped the boat; had it been a man, Captain Cole would have swarmed ashore and lit into him like a whirlwind on a haystack.

The *Canemah* had all the troubles steamboats were heir to, but her greatest was fuel. Though she drew only 17 inches loaded and

WILLAMETTE RIVER

"could run anywhere it was damp," according to her owners, she had to hug the bank if she lacked cordwood for the furnaces. Steamboatmen paid five dollars a cord but farmers along the bank remained uninterested, and during the first years of steamboating only a few wood yards were established. A steamer might start hopefully on a run, trusting to find a farmer willing to sell wood. If it did, the Captain dickered and the crew loaded; if it did not, the boat turned back, used steam as sparingly as it could, and took advantage of the current. Or a boat could start a run with enough cordwood aboard to last the trip.

Soon the Willamette was busy with four or five steamboats on the run between Portland and Oregon City and about the same number running to Dayton, Salem, Albany, and Marysville. Steamboatmen recognized that some order had to be brought to their operations, that free-and-easy competition had to stop. There were two short-lived companies started in 1853: the People's Line operating the *Multnomah* and *Portland* between Oregon City and Portland, and the Defiance Line which ran a daily boat, the *Wallamet, Canemah,* or *Fenix,* from Canemah to upper river points. This company had a carriage which hauled passengers the mile or two around the Falls between Oregon City and Canemah, where it met the boats. Again it was the *Canemah* that led when in 1854 she became part of the Citizen's Accommodation Line in company with the *Franklin*. The new line ran the *Canemah* twice a week to Corvallis (the new name for Marysville) and the *Franklin* three times a week with local freight for Salem and intermediate landings. Fares and freight charges settled to predictable rates, subject only to price cutting when a rival competed. Freight went by steamer from Portland to Oregon City for $3 a ton; from Canemah the rate was $10 a ton to Champoeg, $16 to Salem, $20 to Albany, and $24 to Corvallis. Beyond there the shipper was on his own, at the mercy of flatboatmen and drivers of ox-drawn freight wagons. Passengers paid $1 to ride from Canemah to Champoeg, $2 to Salem, $5 to Corvallis. Meals were extra at a dollar apiece, but berths were thrown in by the company.

Most of the traffic on the river was between Portland and Oregon City where various routes fanned out to settlements beyond. Head of river navigation remained at Corvallis, for most steamboatmen believed that the river above was too shallow for steamboats, and of course Corvallis merchants and freighters were in enthusiastic agreement. What traders and farmers at places like Peoria, Harrisburg and Eugene thought could not be politely expressed, and they had to suppress their wrath and load their freight on the flatboats or the creaking wagons. Either means was expensive and slow, but the freight wagons were the worst—they bogged down in the mud during five months of the year and ran hub deep in dust the rest of the time.

Finally a couple of merchants at Harrisburg moved to act. They were the McCullys, and they had the usual trouble getting merchandise for their store. Moreover, in 1854 Captain Leonard White took his steamboat *Fenix* all the way to Harrisburg and showed that it could be done, regardless of what other river men said about it. Half of steamboating in the Oregon country was to do the impossible; the other half was to do it at a profit. With high costs of operation and uncertainty that freight would be offered, rates stayed high and steamboats went regularly only to places where they were sure to find business. Only a year after the Citizen's Line started, Salem's merchants yelled at the rates until Captain Archibald Jamieson organized a rival line, using his *Enterprise,* but he found he had to keep his charges at about the level already set in order to break even. Jamieson firmly refused to send his steamers above Corvallis, and when the McCullys tried to bill freight direct to their landing they had their cargo unceremoniously dumped ashore at Corvallis, Jamieson not risking the wrath of the Corvallis merchants or the dangers of the river. The McCully temper flared, and when a McCully temper flared, it lit up the skies of the whole upper valley.

Living on lean pickings along the Yamhill route was the new stern-wheeler *James Clinton,* a little boat that did not cut much of a figure on the river; but her captain was willing to listen while the McCullys talked. Would he take a cargo through to Harrisburg for some inducement like a guarantee of further freight? Would he, if people bought shares in the boat, say about $5,000 worth, go up to Eugene where Colonel Joseph Teal had trouble getting goods for his store? He would—and he did. Captain Leonard White of the *James Clinton* had been to Harrisburg once and he could go there again. Captain White never was stopped by a river. When he came to a new one, he went up it. That was what it was for.

From Corvallis the *James Clinton* bravely started, her puffing engine drowning out the jeers from the ill-wishers ashore. That was early on March 10, 1857. A day passed, and the steamboat tied up. By the next night she was at the landing at Harrisburg. So far, so good. On the third day she set out again through the twisting channels and chutes and by evening rounded a butte and turned to a landing just below a reef that showed white water. She was a shallow draft boat to begin with, but had the channel given out entirely, Captain White would have hauled her ashore and run her overland to Eugene where the whole town waited on the bank to welcome her and to live up to the agreement by shelling out $5,000. The dominance of Corvallis was over, and besides, Eugeneans seemed instinctively to dislike those who were from the heart of the valley. Heart of the valley, maybe so, but Eugene was the head. However, the analogy should not be pushed too far. For forty years after the *James Clinton* made it, stern-wheelers worked their way up to Eugene, not always regularly, but often enough to suffice.

Steamboating on the Willamette for a time continued to be a cheerful donnybrook. Everybody concerned was out to swat everybody else, and boat after boat went on the river, each advertised that it would break the monopoly established by its predecessor. McCully with some backers built the *Surprise* to supplement the little *James Clinton;* Jamieson, who had irritated the McCully clan to start the fight, countered by selling his *Enterprise* and building the *Onward* to outrun the *Surprise*. New boats went onto the Yamhill run. By 1860 there were too many boats for too little business, and in the meantime tension gathered.

Oregon's becoming a State in 1859 seemed to be overshadowed by the coming presidential campaign of 1860, and all the old sectional feuds of the Eastern States appeared in the Willamette Valley, where the drawling twang of Missouri and southern Indiana and Illinois took on political significance. When Captain Apperson launched a new steamboat at Canemah in 1860 he hinted his loyalty but coppered the bet by naming it the *Unio*. A little later he sold it to Captain Miller who promptly stuck out his jaw, sent for a sign-painter, and had the name board repainted UNION. To hell with the Secesh was his attitude; let them give their freight to other boats.

Order came to the chaotic river business in 1862. Led by the energetic McCullys, a group organized the People's Transportation Company to operate steamers from Portland to Eugene, and began business with the *James Clinton, Relief* and *Enterprise*. By then the Oregon Steam Navigation Company had also entered the Willamette service, and a rate war promptly followed until the People's Transportation Company put the *E. D. Baker* on the run to Cascades, invading the home waters of the big rival. Clearly neither company was getting anywhere and a compromise had to be worked out. In the meantime, people along the Willamette enjoyed the fight—fares from Portland to Salem dropped to 50¢, and to Corvallis a mere $1.50, with meals and berth thrown in. Passengers could ride between Portland and Oregon City free and take freight with them at 50¢ a ton. The test was to see which company went broke first.

The compromise came when the P. T. Co. applied for a right to condemn a strip of land belonging to its rival at the Cascades, in order to build a plank portage road there. That settled it, and the O.S.N. withdrew from the Willamette in return for the P.T.'s abandonment of its Cascades run. The O.S.N. turned over its *Rival, Onward,* and *Surprise,* boats running on the Willamette, to the P.T. Co. and took in return the *Iris* and *Kiyus* built above the Cascades. Not for ten years did the O.S.N. return to the Willamette, and then through a subsidiary company. Then, it might be added, it stayed.

Left alone on the Willamette, the P.T. Co. became powerful although never without competition of some sort. Just as sure as it would buy out opposition somebody would build another steamboat and start nibbling again. The People's Company added rival boats to its fleet and built new ones to handle the trade of the valley, but in spite of good business it made no profits until 1865 when it totted up its books and found surplus to permit a ten percent dividend—and buy three more steamers at the same time.

Boats of the P.T. Co. were efficient rather than elegant. It had nothing to compare to the big *Wide West* of the O.S.N. and seemed not to worry. The Columbia boats were for long runs; the Willamette boats depended on short hauls, local trips, informal and friendly, from landing to landing, carrying mail to the settlements and bringing down cattle, wheat and farm truck to market. To travel them required early rising at Portland, but not so early as to go by O.S.N. If he intended to go up the river, the passenger had to be at the Portland dock before seven when the *Alert* pulled out for Oregon City. A local boat, the *Senator,* came down from the Falls in the morning and returned in the afternoon with local freight and passengers, but the *Alert* was the through boat, connecting with upper river steamers and getting back to Portland in the afternoon.

As soon as the *Alert* came into the lower landing at the Falls, roustabouts went to work wheeling her freight into the warehouse, and her passengers climbed the ramp to the basin where the upriver boats waited. There three times a week the *Yamhill* left for Hillsboro on the Tualatin and the *Union* pulled out to Lafayette on the Yamhill. On Mondays and Thursdays the *Reliance* made the run to Corvallis; on Tuesdays and Fridays it was the *Fannie Patton,* each boat taking a day and a half each way. Once a week the *Enterprise* ran through to Eugene.

Freight rates fluctuated, though in general the P.T. Co., like the O.S.N., reduced the tariff when costs allowed. By 1867 freight from Portland to Oregon City cost $2.50 a ton, or $2.00 in the other direction; to Salem the rate was $8 up and $6 down; Corvallis, $11 and $8; and Eugene $16 and $11. The rates were high, but only half of those charged ten years before. The river itself was a kind of monopoly, for as yet no railroads tapped the valley, and the roads were rough and troublesome. Practically all freight and passengers had to travel on the steamboats.

By 1868 there were scents of danger in the air for the People's Transportation Company, although it had fought down all competition, some of it peculiarly noisy. The Willamette Steamboat Company brought down from the Snake an independent steamboat, the *Lewiston,* dragging her through the Dalles and the Cascades and finally, in December 1867 to Oregon City where she was hauled around the Falls. The P.T. Co. waited until everything was ready for her launching and then quietly got an injunction to prevent her use of the steamboat basin built by them, and she remained high, dry, and useless on the bank. Then someone cried Monopoly and a mob collected, spontaneously perhaps, that with a whoop, a hur-rah, and considerable heaving pushed her into the basin in spite of the injunction. But shortly the *Lewiston* was renamed *Ann* and then significantly *Cowlitz* and hauled around the Falls again. The P.T. Co. this time said absolutely nothing. Nor did it have to say much when the Canemah Transportation Company put the mis-named *Success* on the river; it only had to wait, and six months later the Canemah Transportation Company had enough and the *Success* carried the long banner of the P.T. Co. on her jackstaff.

With organization of the Willamette Falls Canal and Locks Com-pany in 1868, a real threat developed. Led by Bernard Goldsmith of Portland and some steamboatmen who were sure to be in any deal that was aimed at breaking up a monopoly—men like Orlando Humason of The Dalles, Joseph Teal of Portland, and D. P. Thompson of Oregon City—the new company planned to dig a canal and construct locks on the west bank of the Willamette around the Falls. If it did, the monopoly of the People's Transportation Company ended right there, for any rival company could operate through from Portland to Eugene merely by paying tolls. The P.T. Co. had been successful largely because it controlled the only convenient and practical portage.

Passengers had long complained that at Canemah they had to clamber up the steep river bank with "something of the agility of a mountain goat," and then "essay the comfortless two-bit ride in the miserable one-horse boxed-up car over the snake-head railway" as an editor put it. In 1865 the People's Transportation Company built in the slackwater above the Falls and close to the bank at Oregon City a deep basin, protected by dolphins and a breakwater, and on shore an elaborate system of warehouses connected by in-clined planes and ramps. By using the new system, a boat might dock close under the Falls, almost in its spray, and unload into a warehouse its freight and the passengers, who moved up through the building to the second boat in the basin above. Time needed to make the transfer was cut in half, and the whole thing was a marvel of convenience. It had its drawbacks, however, for getting boats in and out of the basin remained difficult. When a steamer approached, a deckhand threw ashore a line which would be fastened firmly to keep the boat from drifting too far toward the lip of the Falls and being caught in the racing current. Next the steamer moved toward the basin, threshing the water with its wheel and straining at the cable. Sometimes during high water a steamboat had to fight the side pull of the river for an hour before it finally got into quiet water, and more than one passenger busied himself praying the cable would hold.

With such a convenient portage, the P.T. Co. viewed with open disfavor the whole idea of locks and a canal, and it whistled in the dark to keep up its spirits, suspecting the truth that behind the new Canal and Locks Company was the O.S.N., ready to try for Willamette business again. Just to show how little it worried, the P.T. Co. ordered a pair of new boats, the long lasting *Albany* and *Dayton*. The Company seemed to have reason for its confidence, for after the organization not much happened in the camp of the Locks Company. No further rivals appeared, and the old ones disappeared. The attempt to use the *Ann* by the Long Tom Transportation Company, which ran her up the sluggish Long Tom River to Monroe and got her back down with a cargo of flour, could be ignored, with reason, for the Long Tom Company had neglected to license the boat and the sheriff sold her. To its fleet, the P.T. Co. added another boat in the class named for towns, this one to be the *Eugene*. All along the banks men and boys whistled a popular song that admonished an insect not to rile the musician, and the Company, bowing to the taste of the day, christened the steamer on launching not *Eugene* but *Shoo-Fly*. Such indignities few towns can suffer in silence.

Then a new force entered the scene, a powerful, rather uncouth force, in the person of Ben Holladay. After having built an empire with his stage coaches on the Overland route, Holladay neatly sold out ahead of the transcontinental railroad and came to the Pacific Northwest to bring together a complete monopoly of transportation. He bought the coastal steamers, the slowly building Oregon Central Railroad, and the Legislature, and he organized a miscellany of ventures in Portland, such as the first street railway. Then he turned to the river, for his Oregon Central, by then creeping along the river bank a few miles above Oregon City, would have to compete with the steamboats as it moved up to Salem and Eugene.

In 1871, just about the time that the railroad got to Eugene, Holla-day bought the People's Transportation Company, securing nine steamboats and virtual control of the river traffic. His interest was not in the steamers themselves but in the power they gave him, and except for the *E. N. Cooke,* he had no new boats built. With the rail-road and the steamboat lines, he could juggle rates as he needed to maintain monopoly; and with a steamboat tied up at Salem, its pantry loaded with fine foods, plenty of wine, and convincing whis-key, and its cabins supplied with other inducements, he could man-age the State Government. He did that so well that he succeeded in staving off the construction of the locks at the Falls by keeping firmly restricted the funds voted in aid of the project—for a time, at least.

Naturally, Holladay ran into opposition, and competing lines continued monotonously to rise and fall. Clearly, as a ruler of the river he was no more popular than his predecessors, and ashore he was not popular either. His trains, the users complained, were poorly equipped and badly run, and as it took up to eighteen hours for one to crawl from Portland to Eugene perhaps some reason for complaint did exist.

Holladay's main trouble came from overambition and overexpan-sion—he had too much railroad and too many steamboats for the amount of freight he could secure for them. All cash went out of the till, and none came in until nothing was left. Then Holladay and his empire in Oregon toppled neatly before the push Henry Villard gave them. The two men were unlike: Holladay, rough, ruthless, expansive, ambitious, a dreamer of empires; Villard, suave, ruth-less, expansive, ambitious, a dreamer too. The difference was in their manners and their education, or rather in Villard's having both and Holladay neither.

While Holladay scrambled for money to keep his system going, more rivals rose. An independent steamboat, the *Calliope,* had been built to compete with the P.T. Co. but found no business on the main river, whereupon her owners sent her up the shallow Santiam to Lebanon landing for any freight she might glean. The *Calliope* went to Lebanon all right, and then found she could not come back; while she was there, the river rose, and the *Calliope's* chimney would not clear Holladay's railroad bridge at Jefferson. The only way to go under was painful, but the crew did it—they scuttled the boat, dragged her along the bottom of the river until she was below the bridge, then bailed her out till she floated, and serenely went their way down the river.

Old time steamboatmen and cautious capitalists shook their heads. Steamboating was over. No longer could the river compete with the railroad, and no more money ought to be risked on hopeful projects like rival boats, especially when the builder was a mere wild-eyed enthusiast. There was one of those around Portland, trying to argue his way into a good job with the big Oregon Steam Navigation, but no one was taking him seriously. His name was U. B. Scott, and he claimed to be a boat builder with a lot of practical experience on the Ohio River. Rumors that two or three had swallowed his story and given him some money so he could build a boat of his own only caused laughter—with pity for the backers.

Down on the river bank, U. B. Scott, unbothered by the jeerers who lined the shore, went to work to put together the strangest contraption any of the boatmen had seen. From an old dredge he had got parts of an engine; now he put together a hull, broad, almost flat on the bottom. On it he built a deckhouse, squarish, plain, downright ugly, looking like a shed. Then he started with the machinery. He had his engine, but no pitmans for the stern wheel; lengths of gas pipe had to do, and they did. He lacked money to buy heavy iron castings for the web of the wheel, so instead he framed it with wood from small iron spindles. As the boat took form, the wonder grew; nothing like this had been seen before, and nothing like her would work. Everyone knew that.

Scott knocked out the blocks, and the boat slid sideways into the river where, the skeptics grudgingly admitted, she at least floated. Scott lit a fire under her boiler and the steam began to rise. When he hauled back on the throttle the engines took hold, the gas pipe pitmans picked up the load, and the wooden wheel turned. So far so good, if not miraculous. He had named the boat *Ohio,* in memory of the place where he had learned steamboating; it was a name those who had sneered would remember. On December 12, 1874, Scott, standing on the roof near the boxy pilot house, ordered the lines cast off. Slowly the *Ohio* nosed into the current and headed up the river to Oregon City. She made her way through the locks and kept going, past the Yamhill, and Salem and Albany. She had no trouble at Corvallis or even Harrisburg where the river shoaled, and at last came to Eugene, without scraping her keel once, and no wonder! Steamboatmen found she drew only eight inches. The *Ohio* would not have to worry whether the river was deep enough—all that would be bothersome was whether it was wide enough.

At Eugene she took aboard seventy tons of wheat and started calmly back down the river. That was a settler. Not only did this jerry-built patchwork of left-overs go anywhere, but at a profit. When Captain U. B. Scott came back to Portland, those who had sneered were waiting with checks in their hands. They were wrong, and they wanted to profit by it. Scott smiled, but at the moment he had some repairs to make on the *Ohio*, because she was jerry-built, and now and then she tended to come apart at the seams.

Travelling on her was always an adventure, because no one could predict what she would do next. Now and then as she headed toward a wharf, the pilot would yell to back the engines. The engineer would oblige, but the pitmans, revolting at the strain, would bend, leaving the engine and wheel locked in dead center. Whenever that happened, the *Ohio* swept grandly into the dock with a satisfying crash of splintered piling. Cautious wharfboatmen went ashore when they saw her coming. On the river, too, the *Ohio* developed distressing habits. Now and then wooden braces of the wheel would work loose and fall off, letting the buckets drop and the wheel spin futilely. When she was going down river and that happened, Scott would feel the engines suddenly speed and see pieces of the wheel float idly by; then he had to bawl for a skiff to be put overside to catch the parts before they got too far ahead. If he saw them in time, he merely swore and fetched a boathook.

A year later he organized the U. B. Scott Steamboat Company and built the famous *City of Salem;* he had all the money he needed, and the new boat had none of the makeshifts and all of the virtues of the *Ohio*. Moreover she was a comfortable boat with good furnishings and plenty of space in her cabin and generous but not particularly gaudy gingerbread trim on the decks. On her cabin deck forward a pair of locomotive headlights, huge metal boxes with oil lamps, lit the freight deck for night work at landings. All along the river, the *City of Salem* prowled from landing to landing, picking up freight. Scott liked her, and in a few years gave her new engines. The old ones he put in the *Ohio* which quit its balky habits promptly. Eventually William Reid bought the *City of Salem* to be part of his system of narrow gauge railroads and steamboat lines; for him she ran from Ray's Landing and Dundee to Portland, carrying freight and passengers for the Oregonian Railway. She aged gracefully and finally, after breaking a shaft in 1884, slammed into a reef near Rock Island Rapids while under tow. Along the river old patrons regretted her passing.

While Scott's system grew, Holladay's fell, leaving the former People's Transportation Company to be picked up shortly by Villard. New companies and new boats kept fighting for business, and of the boats the *Willamette Chief* was perhaps the best of the lot, the pride of the Willamette River Transportation Company. She had been launched at about the same time as was the *Ohio,* and had been intended as another monopoly breaker. On her first trip down from Corvallis, she carried 200 tons of wheat, thirty farmers and Joseph Teal, heading for the wharves at Astoria. Teal had become an inveterate speech maker and hopeful breaker of monopolies and was always around when a new steamboat company tried to elbow its way into the business of the river. On the *Willamette Chief,* he made a speech, envisioning things to come when all the valley wheat from all the valley farms would go direct to Astoria for only four dollars a ton, there to be shipped to the hungry world. Prosperity would follow, and the voice of the turtle be heard in the land. Somehow both prosperity and the dove got lost in the shuffle.

When Holladay disappeared from the river, the O.S.N. came back. Now that the People's Transportation Company no longer existed, the O.S.N. reached out for business; first it assumed open control of the Willamette Locks and then of the Willamette River Transportation Company until it had everything on the river except Scott's boats and a few negligible traders and peddlers. Then the O.S.N. itself became Villard's Oregon Railway and Navigation Company, its name showing a shift in emphasis. In the future steamboats would be secondary to the railways. Yet for many years the O.R.&N. boats kept running up the Willamette, leaving Portland daily for the Yamhill and the upper river to towns like Salem, Albany, Corvallis, Peoria, Harrisburg and Eugene, and little landings like Butteville, Buena Vista, Eola, Independence, and Lancaster. Then, as time went on and business declined, the runs turned back at Corvallis. Next Independence became terminal for the line, and then Salem, until finally only the boat to Dayton on the Yamhill remained in service, with one or two other standby steamers for seasonal traffic, such as the *Ruth* and the last of the fleet, the *Modoc.* They held out until 1916 when the O.R.&N.—the last of the O.S.N.—withdrew its boats from the river.

That is not to say steamboating vanished with the O.R.&N—far from it. In 1894 at Portland F. B. Jones launched the *Eugene,* intending to use it on a run to the town for which it was named, and other light draft independent boats were built as late as 1906. Usually such steamers made a run or two before they dropped down to Portland to pick up a living as towboats, and ordinarily their main purpose was to force the railroad to lower rates. The last stern-wheeler touched Eugene in 1905, and above Harrisburg the river fell silent—the river that a steamboat once climbed on high water all the way to Springfield. In 1906 the *Mathloma,* the Army Engineers' stern-wheel snag boat, worked on the channel; though Eugene felt hopeful that steamboating might revive, the *Mathloma* turned back, and the Engineers officially abandoned the channel above Harrisburg. When the Oregon Electric built south through the valley in 1912, Harrisburg had a little more of the old days for a time while the *Leona* brought up loads of supplies for the railroad, especially steel for the bridge—a fine one with a lift span that hung between tall towers. Alongside was the Southern Pacific bridge with no draw at all, only a span that could, should occasion demand, be rebuilt to swing. The occasion never came.

One company that rose late made a go of Willamette steamboating for thirty years. In 1889 the Grahams, father and sons, organized the Oregon City Transportation Company to run boats from Portland to Corvallis and put their first steamer, the *Latona,* on the run. They knew what the public wanted and their boats, each one easy to recognize by its stack with the broad yellow band, were comfortable, pleasant, and dependable. The Yellow Stack Line soon had other boats on the river, each with a name ending in *-ona: Ramona, Altona, Leona, Pomona, Oregona,* and *Grahamona,* and passengers liked them. So did shippers, especially the valley hop growers. The Grahams met competition where they found it, and they found it in odd places. In 1893 a new electric interurban railway started running between Portland and Oregon City and promptly took the cream of the casual passenger trade; in reply the Yellow Stack Line cut its rates so that for a time there was the odd spectacle of a rate war between a steamboat and a trolley car. Eventually the two compromised by an agreement whereby excursionists to the pleasure park above the Falls at Canemah (how the mighty had fallen!) might go one way by electric railway and the other by steamboat, on which they had a chance to go close up to the Falls themselves. It was a trip worth making, because the water still roared and crashed over the black rocks and not yet was confined behind concrete weirs and sent protesting through penstocks to turbines.

In 1915 everyone in the valley expected that the newly opened Panama Canal would bring instant prosperity and a great seaborne traffic to the Pacific Northwest. Somehow the traffic, and the prosperity, remained behind schedule; the war in Europe set up a call for steamers, and business remained uncertain. On the Willamette the O.R.&N. boats like the *Elwood* and *Elmore,* that long were popular, became memories, but the Oregon City Transportation Company boats still made their daily runs, although by then they had deserted Corvallis and were turning back at Independence. The Yellow Stack Line was an institution along the river, something to be taken for granted. Suddenly, in 1919 when automobiles and trucks began to offer the worst competition the steamboats had encountered, the Oregon Transportation Company withdrew from the Willamette, tied up its *Oregona* and *Pomona,* and started to refit the *Grahamona* for service on the upper Columbia. Hastily, employees chartered the *Pomona* and under the name of the Capital Navigation Company put her back on the Willamette. A year later, Captain Graham organized the Inland Empire Boat and Truck Company, and put the *Oregona* and *Pomona* on the Willamette, and the *Grahamona* on the Columbia and Snake rivers, to operate in conjunction with lines of freight trucks radiating from the landings. Somehow, though the idea was good, nothing came of it, and after some uncertain shifting about the *Pomona* continued working as far as Independence, the *Grahamona* went to the boneyard, and the *Oregona,* renamed *Interstate,* ran to Longview and Kelso, but could, when any need showed, run to Dayton.

The *Pomona* finally emerged as a towboat, to be joined by *Interstate,* both working on the Columbia; then the *Grahamona* was hauled out for patching, renamed *Northwestern,* and fitted out as a floating crew barracks and work boat for the Pacific Telephone and Telegraph Company which was stringing new cables through the Columbia Gorge. Under Captain Raabe she finished that job and, by one of those feats of corporate legerdemain, reappeared on the Willamette River, running for the Salem Navigation Company as a freight boat until 1940 when her owners finally gave up. With her last run from Salem, stern-wheel service on the river ended. The *Northwestern,* however, had other jobs ahead. Her bulkheads and cabins reinforced, she obediently followed a towboat up the coast to Alaska, where she still runs on the Kuskokwim River.

Except for an occasional towboat with a barge that passes through the locks, or some steamer that takes a load of veteran steamboatmen to the annual picnic at Champoeg Landing, stern-wheelers have disappeared from the upper Willamette. Yet the river is busy with small gasoline tugs hauling booms of logs down to the mills. Merely one day has gone, and another day come.

Chapter 6
THE PORTAGES

THE RIVERS were highways striking from the sea deep into the back country, but the highways had detours. Both the Columbia and the Willamette were crossed and fretted by barriers that either handicapped navigation or stopped it entirely. Steamboats could come down over the rapids at high water, but no captain in his right mind made plans to do it regularly. At Willamette Falls, at the Cascades, at Tumwater, at Little Dalles, and some of the other places on the river boating became impossible and everything had to be unloaded, toted around the falls or rapids, and reloaded on another boat. To reduce the troubles, steamboatmen tried all kinds of devices at the obstructions.

Hudson's Bay voyagers had the simplest means. When they came downstream, they rode the spring freshet, and with skill and an overdose of luck could steer the bateau over most of the rapids; where the river was blocked, the boatmen, following the old custom of their trade, climbed ashore and lugged first the goods and then the boat itself around the barrier on the *portage*—the carry. Where the portages existed Indians gathered, as at Celilo where the Wishramites lived as trading people at the meeting place of the tribes. Wishram, in fact, was something like Erie before the railroads to the town had a single, standard gauge.

[67]

The emigrants followed the Indian trails around the rapids, but the more emigrants used them, the more troublesome and rough the trails became. The trails widened to roads, while the ruts deepened. It became only a question of time before someone with initiative and an eye to profit made improvements. That someone arrived at the Cascades in 1851, in the person of a man named Chenoweth who promptly busied himself by constructing a tramway on the north or Washington bank around the rapids. The *Oregon Statesman,* never chary in its praise of improvements, called Chenoweth's project "a great service to emigrants," and by fall Chenoweth's wooden railroad, on which a single car hauled by a skeptical mule carried the goods, was in operation, taking the emigrants from the pioneer *James P. Flint* above the Cascades to the veteran brig *Henry* below. Chenoweth charged seventy-five cents for each hundred pounds of freight, and kept busy. In time he sold out to the Bradfords who owned the *Flint,* and in 1855 they began renewing the railway. Chenoweth's track construction was flimsy, but it served until 1855 when the rush of miners toward Colville and the Army toward the Indians required better service. When the attack came at the Cascades in 1856, the Bradfords had crews rebuilding the tramway and extending it to the lower landing. The road was six miles long, but still moved freight on small flat cars hauled by mules.

Not long afterwards a similar road was built on the Oregon side of the Cascades by J. O. VanBergen, a rival to the Bradfords, to connect with his steamers *Wasco* and *Fashion.* To meet this threat the Bradfords gained dignity by incorporating their line as the Cascade Railroad. VanBergen sold out to Ruckle and Olmstead who retaliated by naming theirs the Oregon Portage Railway. Both served, after a fashion, until the great flood of 1861 when the Bradford road went under water, while the other survived.

By then the Oregon Steam Navigation Company, trying to keep up with the rush of freight offered it, had to do something to increase the speed of transfer at the portages. It had planned a thirteen mile railway at Celilo and made agreements with the Bradfords and Ruckle and Olmstead. When the Cascade Railroad went out of operation the Oregon Portage Railway was hard pressed to carry the traffic, and the O.S.N. faced a real problem. It had the boats, it had the business, but it did not have the portages; whoever controlled the portages controlled the river. The railways charged high rates for the short haul, and in addition the crews regarded their

At a Snake River landing, the *Annie Faxon* loads sacked wheat.

Above. The *Lewiston* on the Snake River before she changed her name to *Barry-K* and went to Alaska.

At Dayton, on the Yamhill, the *A. A. McCully* loads wheat from a warehouse high above her on the bank.

Below. Landings were no problem to the *Chester.*

jobs as offering certain perquisites. Captain Ainsworth of the O.S.N. Co. had been plagued by claims for missing freight and had suspicions that he knew where between Portland and its destination the freight disappeared. In 1862 he wrote sadly to Olmstead of the Portage Railway that a friend, just off the *Carrie Ladd,* "saw three of your men stop with two freight cars and take a box and hide it in the bushes." Later the box had been found where it lay hidden. "This," Ainsworth went on, "is only another proof positive that a large portion of our losses occur on the Cascades." Would Mr. Olmstead do something about it?

To help in constructing the projected portage railroad at Celilo, the O.S.N. ordered a very small locomotive which finally arrived and was hoisted out onto the dock at Portland. Not yet ready to use it at Celilo, the company sold it to the Oregon Portage Railway and shipped it along with some strap rail to the Cascades where Engineer Goffe, sent from San Francisco with the engine by the Vulcan Iron Works, tinkered and tried it and got it ready to run. The O.S.N. had decided on the move after the Bradford road had broken down and the freight piled up across the river on the Oregon side. It could spare the locomotive; two more were on the way, one for Celilo, one for the Bradfords. The tiny first arrival, called from the beginning the *Pony,* could meet the emergency on the Oregon Portage Railway.

The *Pony* was not an impressive locomotive. Built to the five-foot gauge then standard in California, it was a glorified toy resting on four connected drivers (in railroad lingo, an o-4-oT). Its frame carried both boiler and tender, neither very large, the boiler being three feet in diameter and five feet long. A steam dome disproportionately large emerged from the center of the boiler, and from the rear rose a slim stack topped by a diamond spark arrester. There was no cab; the canopy that the engine now carries was a later touch of elegance. But it was a locomotive, and on the morning of May 10, 1862, Engineer Goffe fired it up for a trial trip. When it was ready a group of very distinguished personages arrived to take the ride and, refusing the splendor of a private flat car, insisted on clambering aboard the engine itself. There were Colonel J. S. Ruckle, owner of the road, R. R. Thompson and S. G. Reed of the O.S.N., one of the rival Bradfords, and W. S. Ladd, the road's financial godfather, and when all of them were aboard the *Pony,* Engineer Goffe hardly had room to heave chunks into the firebox or to manipulate the controls. Elbowing his way into place he opened the throttle and the engine, with a chuffing sigh, moved forward uncertainly along the wooden track, its wheels clicking and slapping on the strap iron facing of the rails. A soft breeze blew, the passengers smiled, and the engine rolled along—until it came to the first grade where the track climbed around a promontory. The engine slowed and then began to work hard, gasping and coughing smoke, water and firebrands from her stack. With absolute impartiality, the mixture shot down onto the very important personages who had not expected such rugged treatment and were bedecked in broadcloth, boiled shirts and plug hats. At the upper landing the passengers descended limply, the boiled shirts gray, the broadcloth smudged, the stovepipe hats spotted and dented, shoved hard down over their ears. Fortunately the *Idaho* was handy, ready with a restorative, and—though she carried no bar—the steward aboard had a private stock he was willing to sell. Expected to, in fact.

Olmstead and Ruckle had business all to themselves for a time, while the *Pony* shuttled back and forth with its trains, and the Bradfords across the river swore in smothered rage. When they suffered long enough, they demanded a cut of the pie, and the O.S.N. obliged by transferring construction crews from Celilo and rushing work on the Cascade Railroad. That was enough for Olmstead and Ruckle, who promptly sold their Oregon Portage Railway, lock, stock and barrel, to the O.S.N.—two wharf boats, twelve mules, five horses, twenty freight cars, one passenger car (a flat car with benches under a canopy), three wagons, and the *Pony,* the last not yet paid for and owned all the time by the O.S.N. Within a few months the Oregon Portage Railway would fall into ruin after the business shifted across the river to the Cascade Railroad.

The *Pony* did not serve long, but it was a portent of things to come. When it chugged along the wooden track, its piping whistle hooting at the surprised Indians, it acted like a real locomotive on a real track, and the people of the country appreciated it. One traveller wrote to the *Oregonian* that "it really seemed like going once more to 'America,' . . . where we had once more had the pleasure of being dragged through mountain gorges on a train of cars drawn by an actual, live, smoking, panting, fire-breathing iron horse," echoing the paper's own rhetorical query: "Who expected two short years ago to hear the whistle of the locomotive, that harbinger of civilization, in these wilds?" And who, it might be added, recognized that the cacaphony of locomotive whistles would in time drive the last wail of the steamboat from those shores?

The Cascade Railroad was built solidly with T-rail on which rolled double-truck box cars and real passenger cars with arched roofs and upholstered seats flanking an aisle. That the seats were hard, the windows narrow, made little difference: the railroad was progress. At each end of the railway was a platform for passengers, and beyond, the track slanted down an incline to the wharf boat. Trains loaded and unloaded their passengers at the top and coasted down to the wharf. Letting the cars roll was dangerous practice; and one day an Indian squaw with her child stepped behind the train just as the brakeman let off the brakes. The cars, moving silently, struck the woman and killed the baby. If they had not been Indians, something might have been done about it.

Up at Celilo another portage railroad was completed at the same time so that the two of them, the Cascade Railroad and the Dalles-Celilo, began operations together on April 20, 1863. Each had a single locomotive, named respectively *Ann* and *Betsy,* grown-up versions of the *Pony* and, if anything, stranger looking. At the front were boilers and drivers, a complete locomotive, entirely housed in a box-like cab and resting on a frame that extended back to a trailing truck, forming a kind of flat car. Similar engines, with the rear extensions built into passenger coaches, were operating as street cars around San Francisco at the time. Later the portage roads bought conventional locomotives built by Danforth and Cooke's works in the East, still small but recognizably engines of the 4-2-0 type. To them were added others, American-type 4-4-0's, until the company had six. That fleet sufficed to carry all traffic until the roads were eventually sold to the Oregon Railway and Navigation Company—the *Pony* having been disused after the closing of the Oregon Portage Railway until it was sold to a San Francisco contractor, and the *Ann* and *Betsy* eventually being leased by Holladay to help him build his Oregon Central south from Portland in 1870.

The Cascade Railroad was largely built on trestle work above the high water mark, but much of the Dalles-Celilo was built on sand. Orlando Humason had hacked out a road for freighting wagons when traffic first developed on the upper river, a road that climbed to the bench and wound around the highlands and over the creeks until it got down to the river again near the mouth of the Deschutes. The railroad, however, stayed close to the river under the bluffs, and that route caused the trouble. For miles, beside the Dalles, the banks are sandy, and the winds, sweeping up the river, drift the sand into fantastic dunes that spread across the tracks.

CASCADES ROUTE

In spite of the sand, the railroad operated regularly. Upriver boats reached The Dalles in late afternoon, but the train to Celilo did not leave until the next morning, the passengers finding it then conveniently waiting in the street before the Umatilla House. Downriver boats reached Celilo in the afternoon, and to insure the presence of a train, the O.S.N. strung a telegraph line along the track. When Celilo wired that a boat was in sight, a train left The Dalles to meet it. Like the trains at Cascades, these were real ones, with the coaches and baggage cars brightly painted and the company's initials, "O.S.N.", blazoned above the windows on the letterboards.

At either terminal, the landing was well below the track, and again inclines were used, but cars were raised and lowered by cables wound on large drums turned by steam engines. Everything moved smoothly, casually (some complained that it took forever and a couple of extra hours for the conductor to stroll out of the small shack or depot, wave a languid highball at the engineer, and get the train under way). The passengers took this road for granted; any interest they had in railroads was satisfied by the railroad at Cascades. This one was just another part of the trip. Of course, the ride was spectacular as the train wound along the river below the towering cliffs, but many found it a bit too intimately geological for untrained taste.

Like the Columbia, the Willamette had its interruptions so that traffic on it broke into three clearly defined routes—downriver from

Portland to the Columbia and points on the larger stream; upriver from Portland to Oregon City, and above Oregon City as far as Eugene. Fortunately, the portage at Oregon City was short, not over a mile, and a fairly decent road could be maintained. Finally in 1862 a horse railway was built from Canemah to Oregon City, but by then the country had become sophisticated and resented its inefficiency. There had been a warehouse and tramway on the west bank, through which freight could be moved mechanically, but the flood of 1861 had washed that out, and the horse railroad on the east bank remained the fastest means for transfer. Then in 1865 the People's Transportation Company completed its basin and transfer warehouses at Oregon City, and that system served until the locks and canal were built on the other side of the river.

Sometimes the portages became rather complicated, like the one developed by the Sucker Lake and Tualatin River Railroad in 1865. The purpose was to shorten the trip up the Tualatin by avoiding the Falls, but in practice, the passenger was made dizzy by the number of changes and interruptions in the journey. He landed from the Portland boat at what is now Oswego, shinnied up the bank to the lake, and there found a tiny steamboat, the *Minnehaha,* waiting for him. He boarded it to ride the few miles across the lake to the railroad. There he found a tramway, with the usual five foot gauge, on which were platform cars ten feet long and eight wide, each drawn by two horses. He could ride one if he wished, but it was hardly worth the effort, for it was only a mile and a half to the Tualatin River. There the *Onward* waited to make its weekly trip up the Tualatin to Hillsboro, Forest Grove and Centerville Landing. Usually passengers did not go to so much trouble, preferring to take the stage coach out the plank road from Portland, but logs were in no hurry, and logs formed the main part of the freight, going down to the lumber mill the railroad company owned on the bank of the Willamette.

Down in the Coos Bay country was still another portage, like that of the Tualatin, a cut-off to enable freight and passengers to move by water as much as possible. It was a country admirably adapted to steamboating, with its quiet sloughs and long penetrating inlets from the bay, and its rivers; and so, long after other parts of the State turned to railroads, the steamboats continued to ply their trade on the Coos and the Coquille. Some were tiny boats like the *Coos,* built in 1874, a side-wheeler only 58 feet long, that could inch its way up any winding slough, carrying freight and passengers. From Empire and Marshfield on Coos Bay to the towns of Coquille and Prosper on the Coquille River the route by sea or land was long and tedious, but the Isthmus Slough, an extension of the bay, winds its way south through the hills until it comes to an end in a marshy shallow, while only a couple of miles across a low rise is one of the sluggish sloughs of the Coquille River. In 1869 a tramway, powered by horses and mules, covered the two mile gap, hauling small cars, one of them fitted with seats and covered by a kind of awning or canopy for passengers. By 1874 a steam locomotive was brought in for the road, now called the Isthmus Transit Railroad, and continued to operate until the 1890's when the Coos Bay, Roseburg and Eastern Railroad took over and extended the line north to the towns on the bay and south to Coquille, putting an end to the portage. Steamers, however, continued to run on Coos Bay until the 1920's and on the Coquille River until the 1930's.

On the Columbia, the portage railroads went through a series of changes and vicissitudes. When Villard purchased the Oregon Steam Navigation Company and made it the nucleus of his Oregon Railway and Navigation Company, he promptly decided to extend the railroad from Celilo to Wallula and then beyond to connect with a transcontinental line. His first plan was to build the popular narrow gauge of three feet, with a third rail between The Dalles and Celilo to permit through travel. However, after a temporary track was laid to narrow gauge, he decided to use standard gauge, with four feet, eight and a half inches between the rails, and the road was rebuilt, opening in 1880. The old portage at the Dalles then became part of the through line and went out of existence as a separate road.

At Cascades a somewhat different situation arose. Construction of the through railroad began at The Dalles, leaving the steamboat connection from there to Portland still necessary. In 1880, to make equipment usable in all parts of the system, the gauge of the Cascade Railroad was changed from its original five feet to standard, and then three years later the job was done all over again when the railroad was made narrow gauge in order to use surplus locomotives and cars left over from a recently converted narrow gauge road near Walla Walla. To the end of its days, the Cascade Railroad remained narrow gauge, its equipment comfortably aging and wearing. In fact, there was very little work for it to do once the main line railroad was extended along the Columbia to Portland. The O. R.

& N. continued steamboat service for a time and then dropped it, retaining the Cascade Railroad to carry freight and passengers of independent and rival steamboat lines. Of course, the Cascade Railroad supplied the required portage service, but the Cascade Railroad naturally did not strive officiously to do it well. When the flood of 1894 came down the Columbia, about half of the railroad washed into the river, and the owners leased what was left to a fish cannery which used it for carrying salmon from the wheels to the plant.

Steamboatmen for years wailed at the poor service and high tolls charged by the Cascade Railroad, and the locks, intended to open the river, never seemed to be completed. Finally the boatmen carried their problem to the State of Oregon which established in 1891 a Board of Portage Commissioners, charged with building a State-owned railroad at the Cascades. There were tracks already at the proposed locks; the Corps of Engineers had narrow gauge construction railways on the scene, and in order that the line be built easily, the Commission decided to use the same gauge. By September, 1891, the Oregon Portage Railway was in operation, with all the usual facilities: a wharf boat at the lower landing, inclines at both landings, and enough second-hand equipment to handle all expected business. Rates were not heavy, but neither was traffic. The single line of steamboats making use of the portage railroad did not seriously cut into the business of the O. R. & N.'s railroad and thereby save the Inland Empire from the throttling monopoly—as the State-owned portage sponsors had hoped. Wheat, railroad iron, and hay "in common bales" formed one class of freight which was charged forty cents a ton. Only coal and shingles had a lower rate, and everything else paid sixty cents. An emigrant wagon, set up, cost a dollar. The rate on cattle was three dollars for each carload, but single stock paid a separate tariff. Charges were based on actual rather than measured weight. Boats lingering at the landing more than three hours after loading or discharging cargo paid a wharfage fee of two dollars per ton of registered tonnage—that to keep some evil company (like the O. R. & N.) from tying a boat to the wharf and keeping competitors from their chance to unload.

In the first year business was fair; something over eight thousand passengers and ten thousand tons of freight passed over the road. Most of the tonnage was wheat, moving in the fall and winter months. The first statement of earnings for a little over a year of operation showed receipts totalling $7,039.91 and a net income after disbursements of $837.62. It was not big business but it at least opened the river to competition. Then freight traffic began to decline, and in 1893 the portage carried but five million pounds of wheat and flour and eight and a half million pounds of general merchandise, including the heavy wool clip. Only seven thousand passengers moved over the line that year, and in 1894 the number dropped to sixty-two hundred. The wheat, in 1894, increased to about seven and a quarter million pounds, and general merchandise to nine million pounds, and receipts rose slightly. But added costs made the road barely break even: the track had to be relocated in order to avoid interference with work on the locks, and the lower incline had to be rebuilt after the flood of 1894 had washed it out and put the whole line out of commission for several months.

In 1896 the end came. First, the Army Engineers refused further joint use of trackage; second, the locks were ready to be opened, and so the railroad ceased to operate in May. Passenger traffic had climbed to 10,675 in 1895, but only three and a quarter million pounds of wheat moved over the line. With the final report of the Commissioners went a recommendation that the salary of the caretaker be paid by the State and that the equipment, which had been removed and stored, be sold. In the treasury of the road remained $7.13, but the monopoly had been broken.

The monopoly extended to Celilo and of course came in for the same sharp attack. In 1882 a boat railway was proposed at the portage, a popular device, for boat railways were a dream at the time, stemming from the elaborate proposal for a boat railway across the Isthmus of Tehuantepec. They were cheaper to build than canals requiring locks, and their advocates fondly believed they were practicable. A boat railway was simply two or more parallel standard gauge railroad tracks extending around an obstruction in the river to quiet, deep water above. On the tracks would be placed a car, built like a ship-cradle, wide enough and long enough to accommodate any river boat and rolling on a multitude of ordinary railway trucks. When a boat approached the obstruction, the car would be let down an incline into the water, the boat would be floated over the cradle, and secured to it. Then the cradle-car would be hauled up the incline. At the top of the incline regular locomotives would be coupled on and proceed merrily down the track to the other incline where the car would roll into the water, and the boat would float free to continue its run on up the river. By the device no unloading and reloading of cargo would be needed, and the time required for transit naturally was far less than that of an ordinary portage and not much more than a passage through locks and a canal. It was a beautiful idea, resplendent in its economy in time and money, and Congress liked it, appropriated money for one of the contraptions at The Dalles, yet nothing came of it.

With the great boom that swept Central Oregon shortly after the turn of the century, there were indications that cheap means for moving bulk wheat down to shipping terminals at a seaport were needed. Again the cry of monopoly was raised and the State was belabored to offer help on a portage at Celilo. Again the State, in 1903, answered the call and appropriated money to build and operate a railway around the Dalles. From the beginning, in spite of the most vocal enthusiasm that proponents of the plan could muster, the railroad ran into trouble. First, the officials of the Oregon Railway and Navigation Company, now controlled by Harriman's Union Pacific, showed an understandable lack of enthusiasm for the whole idea and seemed not at all anxious to help the project, although finally they granted a right of way paralleling the O. R. & N. Then there were other problems: surveys, rights of way, and contracts; but in September 1905 the job was finished and the railroad ready to operate—after the Open River Association had advanced money to pay for equipment.

This line, called the Oregon State Portage Railroad, began at Big Eddy, four miles above the city of The Dalles, and followed the original portage route to Celilo and slackwater just above Tumwater Falls. It was a standard gauge road that owned a couple of locomotives, a passenger car, a few box cars, and some flat cars, all second-hand equipment that looked second-hand. At Big Eddy was the usual incline, rather sharp and requiring expensive trestlework, down which cars had to be lowered on a cable, but at Celilo the grade was easier and steamboats came close to the gently sloping trestlework terminal. The tariff, adopted before the road began operations, called for twenty-five cents a ton for wheat, and fifty cents for all other freight. Passengers paid twenty-five cents for the eight mile trip. Upriver freight, in some classifications, paid as much as a dollar a ton. When the road started, one of the boats of the Open River Company came up the landing with a party of derby-hatted dignitaries and was met by a train, made up of Locomotive

Number One (it was impossible to miss it, with a large, vivid "1" on the smoke box), a string of flats and the coach. The train backed down the incline to let the crowd come aboard, then climbed to higher land where there were some hopeful trees, and the speeches began. Joseph N. Teal made one, and under the spell of his words the audience saw the Inland Empire blossom as a rose, and each petal become a fine white steamer floating down the Columbia River, freighted with the golden grains of nutritious wheat destined for the hungry of the wide, wide world. Altogether, it was quite a party.

However, the golden grains neglected to come, probably because the Union Pacific took the hint and reduced the freight rate. When the State Portage road at Cascades opened, the O.R.&N. had cut its rate from $3.50 per ton from the Inland Empire to $2.00. Now again, the rate, which had been $2.90, went down to $2.50 for wheat. Moreover, the steamboatmen were reticent. The Big Eddy terminal was hard to approach, and anyway The Dalles was the natural head of navigation. Would the State oblige and appropriate money to extend the road to The Dalles?

The State would and did at the 1909 session of the Legislature, so that the Portage Commissioners hoped to have the extension ready by March of 1911. The extension cost $24,578 (the whole line at the Cascades had cost in the 1890's only $2,000), and $14,666 more would be needed to build another incline at The Dalles. All totalled together the cost of building the Oregon State Portage Railroad came to $74,821. In the four years remaining for operations, that money would not be earned, but the Open River Association pointed to indirect benefits—the North Bank road, the proposed electric railways, the increase in traffic and business, the reduced railroad rates.

Wheat naturally formed a large part of the freight carried between boats above and below the line. In only four months of operations in 1905, the road carried 2,165 tons of wheat, and during the next year 3,388 tons, but in 1907 only 81 tons went over the road. Business picked up somewhat after that bad depression year, with about 1,000 tons passing over the line in 1908 and 3,500 in 1909. After that another decline set in and general merchandise rather than wheat, provided the most tonnage, the road carrying 13,486 tons of merchandise and only 5,425 tons of wheat during its eight years of existence. That it was not a popular route for passengers is clear. During its first four years it carried 305 passengers, and after that it quit worrying about them or forgot to count them. In 1915 the line finally was abandoned—the opening of the Celilo Canal and Locks made it unnecessary.

While the Oregon State Portage had been languishing, the Cascade Railroad suddenly came back to life. Faced by the threat of Jim Hill's forces to build a railroad along the north bank of the Columbia, the Union Pacific suddenly remembered the Cascade Railroad. The Union Pacific still owned it, and though it had no purpose, no business (even the fish cannery had quit using it), its right of way did have a distinct nuisance value. Once it had controlled the river. Now again it might—properly handled. And so a new superintendent was appointed for the ruined line, to meet the threat which arrived in 1906 when the Hill railroad, the Portland and Seattle, applied to the court to condemn a right of way that crossed the Cascade Railroad at four points. The moves and countermoves became dizzier and dizzier. Hill's forces were trying to build on the north bank to offset possible construction by the oncoming Chicago, Milwaukee and St. Paul, but if Hill built on the north bank he would be coming dangerously into Harriman territory. Back of it all was the determination of the railroads to secure the water level route from the Inland Empire to the sea—or, simply, to hold the river and to use the gorge and pathway it had cut through the mountains.

Hill's forces won, although the Union Pacific fought the whole case to the United States Supreme Court. In 1908 the Portland and Seattle built the railroad it wanted—and then, following orders, rebuilt the Cascade Railroad, giving it a slightly different alignment, and crossing it only twice. The Cascade Railroad was a nice, new railroad by then, but it had no business and no further function so the Union Pacific let it die. Traces of the grade may be found, but that is all. Across the river, boats passed through the locks at will.

Chapter 7

TO THE FARTHEST REACH

THE UPPER COLUMBIA begins above Tumwater Falls at Celilo and extends generally north, winding through Washington and up into Canada, doubling back on itself, and, finally, by coming within shouting distance of one of its tributaries, almost forming a complete circle. Paul Bunyan may have got his idea of the circular river from it, or maybe Paul made it in one of his playful moments in the north woods. At one time or another stern-wheelers ran on most of the long stretches of the upper river and its tributaries, the Snake, Okanogan, Clark Fork, and Kootenai.

Steamboating above Celilo started in 1858, naturally under Leonard White, who, it would seem, commanded steamers on every out of the way piece of river. During the Indian wars R. R. Thompson and L. W. Coe were running supplies from Celilo to the Army posts at Walla Walla and beyond, using small scow-like boats, rigged with sails, that beat their way up and down the river. Eventually business became so good that after the discoveries of gold in Idaho, Thompson and Coe decided on a steamboat, to be built there in the wilderness to do the job. With a freight rate of $100 a ton on their boats, they could afford to build a steamer, which they called *Colonel Wright* after the popular hero of the Indian war. As Master they secured Leonard White who had taken boats as far up the

Willamette as there was any water to float them, and then they turned him loose to see what he could do.

When the stern-wheel *Colonel Wright* was all assembled at the mouth of the Deschutes River, Captain White, just to be sure, rigged a mast and hung a square sail from it, thus preparing for all eventualities. By the time he was ready to take her out for her first run, plenty of tonnage already had piled up waiting for her, so much so that Thompson and Coe cut the rate to a mere $80 from Celilo to Wallula. White set out up the river, stopped at Wallula, and came back safely. On the next trip he kept going until he nosed the boat fifty miles up the Snake River and entered new territory. It was clear that steamboating would pay in those parts, and in 1860 a larger boat, the *Tenino,* joined the *Wright.* Business was still booming, and the *Tenino* made money as fast as the purser could collect it and stuff it into a carpetbag. On a single upriver run in May, 1862, when the gold rush was at its roaring best, the *Tenino* gathered in $18,000 for fares, meals, berths, and incidentals—the bar. The *Colonel Wright* kept pace, taking as much as $2,500 a trip for passenger fares alone.

Then the *Colonel Wright* went venturing again, passing Lewiston and going up the Clearwater almost to the forks. The Snake and its tributary are swift rivers, and the boat spent several sweaty days working her way up the three hundred miles she did, but when she turned around and started back, she came a-whooping, taking only twenty-four hours to make the run downstream to Wallula. She tried other waters around there and shortly had a companion, the wheezy little *Cascadilla* that began running from Lewiston to Fort Lapwai. In the meantime, the *Colonel Wright* kept at its chores, but in 1865 Captain Stump, who had replaced Captain White and who was about as daring, set out upstream once more, heading for Farewell Bend, on the border between Idaho and Oregon at the point where the overland trail crossed the Snake. For eight days Stump kept the boat clawing at the rapids of the Snake, inching her way until she had gone a hundred miles upstream before he turned her bow back down the river. Downstream she shot, in five hours, to Lewiston, but she never recovered; her aging hull was strained, and her owners, the Oregon Steam Navigation Company, ordered her broken up.

Beyond the canyon of the Snake certainly ought to be business; a mining boom had broken out around Boise, and miners were moving into the country in hordes. To carry them on their trips, the O.S.N. decided that, if to take a steamer through the canyon were impossible, one could be built above it. In 1866, therefore, the O.S.N. had the large stern-wheel *Shoshone* built at great expense at Old Fort Boise and launched into the river. As she drew less than two feet, the *Shoshone* had no trouble on the maiden voyage to Old's Ferry, and the company had high hopes. Then, too late, the discovery came that the river boom was over, for miners found a shorter route; the *Shoshone,* her occupation gone before she ever had it, slid up to the bank, made fast, and settled down to wait for something to happen. Nothing did, or practically nothing. One night a year later the watchman aboard awoke to hear guns banging away on the bank and, as he soon discovered, at the boat, but it was only a roving band of Indians with a mad or a binge on. Two years more she waited before the company took her away from there.

The upper Snake above the canyon clearly was not steamboating territory, at least until enough people moved in to make a sociable game of cards with the steamboat crew. At last the population arrived, encouraged by the building of the Oregon Short Line and the lively advertising Bob Strahorn issued about his townsites. When that happened, steamboatmen tried again. In 1890 came the *Gold Gatherer,* a husky, unlovely scow shoved along by a stern wheel, but the *Gold Gatherer* was not built to entice passengers. Her owners planned to use her to dredge gold-bearing sand from the banks and to work up and down the Snake from Huntington, panning all the remote bars. That the railroad bridge at Huntington was without a draw—when it was built no one had expected any kind of steamboat to come puffing along—had been overlooked, and *Gold Gatherer's* stack would not go under the bridge. There were words, very ponderous words, about it when the boat's owners sued the railroad. No one seems to remember how the suit came out, and maybe it did not matter, but the *Gold Gatherer* kept at her job for some time, keeping alive a western tradition of enterprise. How could she avoid it when her official place of building was named Whiskey Bottom.

Next came *Norma,* built by Jacob Kamm at Huntington in 1891, and the *Norma* learned all over again the lesson of the *Shoshone* a quarter of a century before: that nobody seemed to be in need of steamboats in those parts. So the *Norma* followed the *Shoshone* down the river in a few years, to find something to keep her busy at Lewiston.

Snake River running had fairly quickly settled down to the trip from Lewiston to the mouth, and some short runs up the Clearwater to Lapwai and up the Snake to around the Grande Ronde River. Miners and their supplies, gold dust, and groceries had to be carried, and later wheat, lots of it, after the farmer discovered the country on the tops of the bluffs. Rates went down sharply; by 1866 freight travelled from The Dalles to Lewiston at only $60 a ton. By then more boats were on the route, the *Spray, Webfoot, Yakima, Nez Perce Chief,* and the old *Tenino.* One of the stern-wheelers headed upriver from Celilo every other day, starting at 4:30 in the morning and arriving at Lewiston two days later. When the boom was over and traffic fell off, the service accordingly slackened, so that during low water, Lewiston had a boat only about once a week. Then the railroad built north from Walla Walla to reach Spokane, crossing the Snake at Texas Ferry, or Riparia, and the run between Wallula and there was dropped, boats covering only the stretch above the crossing to Lewiston.

With the rise of wheat growing, newer boats went on the Snake. In 1894 came the *Lewiston,* and in 1899 the *Spokane,* big boats, both built primarily for wheat carrying between Asotin, above Lewiston on the Snake, and Riparia. As they worked together, so they died together. Early on the morning of July 12, 1922, when the two stern-wheelers were tied up side by side at the dock in Lewiston, their watchman spotted a fire where no fire should be. The boats were cold, their boilers empty and furnaces out, but their upper works were tinder dry from the summer heat; so the fire spread, snapping at the heels of the watchman, and in an hour both boats were hulks. The *Lewiston* had been rebuilt in 1905 with a new hull and engines, but this time there was little to salvage, except some of the machinery, and, to replace her, an entirely new boat had to be built by her owners, the Union Pacific Railroad, successors to the O.S.N. and the O.R.&N.

The new *Lewiston,* for the name was retained, came down Supple and Martin's ways at Linnton in February 1923, a little smaller than the old one, but more powerful, and better built. Intended to carry a load of three hundred tons, the boat had the engines of the older *Lewiston* and was fitted solely as a freight hauler. The lower deck was left free, having only quarters for the firemen on it, equipped with showers and wash room. Her lower house extended to the guards, but the upper cabin had wide decks and housed the officers, stewards, and deckhands. Hot and cold running water was furnished the crew, to be about twenty men, and the accommodations were for their comfort. When she completed her trials, she set out to her station, there to relieve the *J. N. Teal*, that had been brought in to replace the burned boats.

After 1930 the new *Lewiston* had little work to do, so that she spent most of her time aging gracefully at the dock. Finally the Union Pacific abandoned its last river service and sold the *Lewiston* down the river to Portland where, in March 1940, she lost her old name and became a towboat, the *Barry K*, picking up odd jobs on the Columbia and Willamette. Eventually the Army had need of a boat like her in Alaska and sent her north in 1943 to join the fleet of stern-wheelers run by the Alaska Railroad on the Yukon and Tanana. She was a railroad boat all her life, except for the few, plodding years around Portland.

The *Colonel Wright* wore herself out on the Snake, and anyway the O.S.N. had use for her engines. Another gold rush began in the middle 1860's to Montana; one route, the Company decided, might be just as good as another, but better if the O.S.N. controlled it. Unfortunately, the O.S.N. had no such route handy, but it made one. First, the miners would go from Portland to the Snake River, riding elegantly on company boats; then they would travel by stage to the head of Lake Pend Oreille and take another company boat across the lake. From there, another stage or portage at Cabinet Rapids on Clark Fork would get them to still another company boat, and another portage to another boat, far up on the headwaters of the river. Beyond there the miners were on their own; the O.S.N. had run out of rivers. To open the route, the O.S.N. gave aid to a pair of builders at Lake Pend Oreille who put together the *Mary Moody*, using the engines of the dismantled *Colonel Wright* after they had been hauled overland in freight wagons. The little steamer made her first trip in March, 1867, crossing the lake to the mouth of Clark Fork and up the Fork to the foot of Cabinet Rapids. There she put ashore a party that set to work hacking a portage road through the woods. At the time another pair of steamers were under construction at Heron Rapids at the head of Cabinet Canyon, and until they were ready, the *Mary Moody* ploughed back and forth across the lake, carrying passengers and pack mules at $4 a head and pack mules with loads at $5. The three steamers were controlled by the Oregon and Montana Transportation Company,

Even as a ferry boat on San Francisco Bay, the
Telephone had lost none of her speed.

The *Olympian* was the biggest—and most expensive—boat
that operated on the Columbia River.

With boiling rapids abeam, the *Charles R. Spencer* edges
her way into the Cascade Locks.

Wilson Collection

Speed on the river. The *Hassalo* runs through the Cascades.

organized as a subsidiary of the O.S.N., and were advertised for their superior advantages. This route, according to the proprietors, opened to the public "the only route from the Pacific Coast over which Freight and Passengers can be transported any great distance by water," and put down its patrons a mere hundred miles from Missoula, charging them only $32.50 from Wallula for the trip. Freight moved at seven cents a pound, which sounds a lot cheaper than $140 a ton.

Like many booms the Montana boom faded, so that by the summer of 1867 it became depressingly clear to the owners of the Oregon and Montana Transportation (the owners of the O.S.N., that is) that the new boats would never pay for themselves. Rather than throw any more money in their direction, Captain Ainsworth wrote to the manager at Lake Pend Oreille to tie up the new boats and leave well enough alone. Mail was slow, then, and the letter got to Idaho too late—already the new boats were moving, but slowly. In mid-June the first of them, named *Missoula,* lined over Heron Rapids and went up to Thompson Falls to pick up business. But there was none, and, chastened, the *Missoula* crept back to Rock Island. The lack of patronage extended by eager miners was simply overwhelming, and the two boats, the other being the *Cabinet,* which was built to run between Heron Rapids and Rock Island Rapids, were tied to the bank and turned over to the mercies of watchmen, while the *Mary Moody* disconsolately kept at work on the lake. At last, in 1869, Ainsworth sent a crew to bring the *Cabinet* and *Missoula* through the rapids to the lake. Cabinet Rapids were too much, though, and at its head the two steamers were laid up. Below, on the lake, the *Mary Moody* tied up at the bank, and the saplings began to spring up in the portage roads.

While all this was going on, Captain Leonard White was at it again. After getting the *Colonel Wright* up the Snake and keeping boats going through all kinds of water, Captain White felt he was earning the monthly $500 that Coe and Thompson had paid him and that the O.S.N., when it took over the *Wright,* continued to pay him. Captain Ainsworth, who was no slouch of a steamboatman, thought otherwise; the idea of paying good wages was one of his pets, but there was no use overdoing a good thing. Captain Ainsworth suggested that a couple of hundred dollars be lopped off the salary to bring it down with other O.S.N. captains' wages, but Captain White in no uncertain terms said he'd be damned if he'd take a cent less. Captain Ainsworth was firm; Captain White was firm, but as the former had the money, the latter had a choice. Captain White stomped ashore, and Captain Stump stalked aboard. Captain White kept going, finally stopping due north of his starting point, at Little Dalles near where the Forty-ninth Parallel crosses the Columbia River. There he decided to build a steamboat, and Captain Ainsworth, who knew good steamboatmen and bore no grudges, supplied the machinery (from the old *Jennie Clark*) and some money, especially because another gold rush had broken out up in British territory around the Arrow Lakes. Captain White had his boat, called the *Forty-Nine,* ready at Colville Landing by December, 1865, and taking aboard some miners and their provisions started up the Columbia. The *Forty-Nine* made it through the rapids and to Fort Shepard, a Hudson's Bay post a mile above the Canadian boundary. Then, using a line, White worked her over Little Rock Rapids and reached the mouth of the Kootenai. The next day, however, near the head of Lower Arrow Lake he ran into ice and turned back after landing his load. Again, the next April, he set out, this time with fewer passengers, and got 270 miles above Colville Landing, steaming through both Arrow Lakes and up the river beyond as far as Death Rapids, now Revelstoke, B.C. This time there was a rush all right, but in the wrong direction, and on her third trip the *Forty-Nine* carried three passengers north and came back loaded to the guards with miners intent on getting out of that whole general country—the mines had not panned out well. White kept the boat going, running upriver light and coming back loaded, but with passengers too broke to pay. The hard work and cold had been bad for the Captain whose health failed, forcing him to go to the coast. In a year he was dead. Rarely had a more adventurous, determined spirit been on a river. Captain Leonard White deserves a monument, at least to his daring.

His steamboat did not survive him long. Hardly had he left before the *Forty-Nine* hit a rock and had to be beached in shallow water to keep her from sinking. Ainsworth in Portland viewed the disaster calmly and wrote to Captain Pingstone, White's successor in command, "As far as our interest in the boat is concerned, we are willing to dispose of it, or do most anything in reason that would enable the boat to be raised, *except it be to pay out any money.*" That was final, but Pingstone raised her and patched her anyway, so that she kept running, at least occasionally, for a few more years.

The upper river was not ready for steamboating. Curiously, the upper river had to wait for railroads before it had steamboats; on the lower reaches, it was the other way around—when the railroads came, the steamboats went.

Take Lake Coeur d'Alene, for example. The Northern Pacific built its line in the neighborhood in 1883 and promptly the Coeur d'Alene Transportation Company sprang into existence with a fine stern-wheeler, named, without imagination, *Coeur d'Alene*. The steamer served settlers on the lake shores and reached the old Mission on the St. Maries River above the lake. Soon the steamboat's owner sold out to the Northern Pacific, which kept it running across the lake. Later, in 1892, the *Coeur d'Alene* was replaced by the *Georgie Oakes*, as pretty a stern-wheeler as ever churned inland waters. She was an elegant boat looking like a boiled down version of the big *Wide West* on the Columbia, and she went about her daily round trip between the railroad and the Mission promptly, scooting along at as much as eighteen miles an hour, a really good clip, for there were few on the lower Columbia that could do better.

While the *Georgie Oakes* was being built on Lake Coeur d'Alene, the *Katie Hallett* was building on Clark Fork, to be used primarily to carry supplies for the railroad construction along the river. When the railroad was finished, her job was done and her engines were put aboard a new steamer built at Little Dalles and named the *Kootenai;* for finally, after fifteen years, there was reason for steamboating above the boundary.

Part of the reason was the general growth of the country, but fairly shortly the steamboats became weapons used by rival railroads to secure business. To the north the Canadian Pacific was building its line to the coast and throwing feeders down along the headwaters and branches of the Columbia; to the south were the Northern Pacific, and a little later the Great Northern, also sending branches into the upper Columbia country. Between were the lakes of British Columbia—Okanagan, Arrow, Kootenay, cut off from railroads, but rich and prosperous with mining suddenly developing as new methods were introduced. The *Kootenai* like her predecessor, *Katie Hallett,* was built to carry construction supplies for a railroad. Beyond the border, on Kootenay Lake and the Columbia in Canada, small steam launches and propellers appeared at the same time. In 1890 a number of steamboat owners joined to form the Columbia & Kootenay Steam Navigation Company, receiving encouragement from the Canadian Pacific, which saw the Spokane Falls and Northern Railway, one of Jim Hill's many projects connected with his Great Northern, creeping toward Little Dalles, where it would tap the business of the region. The new steamboat company fetched a shipbuilder from Victoria and set him to work on a stern-wheeler, the *Lytton,* which he finished in 1890, and at the same time it bought the *Kootenai,* tied up at Little Dalles since her job ended in 1886. The *Lytton* started service below Robson, going down the swift waters of the Columbia to Little Dalles; above Robson, the *Kootenai* took over the route and ran up to Revelstoke, except when the water was too low.

The railroad rivalry was sharp; first the Great Northern reached Little Dalles, then the Canadian Pacific got to Robson, and the Great Northern built to Bonner's Ferry and Nelson on the Kootenay River. Settlement increased, and many emigrants from the States moved toward the Canadian plains by way of the railroads and the steamboats. Quickly, to meet the increased business, the Columbia & Kootenay Steam Navigation Company built new boats, or bought those already at hand, adding the *Columbia* and *Nelson* in 1891, and the *Spokane,* the big *Nakusp* and others until a good-sized fleet worked back and forth on Kootenay Lake and River down to Bonner's Ferry, and on Arrow Lakes and the Columbia River. Farther west on Okanagan Lake a fine stern-wheeler, the *Aberdeen,* went in to service in 1893.

On the upper Kootenay River a steamboat also appeared, the *Annerly,* built at Jennings, Montana, to run up to Fort Steele in the Province. Another one, the *North Star,* under Captain Armstrong, who seemed to have something of Captain White's spirit, started at Jennings and kept going, up past Fort Steele and on to Golden, on the Columbia. That was something of a geographic miracle: to start toward the headwaters of one river and end on the headwaters of another, but it could be done—for a while, anyway. Near Columbia Lake in Canada, where the Columbia finally finds a source, the ground is low, with an imperceptible divide cutting the Columbia, which there is flowing from south to north, from the Kootenay, there flowing north to south, and only a mile or so apart. During part of the development one promoter cut a canal between the two rivers, put in wooden locks, and succeeded in making the whole Selkirk range of mountains an island. Through the locks, Armstrong took the *North Star,* and the job was done—headwaters of the

Kootenay to headwaters of the Columbia in one easy operation. Armstrong kept steamboats running around Golden, on the far upper Columbia, as long as traffic held out, or rather until the railroads came in, built branches, and took business away from him.

Farther downstream, the Columbia & Kootenay Steam Navigation Company found the railroads crowding in, too, but the Canadian Pacific bought out the steamboats and made them part of the railroad's own operations, adding to the fleet still more boats, like the *Kokanee*, and a new *Kootenay* to replace the original *Kootenai* (the Canadians, with singular perversity insist on spelling the name with a *-y*; and the Americans, with equal singular stubbornness hang onto the *-i*. Either way it is spelled, it comes out about the same). To meet increasing business, a pair of stern-wheelers, *Minto* and *Moyie*, which had been intended for northern waters to meet another gold rush, this time to A ska, were brought in and assembled, the *Minto* going to work on Arrow Lake, the *Moyie* on Kootenay. That pair still survive, graying as they approach the half-century, but still doing their work, *Moyie* running from Proctor to Kaslo every Saturday, touching all the way landings informally, and bringing to little, isolated lake settlements their mail, groceries, and visitors, stopping briefly to chat while the cargo is transferred, and going casually on. At noon everyone finds a good place on deck, breaks out a lunch basket, and sets to, since the *Moyie* no longer has the refinement of a dining room. But *Minto* still has one and needs one, for her run is longer, the length of Arrow Lakes and a strip of the Columbia down to Robson, a trip lasting about two days. There were other stern-wheelers in the fleet, newer than the twins, but they did not have such powers of survival. Perhaps their names were too much for them—*Kooskanook*, for example. However, *Nasookin*, built in 1913, by coming down in dignity a bit, kept at it until 1946. Her time seemed to come in 1931 when the railroad no longer had any use for her, but the Province reprieved her by buying her to serve as an auto ferry across the lake. At last, in 1946, work started on her successor, a twin screw ferry, and *Nasookin* was through, the last except for *Minto* and *Moyie* of the old stern-wheelers.

Many of the Canadian stern-wheelers had been built by Captain James Troup, inveigled to come north from the lower Columbia where he had a reputation for boat operation and design. Each new boat was built to fit a particular service or condition, such as the *Trail*, which Troup designed and built in 1896 especially for barge hauling, a form of business that was becoming important on the upper waters.

The first of the fleet, *Columbia,* caught fire at a woodpile and went up with a roar, but not until she had passed her name to another, not a boat. On one of her trips, crowded with settlers moving north, a baby was born on board, whereupon the Bishop of Westminster, by chance a passenger, got out his canonicals and in full regalia of his office, before an improvised font, intoned the christening, ending with the baby's name: Columbia Florence Holliday. Sometimes other excitement would break out. Now and then a rival boat would appear, and fight for advantage. The Great Northern quietly backed the entry of the American registered *State of Idaho,* a fast boat that soon showed her heels to *Nelson* or any other steamer on Kootenay Lake. The *State of Idaho* spent a glorious summer in 1893, racing the hapless *Nelson* and incidentally gathering in most of the business for the Great Northern, before the end came. One foggy trip her pilot missed his bearings and piled her up ashore where she was hastily surveyed and ruled a total wreck. Shortly afterwards she was repaired, put under Canadian registry, and went back to work, less spectacularly, under the name *Alberta.*

North of Little Dalles on the Columbia there is swift water to Robson, and more swift water above Arrow Lakes, the lakes breaking the rapids by some quiet water. Yet even the lakes could be ugly, as they were one cold night in 1895 when the little propeller *Arrow* caught a sudden squall in the Upper Lake and capsized, her crew drowning. South of Little Dalles the river is spotted with shoals and rapids, sometimes separately, sometimes together. There are short stretches of smooth water, but steamboating over the whole length down to the mouth of the Snake is at least hazardous, if not practically impossible. When something offered, a steamboat would go up as far as Priest Rapids, where the rough water began, take on the freight and return, but not on regular schedule. Then by the 1880's farmers who had taken up land along the Columbia found the Wenatchee and lower Okanogan country good for something besides mining. Finally, enough settlement to make steamboating profitable having gathered along the banks, Captain William Gray, who had been Stump's pilot on the *Colonel Wright* during the attempt to run up the Snake Canyon, was given the chance to try a regular run on the river above Priest Rapids. If anyone could get a boat through, he could.

For the new service, a new boat, named appropriately the *City of Ellensburgh,* slid into the river at Pasco, and as soon as the trial runs showed that everything was all right with her, Captain Gray loaded her with cordwood and headed upstream. Priest Rapids broke the river badly, but Gray got out a line, rigged tackle, and by using the capstan, hauled the boat over the rapids to where her wheel could get a grip on quiet water. Then the *City of Ellensburgh* chugged on upriver, passing safely through rough Rock Island Rapids, to Wenatchee. Behind her came a sister, the *Thomas L. Nixon,* built for the same owners, but lined around the rapids. The *City of Ellensburgh* was the smaller boat of the two and might be expected to be more agile. After 1888 the two stern-wheelers worked back and forth on the stretch between Wenatchee and the mouth of the Okanogan some eighty miles above.

For a number of years the pair had the river there largely to themselves, until the Columbia & Okanogan Steamboat Company put a fleet of boats to work handling the business that rapidly grew after the railroads began to bring in settlers. These were the *Oro,* the *Camano,* the *Selkirk,* and the *Wenatchee,* none very large and all built primarily for trading along the upper river. They were followed by the *Chelan, Enterprise, North Star,* and *W. H. Pringle,* the last being the largest yet put on the upper river.

A river boat working out of Wenatchee could not expect a long and comfortable life on those waters. There were quiet reaches occasionally, but there were also swift ones, and shoals, and rapids, scattered the length of the stream. Finally, the Army Engineers improved the river, blasting out occasional boulders and snags, but confining themselves largely to navigation aids—simple gadgets, made by embedding in firm rock ledges large iron ringbolts. To them a line was secured above the rough water and the boat reeled itself in, or rather over, the rapid. At the lesser rapids, where such heroic methods of steamboating did not have to be used but where the current moved faster than the best speed the boat could muster, another system came into use. When one of the little trader boats came to the rapid, it sent a line ashore and fastened it to a string of horses that waited with a driver. That done, the boat drifted into the channel, piled on all the steam its boiler would hold, spun its wheel furiously, and headed into the rapid. Ashore, the horses surged against their collars as they moved along a towpath by the river, and between the horses and the steamer's engine, both panting with exertion, the boat was able to scramble over the rocks. Going downstream when the water was high was easy; all the pilot had to do was remember where the channel ought to be, head for it, and pray that an eddy did not toss the boat onto a rock. If the water happened to be low, the captain fastened a line to a handy ringbolt, and the boat let itself down the rapid, practically hand over hand.

Those were the routine methods. Sometimes they failed to work, and a boat would not quite make it. Now and then the steamer would go browsing to one side or another and fetch up against a rock that the pilot had not noticed, and there she would hang until she could be floated off or pried loose. Or she would go hard aground on the rocky bank and refuse to be coaxed off, hauled off, or walked off. When a boat grounded, a pair of spars, fixed to either side of the boat, would be let into the water to the bottom; then the boat would be lifted on the spars, as if on a leg-derrick, until she was free. Steamboating in shallow water was hardly a sport for an inactive man; certainly it was not a sedentary occupation for the contemplative. A steamboatman on these waters seemed to be walking as much as he rode, and occasionally he had a long walk, unless he preferred to build a fire and wait for another steamboat to come along.

The casualties were heavy. Though a good many boats at one time or another worked out of Wenatchee, they came and went, only a few running at the same time. The *Alexander Griggs,* built in 1903 by the Columbia and Okanogan Steamboat Company, smashed herself on Entiat Rapids in 1905; the next year the big *W. H. Pringle* piled up at the same place, and the *Selkirk* bashed herself to pieces at Rock Island Rapids. Curiously, the old *City of Ellensburgh* watched a lot of her younger companions go to smash and then was herself quietly dismantled in 1905, her usefulness gone. That is not to say the *Ellensburgh* or the *Nixon,* which had been broken up in 1901, escaped without a scratch. Obviously they did not—a steamboat could not scrape along over the rapids and shallows without showing it, and new planking replaced splintered every time a boat came to the dock yard. For a boat to be grounded during high water meant not much more than a long wait until the river fell so that she could be shored up, patched, and worked back to the water on rollers.

A decline in boating came with the slowing of settlement after 1910 so that the C. & O. S. Co. had only four vessels in its fleet by

1915, the *Columbia, North Star, Okanogan,* and *Chelan.* Of them, the *Chelan* was the oldest, having been built in 1900, with accommodations for 110 passengers and a good cargo of freight. Before the Great Northern ran its Oroville branch along the Columbia and Okanogan rivers above Wenatchee, steamboats needed plenty of passenger space, for everyone moving north had to go by boat. *Chelan* was the favorite with passengers, as she was the fastest of the fleet, although *Okanogan* was larger and better equipped. As the summer of 1915 advanced, business declined, and all of the fleet lay at Wenatchee together, *Chelan* tied closest to the bank, with the other three clustered alongside. The *North Star* was moored farthest out, for the company planned to sell her to Captain McDermott for use on the Columbia up around Bridgeport. In fact, the sale waited only for the arrival of the federal inspector to approve her condition.

It was July, and the boatyard was deserted, except for the watchman Reeves and his son who did the maintenance work on the boats while they were idle. Neither Reeves nor his son smoked, and they were careful about fire and matches. A steamboat in summer is practically explosive with all its dry, light woodwork in the cabins. Early in the morning of July 8 Reeves was on duty when he spotted fire on the *North Star.* He rushed ashore with the alarm, but in five minutes the boats were gone—from the *North Star* the fire leaped quickly to the other boats and sent a spire of flame and golden sparks high into the sky. By the time the fire department clanged down First Street to the yard, the boats were burning from stem to wheel, their tall stacks sagging and the cabins folding back into the flames as if they were cardboard cutouts tossed into a bonfire. The firemen unreeled their hoses and went to work, not on the boats, which were gone anyway, but on the buildings of the yard. Then, almost as quickly as it had started, the fire was over. Inshore, the *Chelan* survived; her cabins scorched and in part burned, her back apparently broken when the hog-chains gave way. Beyond her were hulks; everything above the waterline of the three other boats had gone, and the engines and boilers had dropped through the charred ribs into the water. The Columbia and Okanogan Steamboat Company had literally passed out of existence. Only a short time before the company's insurance policies had lasped; want of business had made premium payment impossible, at least until the sale of the *North Star* was completed.

Even the *Chelan* was beyond repair. Ironically, the *St. Paul,* one of the few boats not owned by the company, burned the same year at Wenatchee, so that it seemed fire was bound to do what the river could not. A few boats survived. Captain McDermott had intended to run the *North Star* beyond Pateros as a companion to his *Enterprise,* which he had leased from the C. & O. S. Co. and operated between Pateros and Bridgeport. Then, on July 12, 1915, just four days after the big fire, the *Enterprise* quietly foundered at Brewster's Ferry. The *Del Rio* and the *Robert Young* were still on the upper river and would last about ten years, and in 1917 came the *Bridgeport* that lingered around Bridgeport for a long time.

Downstream, around Pasco, another attempt to develop river navigation started sometime after the turn of the century. Steamers were expensive and required a fairly large crew—captain, engineer, purser, steward, firemen, and deckhands, and a big boat had to have a crew of a couple of dozen or more if passengers were to be accommodated. Then came the *Mata C. Hover,* a boat intended to operate in shallow water at the slightest possible expense. Her forerunner had been the *Leona,* a light draft scow, built for the Cowlitz River, powered by a gasoline engine that by clutch and gearing eventually turned a stern wheel. One man could operate a gasoline driven stern-wheeler, if he kept his wits about him and remembered to watch the channel, shift gears, engage his clutch, advance his spark and throttle, and go through other operations—not the least of which was a periodic trip to the bank for a session of tinkering with a recalcitrant motor. A number like her went to work after 1906, carrying wheat from White Bluffs down to Celilo. The idea was a good one, a bit early for a gasoline motor but a bit late for a stern-wheeler, because it lasted only a few years, while the wheat went down the river in railroad box cars or barges.

All of the Columbia boats were built to carry freight, although now and then they found too late that no cargo crying to be taken somewhere happened to be in their neighborhood. With the *Swan,* down on the Umpqua, things were different—the *Swan* was built to convince Congress that the river was navigable. Of course, no one would deny that the lower reaches of the Umpqua were good for steamers. Once a ship gets over the nasty bar at the mouth, it is in wide Winchester Bay which curves back from the sea so that it is a sheltered harbor, rimmed by low green forested hills. The Pacific Mail Steamship Company had considered making the bay its northern terminal from whence the mail could be sent by pack train to the Willamette Valley. By the mid-1850's Gardiner, the town on the bay, was busy with much shipping. Beyond the estuary, as the river moves back toward the mountains, it is broad, deep, tidal. Twenty miles upstream it narrows and shallows, and there at the ordinary head of navigation the Hudson's Bay Company had placed a minor post, recognizing that from it trails could fan out north and south. Later a town, Scottsburg, grew at the place. With the growth of mining and settlement in the Rogue River Valley, Scottsburg and the river became so busy that in 1853 a merchant at Scottsburg, Captain Hinsdale, went to the Willamette, bought the iron propeller *Washington* and took her to the Umpqua where he put her to work on occasional towing jobs in the bay and on regular runs up and down the river. The *Washington* kept at it until December 1857, when one day, just below Scottsburg, her boiler let go with a crash and scattered pieces of her all over the township.

The decline of the gold fields in the Rogue River country reduced the importance of the route, but settlers along the upper Umpqua were numerous enough and vocal enough to demand service. Not much was left of Scottsburg; in 1861 a flood came ramping down the canyon and took the row of warehouses and refined deadfalls by the bank and almost everything else in town, except buildings that had been perched high on the slope. But Nicholaus Haun had an idea that eventually became a steamboat. Haun urged that if a steamboat could reach Roseburg at least once, perhaps an appropriation might be obtained to clear and deepen the channel for other steamboats, which, in turn, would bring prosperity to the whole region by providing the farmers with an outlet to market their crops. Costs of transportation would fall, and the whole valley would flourish. Haun organized the Umpqua Steam Navigation Company and went to work.

So the *Swan* was built to go to Roseburg. From Gardiner she set out on her voyage upriver on January 20, 1870, and got to Scottsburg, a feat not particularly notable because any steamboat could do it. Beyond Scottsburg she was on her own and promptly ran into some rocks, smashed both her rudders, and had to tie up to a handy tree by the bank while the crew built new ones. That took a full day, but on the next she got to Mill's Ferry, twenty-two miles upriver from Scottsburg. There her boiler gave trouble, and as the river continued low, without a normal stage of water, her captain turned her around and took her back to Gardiner where she waited three weeks before trying again. The second time she had better luck, only knocking off one rudder and breaking her capstan. Undeterred by such minor irritants, the *Swan* swept on up the Umpqua and made it to Roseburg, taking a mere eleven days to cover the less than one hundred miles. Swifter navigation has been recorded, and swifter travel ashore—a man on horseback could have made it in a couple of days, and a team and farm wagon in four or five. Still, the *Swan* was under a handicap; she had to stick to the river. If she had been able to go ashore and cut across the fields she would have travelled a good deal faster. It is not exactly truthful to say that she navigated the Umpqua; part of the way she walked, and a fair share of the way she was hauled bodily along, especially where the river was so shallow that anyone who fell overboard from her was liable to raise a cloud of dust when he landed. Urged by ropes tied to trees and wound on the capstan, by pry-bars, and by teams of horses brought down to help by the farmers along the river, the *Swan* inched upstream. Why Haun failed to jack her up and put rollers under her is hard to explain; maybe, in fact, he did. But he made it, acclaimed by crowds the length of the river. At Cole's Valley, one of the places where the boat tied up after a hard day, the farmers swept out a barn and held a dance that lasted, as was usual with such dances, all night. (There was no use going to the trouble of piling into a farm wagon and riding for hours just for a short party—might as well have a real hoe-down when the chance came.) At Roseburg when the *Swan* crept up to the landing, a bit worse for wear, the citizenry gathered there banged away with anvils until the powder ran out. Then they cheered, and that dried their throats so much the celebration adjourned to a place where a man could prop his foot on a brass rail and brace himself while he hoisted a few.

The *Swan* got back down without much trouble, and the Umpqua Steam Navigation Company published its tariff for freight to Roseburg. Word went to Washington of the feat, and Congress, suitably impressed, appropriated $70,000 for improvement of the channel of the river. The project called for removing the worst rocks and snags but meant mainly that the whole sum would be spent in the valley, to the accompaniment of impressive bangs from black powder. The valley appreciated it: seventy thousand dollars made the whole country quite prosperous for a time. The *Swan*, meanwhile, preened her ruffled feathers and then set about a more graceful job running between Scottsburg and Gardiner. She must have been a staunch boat, for after all the battering and straining she took, she kept running for several years.

The Umpqua was not the only river with ambitions in Oregon. Almost every town by some stream or body of water that could not be jumped by an agile boy had ambitions to own a steamboat. Once it had a steamboat, commerce would come to its wharf; business would expand; the outside world would be at hand. Eventually, some sort of steamboat poked its prow up most of the weedy sloughs and narrow rivers—the Coos, the Coquille, the Siuslaw, the Yaquina—and appeared on such lakes as Klamath, Goose, and Wallowa. Even such an unlikely river as the John Day in central Oregon is said to have had a steamboat.

At Yaquina Bay, an estuary something like that of the Umpqua mouth, a port developed to serve settlements along the Yaquina River, and with the promotion of the Oregon Pacific Railroad, the harbor town, Newport, for a time rivalled Seaside. Regular steamers came there from San Francisco bringing tourists to the big hotels at the waterfront, and over the hills the trains brought more visitors from the Willamette Valley and Portland. From the end of the railroad above Newport passengers were carried to the resort by boat. Settlements on the south shore needed service too, yet in spite of the apparent chance for paddlers, not many were ever put to use. The *Oneatta*, a stubby little side-wheeler, appeared in 1872 but lasted only a short time until she went to the Columbia. The *Mollie* was another paddler, built in 1874 and lasting into the late 1880's, but most of the steamers there were propellers.

Klamath Lake needed boats to carry freight and passengers from the town of Klamath Falls on the Link River up to settlements and logging operations on the north and west shores of the lake, but not until 1879 did the *General Howard*, a small propeller, begin running. Eventually finding that screw vessels drew too much water for operation along the lake, a man who had a contract for hauling supplies up the lake built a flat bottomed stern-wheeler he called prophetically the *City of Klamath Falls* and put it to work in 1884. After that, as business, especially logging, increased, more boats followed, culminating in the big *Winema*, a three-decker stern-wheeler that was 125 feet long with a draft of less than two feet.

With the *Winema* every cove of the lake could be reached, and the boat was kept busy after her building in 1905. When she was not carrying produce and general freight and passengers from place to place on the lake, she carried excursions out of Klamath Falls, for in 1906 the town was booming. It had a railroad, the California Northwestern, and it had a horse-car line. With the *Winema* progress was complete, and Klamath Falls could look forward only to paving and population for improvement. On one trip, running light, the *Winema* ran into a gale of wind that caught her superstructure, looming high and not well anchored by the shallow hull, and was neatly capsized in a dozen feet of water. As she went over, crew and passengers catted over the side and hung on to the part that stayed above the water while the Captain, getting a skiff loose, rowed ashore for help. Righted, patched, and her top deck removed to give her less wind resistance, the *Winema* kept going until 1925. By then a major highway skirted the lake, the railroad was building beyond Kirk, and motor tugboats hauled barges and logs. That was the usual fate: the steamboat pioneered, took aboard passengers and freight, and generally opened up a region. A railroad came in, and business slackened for the steamer. Then a highway followed, with trucks on it. Business slackened in turn for the railroad—and disappeared for the steamboat.

Chapter 8

THE WHEAT FLEET

GOOD WHEAT LAND, the settlers arriving by wagon train called the Willamette Valley. Good wheat land, with its wide plain and gentle slopes of unbroken soil, its long growing spring and hot, ripening summer. Good wheat land said the settlers, looking out of the car windows of the Northern Pacific, and the Great Northern, and the Union Pacific, at the high rolling plains of the Inland Empire. You could bet your boots and bottom dollar that the Oregon country would grow wheat.

From the time the first farmers broke the prairie and shared their crops with the patron Hudson's Bay Company, the Oregon country was good wheat land, passing through the yearly cycle of planting and growth and harvest. It was anybody's land, free for the asking by fulfilling a few rules that regulated the donation claim or the homestead, or at the worst later it was still fairly cheap. East of the Cascades it was open prairie, just waiting for the plow; and in the Willamette Valley the farmer did not have too much trouble clearing it. First, he hacked down the brush—small trees, bushes and bramble thickets, leaving them where they fell. That job he started in the spring, and by late summer the slash was dry for burning on the fields. Long poles of saplings might be saved for firewood or fencing, but the rest burned where it lay, until over the land spread a blanket of gray ash. In September when the clearing fires were burning, over all of western Oregon hung a curtain of smoke that the sun came thinly through with coppery light, and the hills hazed behind blue clouds. Sometimes steamboatmen found the Columbia gorge so smoky that they had a hard time following the channel marks. And forest fires, too, would run without let for miles along the slopes in the high timber. The whang of wood smoke was everywhere.

After the brush burned, the farmer did not bother to plow; instead he broadcast the wheat into the ash itself and then dragged a heavy tree branch back and forth across the ground, working the ash and the grain together into the soil. Next year he would break the ground, driving his plow through the stiff stubble from the first crop, and leaving the fields cleanly brown, or black, or sometimes, if he had picked a farm at the edge of the valley, a bricky red. If he had timed everything nicely, then the rains came, and those of winter, with perhaps some snow in the valley. Spring and the wheat came together, the dark ground showing a furring of green as the seed sprouted in the warming sun. Then through the growing season the green thickened, and the spring winds sent waves of shadow across the fields. Slowly the wheat stiffened, the heads formed and filled, and by summer ripened, turning to pale green, then to yellow, then to the vivid gold that seemed to send back the sun and make radiant the earth.

With the harvest came dust. The farmer of the early years might spend his days swinging the ponderous scythe and cradle, or a little later riding the reaper whose spidery arms circled across the field. Then the wheat was gathered and stacked to wait the thresher, and all the while the farmer watched the skies. Through the long, dry summer the wheat ripened unhurt by rain, and now the fall rains, the farmer prayed would hold off until the grain was in and under cover. Threshing days were events to the small boys, to practically everybody, probably, even if they did mean hard work. Late in the afternoon the machine came, drawn by long teams of horses. Then in the morning, almost before the sun came over the east line of the hills, crews went to work rigging and tinkering the thresher. A team started its slow circular march, drawing the sweep that, through cogs, put the machinery into action. A later improvement was a steam engine, mounted on tall wheels with wide iron treads, that through belting ran the thresher. The engine towed the thresher, too, along the roads, much to the delight of boys. In time came the combine, drawn by horses, steam road engines, or later, heavy tractors, and the combine did everything at once: cut the wheat, sent it through the thresher, cast aside the straw and chaff, and delivered the wheat in bags, leaving the crews only the sewing of the wheat bags. But however the job was done, tall clouds of yellow dust rose from the fields and told where the harvest was going on.

At last the wheat was sacked, and the farmer then had the worst job of all, and often the most expensive—the haul to market. Constantly he sought easy, cheap ways. That is where the rivers came in handy; if he could get the sacks of wheat to the river, he had an easy road down to market, where he could sell his grain and finally perhaps make some money, which was what he had set out to do in the first place. The easier he could get the wheat to market, the more money he could make; to him the economics of agriculture seemed amazingly clear and simple.

Oregon began shipping wheat early. From the farms of the Willamette Valley the Hudson's Bay Company supplied its posts and traded the remainder on the coast. Up to Sitka went wheat as well as flour from McLoughlin's mills to supply the Russians, and company ships carried more flour down to Yerba Buena in California and across to Honolulu. Wheat grew bountifully; in 1844 the valley, then just being settled from overland, had a surplus of a hundred thousand bushels on hand that it wanted to get rid of. The Hudson's Bay Company could not take it all, and the farmers began a continual search for other buyers until the gold rush started in California, when the market turned around and sought the wheat.

Always the river figured in the crop. Those first keel boats and flatboats of 1846 were wheat boats, bringing the bagged grain from landings at Butteville and Champoeg or any place where a farmer found a spot he could stack his sacks. A river of wheat rode on the river itself. Wharfboats overloaded by the weight of wheat on them tipped into the river. Flatboats with so many of the bags piled on them that their gunwales were barely above the water swamped when they ran into rough rapids. Oregon's first river disaster came to a keel boat, too heavily laden, that went out of control in Rock Island Rapids above Canemah and drowned four of the crew.

Then the steamboats appeared. During the harvest of 1851 they were busy, going up the Willamette light and coming back loaded, with wheat piled high on their freight decks. As the valley settled, the boats each year pushed farther up the rivers after their cargoes. At first Butteville and Champoeg were the main landings, but quickly Dayton emerged as a shipping port on the Yamhill. Other new places came into prominence with descriptive names like Wheatland and Fairfield. Salem shipped wheat, and so did Albany and Corvallis. Quickly the wide flat lands of the upper valley boomed, and Peoria and Harrisburg stacked wheat on their landings. To Lancaster came farmers from the country between the Long Tom and Eugene, until a flood swept down the river, cut across an ox-bow, and left Lancaster a mile from the stream. Far up at Eugene, more wheat gathered for the *James Clinton* and the *Enterprise* to carry away.

Every small town that had a stream giving sufficient fall had a flour mill, for flour was cheaper to ship than bulk wheat and the demand was greater. Some mills grew and lasted, like the one at Boston that survived the town. But wherever they were, they cried for river boats to take their product, whether they were on the Willamette or up some tributary like the Long Tom at Monroe, the Santiam at Lebanon, the Yamhill, the Tualatin. The rates charged by the river boats were a constant source of disputes around the general stores along with politics and usually the two subjects somehow got mixed as the talk ran on. How to get the wheat to market and still to make the income exceed the cost of production—that was the endless problem. The farmer was sure the wheat buyers were out to skin him; the wheat buyer was pinched between what the farmer wanted and what Liverpool would pay, and both began a long fight to cut costs, to permit wheat to be laid down on the docks at Portland at the lowest possible shipping charge. The rates went down but the wails of anguish went up at the same time. The editor of the *Oregon Spectator* had cried monopoly back in October 1848, saying:

The last grain crop of Oregon was abundant, and cattle and hogs are also abundant—all of which would command an enormous price at the California mines—yet wheat brings but 62 cents a bushel delivered at the mills in this city, and the prices of pork and beef are nearly proportionate with that of wheat. It is a very difficult matter for those who do not own or control vessels to ship flour to California. Some has been shipped as a matter of *pure grace and favor* at $4 per barrel.

The thing to do, obviously, was to control the boats so far as possible, and the farmers regularly promised trade to any line that would agree to reduce rates below those prevailing at the moment. The *Gazelle* took to the river in 1854 to break the monopoly held by its predecessors, and from then on the monopoly was successively broken and reformed. Companies sponsored by farmers or operated in their name and ostensibly for their benefit continually appeared and were swallowed by larger companies, each leaving behind it as a kind of memory a steamboat it had built. So in 1873 the Willamette River Transportation Company, backed by Bernard Goldsmith, Joseph Kellogg, and Jacob Kamm, among others, built the *Gov. Grover* and sent her as far as Harrisburg, the largest boat to go that far up the river. The company owned the *Vancouver*, too, and the *Beaver*, and at last the big *Willamette Chief*, built specifically to run from the headwaters of the river to Astoria to carry wheat to the sea at a rate of only $4 a ton from Corvallis (the *Gazelle*, twenty years before had charged $20 a ton from Corvallis to Oregon City, and from there the *Wallamet* had added $8 more to Astoria). The invasion of the Willamette Transportation Company helped the farmers temporarily, especially when Holladay's People's Transportation Company entered the rate war with a whoop and for a time charged only a dollar a ton from Portland to Astoria.

Sometimes the farmers used heroic methods to get their wheat to the world outside. On the Yamhill boats could go some distance, but for practical purposes, Dayton was the head. And the roads were unbelievably bad—if they were roads at all. When the wheat boom of the Seventies got under way, the farmers demanded better ways to carry their wheat and hit upon the idea of a railroad to connect with the steamboats.

And so the farmers, aided by enthusiastic organizers like Joseph Gaston, formed the Dayton, Sheridan and Grand Ronde Railroad Company to build their own line from the river at Dayton back to the wheat towns it named. The farmers took shares, receiving in return certificates good for freight shipments, and in 1878 the road gradually took shape. Of course, the company went broke. The farmers shipped their wheat and paid for the costs with their certificates, leaving the railroad no cash income—and the contractors took over, selling out in time to a new group, controlled by canny Scottish investors, whose representative, William Reid, extended it as the Oregonian Railway down both sides of the valley.

There was another attempt to give the farmers an outlet to the sea, although the idea actually came as an afterthought. T. Egenton Hogg, a man of vast dreams and visions, saw a railroad reaching from Yaquina Bay to some vague point on a transcontinental line in Montana or Idaho and set to work to build the Oregon Pacific west and east from Corvallis. His road got to Yaquina Bay all right but never mustered strength to cross the Cascades and had to depend on freight it could collect in the Willamette Valley. To gather what might be offered, the Oregon Pacific organized its own steamboat line, called the Oregon Development Company, bought the *Salem* and *City of Salem,* and built for its service the *Wm. H. Hoag, N. S. Bentley,* and *Three Sisters,* all of which began running in 1886 and 1887. They were good boats, and for the Willamette fairly large; between them they maintained alternate day service between Portland and Corvallis, taking the usual two days for the trip, laying over for the night at Salem. The *N. S. Bentley* and the *Three Sisters* lasted ten years, but the *Wm. M. Hoag* seemed to go on indefinitely, and then undergo reincarnation. She took to the river from a yard in East Portland in 1887 and went through a series of owners for sixteen years before she was hauled out for rebuilding. When the work was finished the old boat had new fittings and a new name—the *Annie Comings,* and went back to work towing, appropriately, wheat ships for the Western Transportation and Towing Company. In 1907 *Annie Comings* collided with the French bark *Europe* in the Willamette and sank; the big sailing vessel, in for a wheat cargo, had too much weight and bulk for the stern-wheeler, but by 1909 the *Annie Comings* had been raised, rebuilt, and put back on the job, and she kept at it until 1941 when her owners took out her engines and boilers.

Along the Willamette, wheat had always been the main crop and continued to be, but in time the Inland Empire came first to be the Willamette's rival and then its master. Settlers for years passed by the high treeless plains bordering the upper Columbia. Eastern Oregon and Inland Empire wheat was winter wheat primarily; the Willamette Valley had lots of winter wheat, but most farmers there preferred to make their plantings in the spring and raise Club instead of white or white velvet winter varieties. Once the hesitation to climb up onto the plains passed, Eastern Oregon and Washington began to produce wheat in quantities, and by 1885 it dominated the region. Of course the coming of the railroad had helped in two ways—it had brought in settlers (attracted by railroad advertising) and it could move the wheat to market.

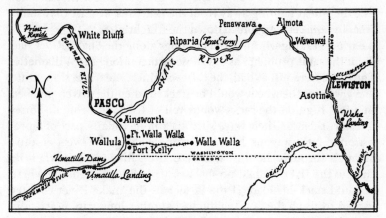

The railroad, as the farmers discovered, could move the wheat to market when it could gather enough empty cars to do the job. Sometimes wheat would be stacked by sidings in long walls, a dozen feet high, for a quarter of a mile, waiting in the sun for trains to haul it down to Portland. The railroads tried, but they could not meet the need—they lacked the equipment to handle so much tonnage in so little time. That is where steamboats might have come in handy, except for the embarrassing fact that there were no steamboats. Confident in its ability to move anything offered, the Oregon Railway and Navigation Company had, after 1883, swept the river clean of boats and taken them all down the river below Celilo, leaving only a few to handle traffic on the Snake where the railroads did not go. After a couple of seasons went by, and the wheat sat by the railroad tracks for days—while prices fluctuated and the farmers, gambling on catching the price at its peak, swore mighty and ponderous oaths, the howl from the Inland Empire roared down the Columbia gorge like a hurricane and shook the brand new dome of the capital at Salem. That was when the cry "Open River!" became the shibboleth of the embattled farmers of the upper river, and that cry would be constant for thirty years. Steamboats came back to the river; The Dalles, Portland and Astoria Transportation Company began to run from Portland through the Cascade Locks to The Dalles, and the Open River Transportation Company started a through line from Portland to Wallula. Some big, fine new boats went into service: *The Dalles, J. N. Teal, Relief, Regulator,* and if they did not take the wheat hauling away from the railroads, at least they sometimes by competition forced down the freight rates.

Farmers taking wheat to the landings along the Snake River had about the same problems as did those farmers along the Willamette. The roads were just as bad, the dust was thick, the travel slow. Onto heavy wagons the wheat would be stacked; then the driver, perched on a seat high on the sacks would yell at the long string of horses and start them on their way. Mile after mile, usually part of a procession of farm wagons, he would trundle along, the sweat eroding channels through the dust that settled on his face. But when he came to the river, he had no short easy pitch to the landing where he could stack his load. If the farmer in the Snake River country wanted to reach the landing, he had another long trip, practically straight down, for the river was below him in a deep, narrow gorge. The road twisted and wound down, down, down, and a loaded wagon had to drag logs, be snubbed, and be held back with ropes all the way from the crest to the landing. A trip or two up and down one of those roads left a farmer exhausted and his vocabulary of cussing pumped dry.

Instead of fighting gravity all the way down, why not let gravity do the work? From the landings up to the top of the canyon wall long covered chutes were built, rising straight, almost vertically; at the top was a hopper into which the wheat could be shovelled, and at the bottom was a bin, large enough to hold several wagon loads, usually fitted with a spout so that the wheat could be sacked at the landing. The first time the chutes were used, the wheat shot down wildly, arriving a bit battered and frayed at the bottom, having almost ground itself into meal by friction and collision during the fall; to slow down the wheat and keep it from going right through the bin into the river, a series of baffles had to be put into the chutes. But time, some patience, and a good deal of ingenuity finally made the device work, and along the Snake River travellers saw pipes rising straight up the canyon wall from each landing. So practical were they that later when the railroads threaded their way down the Snake and the Deschutes canyons, the chutes continued to be used.

When the grain finally got to Portland and was stacked in the warehouses perched on spindly piling by the river banks, the spectacular part of wheat shipping began. The hard work for the farmer was over and now the middleman took over the worry and the job, while all Portland sat back to watch the show, and it was a show—the river filled with ships with tall masts and spreading yards that rose high above the city. That was the wheat fleet, and it ran a season of four months or more each year for forty years and gave Portland a character all its own. There were other wheat fleets eventually—Tacoma, Seattle, Port Costa—but none had the setting for it that Portland did with the river winding through the city.

Though wheat had always gone down the river and out to sea from Portland, not until 1868 did it become a separate spectacle in the harbor. Before then most wheat had been taken down to San Francisco in small coastal vessels or as parts of cargo of the main coastwise steamers, there to be blended with California wheat and reshipped. That in reshipment it was called "California wheat" naturally made the Oregonian unhappy; that his wheat, raised in his country, should bear the alien name was too much indignity, and not until it was discovered that Oregon grain made good flour without blending did his faith and joy return. When the bark *Sallie Brown* from New York, starting a new direct line from the East Coast, came in and loaded wheat, Portland turned out to cheer; but almost on her heels the *Helen Angier* arrived under charter to carry a full cargo of wheat. She was the pioneer, the first of hundreds of successors that brought money and work to Oregon and carried away the crop.

After *Helen Angier* sailed, the fleet took form rapidly. In 1869 the Portland firm of Corbett and Maclay chartered the *Adeline Elwood* for wheat and sent her off to England with it—and with a hundred cases of salmon to try the English appetite and perhaps to extend the market for the new canning industry. The next year five vessels had to be used, and then seven, and then sixteen, so that by 1872 the wheat fleet was in existence. That year there were two American ships and two British, along with smaller barks, all British except for a single Spaniard. The British from the beginning furnished most of the bottoms and gradually edged out the Americans whose merchant marine was going through the long decline that followed the War Between the States. Getting together a fleet took time; ships had to be gathered from all over the world under charter, their masters had to be notified when they touched far off places, and the ships themselves had to be in Portland at a given time. In the days before steam when the ship's way was the wind's way, and the voyages long and slow, and before the cable had reached the strange ports where the tramps touched, the shippers had to allow a year to reach each captain and secure his ship. Usually the vessels were casuals, coming once and then going out, not to return, but a few turned up year after year, like the bark *Barracouta* that came in half a dozen times.

So the fleet grew and as shipping became cheaper and easier, more wheat came down the rivers; in 1870 the Willamette Valley shipped nearly 28,000 tons and felt prideful, but in 1873 it shipped 44,000 tons and took it as a matter of course. In 1877 the export crop brought into Oregon $7,300,000, no small sum, and that year eighty-one vessels were engaged, ranging from the little British bark *Japan* of about 400 tons to the big British ship *Beecroft,* 1600 tons. Surely, agreed everyone who saw her moored in the river, bigger ships never would come upriver, but eight years later the *Tillie E. Starbuck* arrived, and she was rated at 1,931 tons. She had other distinctions, for she flew the American flag at her gaff and was built at the shipyards of John Roach, the only sailing vessel he built. When the *Starbuck* came in the river, she had a heavy load aboard—twenty locomotives for the Northern Pacific, and the fabricated parts for the big train ferry at Kalama. She dropped that cargo and took aboard wheat, made her voyage, and was back in the river again the next year. During the late 1880's over a hundred vessels came in each year for the wheat, but after 1890 the number dropped off, although the cargo they moved did not. More ships, fewer barks accounted for the difference.

Each year the routine was the same. Each year, it seemed, one or more of the fleet would lose its bearings and pile up on the bars that stretched across the mouth of the Columbia, but others took their places. First the tall masts rose over the horizon, and the bar pilot would wait his hail. Sometimes the incoming ship would ride grandly in, picking up its pilot and sailing over the bar as easily as you please, but sometimes there would be fog or off-shore wind, and then the ships would wait, beating back and forth, until they could risk the entry. Once in the river the bar tug dropped its tow, the sails fell limp, the anchor plumped down, and the crew swarmed up the ratlines to make all secure. If the captain happened to be a driver who demanded everything be shipshape and Bristol fashion, he had the yards squared away and the sails tightly furled, but if he did not, the yards rode askew, sometimes festooned with Irish pennants. Then the quarantine inspector climbed aboard to clear the ship, and everything was made ready for the trip up the river to the wheat docks at Portland.

Waiting at Astoria were the towboats which had gathered for the season. Sometimes towboats did double duty: first they hauled the wheat to the warehouses at Portland and then they went on to Astoria to haul the ships up the river to the wheat. When everything was ready, a big stern-wheeler nosed out to the waiting ship, sidled up against its quarter and made fast. When several sailing vessels waited and the towboat was husky enough, two would be placed side by side, and the tug would shoulder in between them. That was the *Ocklahama's* favorite method, and she could do it, husky as she was, with power to spare. The Buchanan Brothers in 1875 built the *Ocklahama,* a stern-wheeler intended solely for towing, but before they finished her, the Willamette Transportation and Locks Company, looking for likely boats to compete with the People's Transportation line, bought her and put her to work. The *Ocklahama* labored faithfully, towing in her time more than any other boat on the river; in 1894, worn out, she was rebuilt so thoroughly that a practically new boat from keel to hog-chains went into service in 1897, but her name remained the same. She was big and strong, and she was tough, for not until 1930, when the towing business had declined, was she abandoned. Over half a century the Columbia carried an *Ocklahama,* a name traditional on the river. Nor was life aboard the *Ocklahama* only routine. She had the usual troubles of towboats, like broken hawsers, and sandbars where sandbars should not be, and cranky moments with the engine, and drifting logs and trash, but those were the commonplaces. In 1886 her time almost came when she was preparing to tow the British bark *Alliance.* Low and squat on the water, the *Ocklahama* was overtowered by her tows, so that when the tall *Alliance* suddenly heeled over against her, there was nothing much *Ocklahama* could do except hang on. When the ballast in the bark had been shifted back and the mess untangled, *Ocklahama* looked done for—her pilot house smashed to kindling and her hog-chains and king post down. But $4,000 and some time at the O.R.&N. Co's shipyard patched her up and she was soon ready for her next scrape.

Promptly she was in trouble again, for one of her tows sank at a wharf in Astoria, caused, so its owners claimed, by the towboat's carelessness. It looked for a time as if the damages, $30,000, would tie up the stern-wheeler permanently, with a government watchman growing old aboard her, but at last she was released on bond and put back in service. Then, in 1889, the *Ocklahama* was not around when the trouble happened. She was clanking up the river, taking one of the wheat ships, the *Clan Mackenzie,* to Portland when her fuel ran low and she had to detour to a woodyard. It was about midnight, cloudy and dark as the inside of a chain-locker, and the *Clan Mackenzie* dropped an anchor, lying at wait in the channel until *Ocklahama* wooded up and returned. Suddenly out of the dark loomed the lights of a liner, the coastwise steamer *Columbia,* speeding along the channel. The *Clan Mackenzie* had swung idly on her chain and her riding lights may not have been too bright, for the *Columbia* slammed into her just abaft the stem, driving the liner's prow in nearly thirty feet and as deep as the keel. When the *Columbia* backed away, the *Clan Mackenzie* took water, so that by the time *Ocklahama* returned, her tow was on the bottom of the river, there to rest for a year until she was raised, patched, and put back to work as part of the 1890 fleet.

Once a tow reached Portland, it had to be shifted alongside one of the wheat wharves, or, if all berths happened to be filled, placed on moorings close to but not in the channel. Towboats kept busy at Portland, bringing in the wheat ships, moving them to wharves and taking them into the river when loaded, hauling them from mooring to berth or stores dock. The early months of each year kept the stern-wheelers constantly on the prowl, handicapped all the time by the high water that set up currents to make the tall-masted ships unwieldy to handle in the river. From any place in Portland, the stately high masts could be seen towering above the city or slipping quietly along as their ships moved. On Christmas the British ships, which always formed the main part of the fleet, celebrated, and Portlanders saw rows of staggered masts, each topped with a small fir tree as a symbol of the season. Ashore, too, the crews celebrated in the joints along Front Street, mingling with the loggers on the skid road, so that sometimes a sailor awoke with a headache and a turkey at some logging camp, and a logger came to with a whopping hangover and an unhappy stomach in the forecastle of an outbound ship. The crimps were impartial whom they shanghaied. But what the hell? So long as a man could get to town now and then, find Erickson's, prop a foot on the rail and an elbow on the bar, and get likkered, it made not much difference whether he came from tall timbers ashore or afloat.

Drink to the past, to the good old days, for by the coming of the new century rivermen and Portlanders in general saw something new on the river—low, rusty ships with lean funnels and a pair of raked masts. They had nosed over the bar and come up the river without tow, using only a pilot, and they found their own way to the wharves. From their sterns flew foreign flags, and they seemed almost sheepish and shoddy, drawn in between the stately ships along the banks. They were the tramp steamers, and before long they carried most of the wheat. Faster, easier to charter, more dependable, the tramp steamer was favored by the shipper; they could be obtained with less trouble, carried just as much cargo, and could reach market before any odd flights of fancy hit the wheat prices. A tramp steamer was no beauty, but she was useful.

The days of glory soon faded when new conditions harrassed the Portland wheat shippers. The domestic crop of the Middle West failed, and the grower discovered he could ship to Chicago as cheaply as he could down the Columbia. The Chicago market cried for Inland Empire wheat, and the railroads, with long miles of unproductive track stretching east, scrambled for the business, offering rates that made the long haul overland preferable to the land or river haul to Portland and export from there. The Puget Sound ports had slowly developed as shipping points for wheat, their cargoes coming by rail from the Inland Empire. Further, the tramp owners kept hiking their charter rates, leaving the exporter at Portland caught between the farmer's natural inclination to sell for the highest possible price and the rate to Liverpool that neatly removed any chance for profit at the exporter's dock. The exporter, and there can be sympathy for his attitude, lacked enthusiasm for his business if he had to conduct it for love only.

Still, the wheat moved, and the tall ships kept coming, although by the beginning of World War I, they were so uncommon that the papers at Portland mentioned them, sighing nostalgically for the past as the Portland papers always do. Yet, if the fleet no longer seemed to be the great event of the year, the wheat continued to come down the rivers in even greater loads—from a low yield of only 9,700,000 bushels in 1892 to 24,700,000 in 1898, and then back slightly as the new century got under way. The opening of the Cascade Locks was supposed to increase the business; the building of the portage railways by the state was to help the wheat shippers, and the Celilo Canal was still another aid to the movement of the golden crop. New companies on the upper river gathered enthusiastic promises of shipments. In 1906 the *W. R. Todd* came down from the Horse Heaven country, her guards nearly awash under the load of sacked wheat, passing Blalock where the *Relief* was being hurried to completion to join the work. Beyond Pasco and as far up as Priest Rapids other boats, some small and gasoline-powered, moved wheat from small landings to larger depots. The gasoline driven stern-wheeler seemed to turn back for inspiration to the noisy *Hoosier* of the Fifties, for its engine turned a gear box that eventually got power to a crank that drove the pitman to the wheel. To meet the new river competition, the railroads cut their rates, until a bushel of wheat could go from Arlington to Portland for twelve and a half cents by rail or eleven cents on boats of the Open River Transportation Company. Possibly the opening of the Celilo Canal might have brought back to the stern-wheeler the main part of the annual crop, but war in Europe confused everything.

After the war, the cry for food rose over the world, and down the Columbia again, part by boat, part by rail, came the wheat; ship after ship, dingy tramps and sleek new war-built steamers run by regular lines, collected at Portland, took cargoes, and rushed off. Among them still lingered occasional square riggers—one or two of them were new, built on wooden hulls that had been intended for steamships but left unfinished when the war ended.

Then something else appeared to dim the glory of the river. Squatty, square barges, riding deep with their loads of sacked grain, now were coming down from as far as Pasco; a single towboat could handle the cargo of two or three stern-wheelers in the unlovely box-like barges it pushed along. Old steamboats fell into disrepair; the last regular steamer line giving scheduled service from Portland to The Dalles retired in 1923, and at about the same time the stern-wheelers found themselves edged aside by low-slung motor tugs, driven by tunnel-screws. The barges grew larger and then were built of steel, nearly a hundred feet long and able to carry 650 tons of wheat each trip. The towboat, usurped by the steamship on the lower Columbia, now was finding its place on the upper river, bringing down barges of wheat and returning with barges of gasoline and oil.

A screw towboat is an unlovely thing, long, low, squat, with two stubby stacks abreast (shades of *Oneonta!*) abaft the pilot house, all plain, all utilitarian. When the towboat bucks the current, there is no spurting of steam, no echoing, cadenced, sa-whoosh, sa-whoosh of the engines, only a dull blunka-blunk-blunka of the diesel, a spindly wisp of bluish fume from the stacks, and a flurry of water at the stern. Still, a Columbia tugboat is not one of the puffy, conceited little vessels that putter around harbors; they are big boats in their own right—the *Captain Al James,* 80 feet long and 26 in beam; the *Defiance,* 86 feet long; or the *Inland Chief,* itself able to carry 850 tons in addition to its tow, a vessel 190 feet long and 39 in beam, drawing 7 feet with load aboard. She may not be the most beautiful boat that ever bucked the Columbia up to the mouth of the Snake, but she is the biggest by far, packing 1200 horsepower in her diesel engines.

And the wheat—what became of it? When the bad Thirties struck Eastern Oregon and the Inland Empire and wheat prices collapsed, field after field lay unplowed, unproductive. Gradually the wheat grew again, but the times had changed. Between 1941 and 1945 the Army engineers kept records of tonnage passing through Bonneville Lock, and year by year it averaged 695,000 tons. Two per cent of that—about 14,000 tons—was wheat. Something had happened during the war years when navigation lights were hooded and the Pacific Coast gradually shook off the chaotic fear and rumors of December 1941. The war took the river for its own, and cargoes that moved on it had to have priorities. Wheat was needed, yes, but not in the Pacific; it could move by rail.

"During the war," says a 1947 publication of the War Department Corps of Engineers, "downstream wheat shipments ceased, but are now up above pre-war tonnage." The wheat fleet has sailed across the bar for the last time, but the wheat itself still moves on the river.

Chapter 9

AS THE SPARKS FLY UPWARD

STEAMBOATS, with luck, lasted a long time, commonly a quarter of a century or longer; then, towed to the boneyard, they would give up parts to another boat and achieve a kind of mechanical immortality. Without luck, a steamboat lived on borrowed time. If no reef, rock, or snag drove a hole in her hull, if no wandering bark ran her down and cut her in two, if her engine did not blow up, if she kept away from fire, if the weather was kind, she had a fair chance of survival.

Sometimes, of course, a steamer did not survive, or was so completely patched up that it returned to the river under a new name. For instance, in May 1853, the *Shoalwater,* a brand new boat on her first trip, had a hex put on her. As she headed in for a landing below Rock Island, the pilot signalled for the steam to be cut out from the engines, and almost immediately something happened: either the safety valve stuck, or the water had been allowed to fall low in the boiler, because a flue let go, blowing back the furnace door and filling the boat with live steam. Luckily no one was fatally hurt, and shortly she was back at work renamed *Fenix,* but Captain Leonard White, her owner, soon had had enough and sold

her. The new owner, Captain Hereford, put her back on the run
between Oregon City and Lafayette but soon found he had inherited the jinx with it. The *Fenix* was a fast boat and tried to race
the big *Oregon* which came up behind and tried to pass in a narrow channel wide enough for one, and the *Fenix* lost—the *Oregon*
was a heavier boat and nudged the upstart out of the way.

Captain Hereford, a member of the Willamette Falls Company
which was busying itself in organizing a steamboat line, with alac-
rity got rid of the ill-starred *Shoalwater,* but too late. The new
steamer the company was building opposite Oregon City, when
nearly completed and ready for launching, caught fire without any
apparent reason and burned.To replace her the company built another boat, the *Gazelle,* and made arrangements to buy the *Oregon*
to operate in conjunction with her. By March 1854 the *Gazelle* was
finished, and on the eighteenth of the month began her trial trip
from Canemah up to Corvallis. She was a side-wheeler, well fitted,
one of the best to appear on the river. She carried a good load of
passengers and cargo, and everybody aboard enjoyed the trip,
especially an Oregon City editor who wrote:

The fine weather and good music tended not a little to enhance the
pleasure of the ladies and gentlemen on board, and all were highly entertained and pleased. Her tables are laden with Oregon's choicest produc-
tions, together with a select variety of imported fruits, etc. Who wishes
for better accommodations, even in this *tyee* day of Oregon refinement?

The editor fell back on an Oregon superlative—*tyee* was Chinook
jargon for "splendid, superior."

While the *Gazelle* was making her maiden voyage in grandeur,
her companion, the *Oregon,* came under the hex. Not far below
Salem she rammed a snag that pierced her hull and sank her in
eight feet of water. Promptly her owners sent the *Gazelle* to stand
by while they salvaged the cargo and lightened the *Oregon* so that
she could be dislodged. Suddenly she broke free and drifted downstream until she heeled over on a sand bar with only part of her
upper works showing and so badly wrenched that the owners
offered to sell her for junk. The *Gazelle,* left alone, turned back to
the Falls to ready herself for service on her regular projected run,
but on the way down she found the river full of drift and in grinding over a log had some buckets knocked from a wheel. Putting in
new buckets is fairly easy, and on the eighth of April, 1858, she was
at the portage road above the Falls, loading for her first regular

trip upriver to Corvallis. At six in the morning her passengers
came up the portage path, scrambled down the bank to the landing stage, and got aboard. Then the *Gazelle* proudly moved up to
Canemah where she pulled in next to the *Wallamet* to load more
freight. Smoke spiraled high from her stack while the work went
on. Suddenly her engineer rushed onto the deck, scrambled ashore,
and headed toward town.

About a minute later the *Gazelle's* boiler blew up and she scattered herself all over the neighborhood. Someone had blundered.
In the roar of boiling water and steam, the upper works burst
apart; pieces of the boat, boxes of cargo piled on deck, and people
were thrown in all directions. As soon as the crash was over, all
Canemah came running. At Oregon City people stopped in their
work at the roar, looked up the river, and headed up the road to
see what had happened. Quickly men began to work their way
through the steam into the wreck, hauling out bodies, carrying
them ashore, and laying them out on the bank. The *Wallamet*
surged back from the blast, her fragile cabins shaken and broken,
her pilot killed by flying wreckage. Men scrambled into skiffs to
pick up bodies blown into the river. At Canemah storekeepers
threw open their buildings so that the dead and injured could be
attended to.

There was nothing left of the *Gazelle* but the hulk, and there,
under piles of junk that had been the cabins, machinery, and
freight, searchers found more bodies, or what was sometimes worse,
only parts. The injured were scalded, or bleeding from flying
splinters. Gradually the count could be made—twenty-eight had
been killed, and some of the thirty wounded were dying. Canemah,
shocked by the tragedy, worked all day treating the injured. Oregon City, suddenly quieted as the news came back, closed its stores,
its iron works, its mills.

The Coroner's Jury met to ask questions. Why had the engineer
rushed ashore so suddenly? And where was he? Some had seen him
after the blast, but he kept moving until he was safe, outside the
Territory. Captain Hereford had been injured but could testify;
the jury found no fault with him. The boiler had apparently been
in good condition (although there were some steamboatmen who
said it was made of brittle iron), and the engines had been well
maintained. So the jury decided that the explosion resulted from
the gross and culpable negligence of the first engineer, Moses

The *Annie Stewart* lies in the locks at Oregon City.

The Bonneville Locks moved the seaways a hundred miles upriver to The Dalles. The *S. S. Charles L. Wheeler Jr.* passes through the Bonneville Locks.

When the Cascade Locks opened, a fleet of stern-wheelers was on hand to celebrate.

Wilson Collection
With the White Collar on her stack and a pair of deer-horns on the pilot house, the *Regulator* was a typical Columbia River stern-wheeler.

The *Bailey Gatzert* backs down from a landing.
Oregon Historical Society

Toner, in knowingly carrying more steam than was safe and neglecting to keep sufficient water in the boilers.

The *Gazelle* provided the worst disaster on the inland waterways of the Northwest, but lived to run again, for by late in the year she had been rebuilt, lined over the Falls, and put back in service. Her name, though, discouraged patrons; so she became the *Senorita* on the Astoria run. Once she towed three ships up the river in one string, and once, her old luck lingering, she had her hurricane deck blown off when she was caught in a gale near the Cascades. Not until 1859 did she go out of service, and then her engines went to the *Okanogan*. The curse seemed to be overcome, because Captain Stump depended on those engines when he took the boat over Tumwater Falls.

Steamboat explosions were happily rare. Now and then a steamer did blow out a cylinder head and came to a clattering stop—even the *Wide West* did that, first with one engine, and then the other; but any explosion at all spectacular became a story often repeated by the steamboatmen. Thus the *Elk* went into the folklore of the Willamette. Three years after the *Gazelle* blew up, the *Elk* followed her example, fortunately with less damage to people. The *Elk* was a little stern-wheeler, methodically chugging along on the Dayton run in 1857 when, just below the mouth of the Yamhill, her boiler turned loose and hoisted itself sky-high, taking the cabin, the stack, and the Captain with it. Captain Jerome's first warning came when the deck below him suddenly rose and sent him soaring high above the steamer, accompanied by the smokestack. On one gyration, so he afterward declared, he could look down through the chimney and see his pilot, Captain Sebastian Miller, sitting calmly on the bank. Captain Jerome then continued his flight, arcing upward and down to land in a cottonwood tree by the river. Captain Jerome had not exaggerated—Miller was on the bank, where he had been tossed a little dazed and barked here and there. Passengers in the cabin watched as a stove beside them suddenly disintegrated and part of the wall and roof vanished, but they did not get a scratch themselves. A few aboard were injured, though not badly, and repairing them was not difficult. Without dignity, Captain Jerome shinnied down the tree. For twenty years pilots on the river pointed out the tree to passengers and told the story of Jerome's flight. Jerome did not. After all, a Captain must maintain some sort of dignity even during an explosion.

Not until 1875 did another bad explosion take place on the river. The steamer *Senator* for ten years had been a faithful boat plodding dutifully on the run between Portland and Oregon City. She was of average size, good for her job, and her engines, that had come from the old *Surprise,* never gave trouble. On the sixth of May she pulled out of her landing at Alder Street in Portland, dropped down to Oregon Steamship Company dock, and loaded some freight and passengers for upriver. Then she turned back to Alder Street, ready to take aboard a crowd for Oregon City. Lying at the dock was another steamboat, the *Vancouver.* The *Senator* arrived abreast the landing and shut off her engines preparatory to coming alongside, her wheel idling, when her boiler gave way. All over Portland people heard the roar. The pilot house, along with the upper works and stack, shot straight up, and the whole cabin forward of the kingpost went to pieces. Crippled, the *Senator* drifted out of control, but the captain of the *Vancouver* got his boat moving and pulled alongside. Toward the bow, dead and wounded lay sprawled in the wreckage; aft, where the passengers had been collected, no one was hurt, although the jolt had stunned them. The *Vancouver* put lines aboard the wreck and rigged a gangplank, its crew hurrying at rescue while the crowds lined the riverbank; when the last person had been taken off, the *Vancouver* dropped away and headed for shore. Seven had been found dead and eight injured. The *Senator* drifted ashore at Albina, where a search showed that only the forward end of the boiler remained, so completely had the explosion ripped it away. Carelessness caused it; the engineer let the water fall low in the boilers, so that when the engines were cut off, the pressure rose too rapidly for the safety valve.

Probably the same thing happened to the *Annie Faxon,* although the fusible plug that should have blown out when the water fell too low was later found intact. The *Annie Faxon* was a big boat on the Snake River run, and when her time came she was sixteen years old, had been rebuilt once and recently inspected. On April 14, 1893, she was making a regular trip down the Snake, picking up passengers and driblets of freight at the landings, performing her usual chores. Captain Harry Baughman, in the pilot house, yanked the whistle to signal for a landing at Wade's Bar, and spun the wheel so that she could round to, with her head upstream against the current. On the bank a young man waited to board her. Purser Tappan in his office cabin gathered up his freight book and nodded to his bride—it was their honeymoon—and started below to check freight and collect a fare, parts of his job when he had no mud clerk to help him. He went down the stairs onto the freight deck and waited at the gangplank, a deckhand standing beside him. The boat swung its half circle and approached the bank, and Captain Baughman rang for the engines to be stopped. Almost immediately a curious, hollow roar came from the lower deck, and Purser Tappan felt a shock, almost a blow. The deckhand beside him fell dead, streaming blood. Tappan spun on his heel to go to his wife and saw that not a trace of the cabins remained. The prospective passenger on the bank had not moved, but stood staring, not believing what he had just seen. The boat had not blown up, he said, but folded quietly in upon itself, so that only the hull remained, and it sank evenly in the slack water near the bank. Evidently the boiler disintegrated, blowing outward to bring down the cabins upon it. Captain Baughman saw his companion in the pilot house beheaded by wreckage. Then he found himself on the bank, dazed and lamed by the crash when he landed ashore. That time eight died, including Tappan's bride who had been blown into the river and drowned.

Fires bothered the boats as rarely as did explosions. Several burned, true enough, but they were usually tied up at a dock or some convenient bank, though there were exceptions to the rule. One was the *Telephone,* a new crack stern-wheeler on the Astoria run. No rival could beat her for speed—or for burning. In November 1887, she was racing toward Astoria with 140 passengers and a crew of 32 when fire broke out in her oil room and, almost before the alarm could sound, swept through the boat. In the pilot house was Captain U. B. Scott, proud of this latest achievement of his in boat-building; as soon as he heard the alarm, he remembered fires on the Ohio steamers, and swung his wheel hard over to head for the shore. The engineer also heard the alarm and, feeling the long, trim boat heel for the turn, opened his throttle wide. Normally that would sweep the fire the length of the steamer, but he took the chance, and the *Telephone* cut for the bank at twenty miles an hour, crunching onto a shore of rolling pebbles that absorbed the shock. Quickly the passengers scrambled over the guards to dry land while the flames roared through the cabins. Captain Scott glanced behind him, saw that the steps to the pilot house had already burned, and promptly dived out the window, barely making it before the whole upper works caved in. By then the Astoria fire department was on hand—

the *Telephone* grounded just above the town—and had its hoses going. There was not much hope, but it saved the hull and in a few months a new *Telephone*, faster, even gaudier than the old, was back on the river. Only one died in the fire, and he was a drunk who befuddled his way first into stupor and then suffocation; everyone else got off safely and only a little singed around the edges.

When steamboats kept from killing themselves by blowing up their boilers or burning to their guards, they found other ways to commit marine suicide. The *Telephone*, not satisfied at having burned herself in 1887, waited until 1892 and then tried smashing herself up. She left Astoria on a foggy night and groped all the way up the Columbia until she came opposite the mouth of the Willamette River; there, her pilot could not see the navigation lights, and, before he knew it, the *Telephone* bashed her bow into the revetment and sank until only a little of her showed above water. She seemed a complete loss, but she was not—the *Telephone* was a hard boat to kill. Pumped out and patched, she floated and went back into service that lasted twenty more years.

A year after the *Telephone* sank herself, the *Orient* came sloshing along the channel and tried to go through the draw of the Morrison Street Bridge. Somehow a tricky current swung the boat off the course and piled it onto a bridge pier, jolting the draw considerably and sinking the *Orient*. She was an old boat giving way at the seams, and raising her turned out to be a long, hard job. Repaired, the *Orient* went back to work, this time on the Cowlitz River where during high water she hit a rock and wedged. When the river fell, the *Orient* sat high and dry, but, as if tired of too much excitement, she waited until crews started to move her; whereupon she caught fire and burned up.

The little *Elwood* had an adventure at a bridge, too. The first of November 1893 began frosty and foggy; to the pilot of the steamer shapes showed vaguely along the banks, and the sounds of the city drifted strangely across the river. Ahead loomed the Madison Street Bridge; the pilot hauled his whistle cord to call for an open draw and rang the engineer to check the speed so that he could drift. On Hawthorne Avenue an inbound car from Sellwood rolled down the grade toward the bridge, the wheels squealing and the trolley sparking in the cold, wet air. On the platform the motorman saw the closed bridge gate and the open span; with one hand he shut off the controller and with the other began to wind up his hand brake to stop the car short of the barrier. But the brake locked and the wheels slid like runners on the frosty rails. The flimsy barrier splintered and the car teetered only a moment at the edge of the open approach before plunging into the river, just missing the steamer.

The pilot of the *Elwood* saw the trolley car fall but there was nothing he could do about it, and his boat slipped quietly over the bubbling wash where the car had gone down. He could not reverse his engines for fear that he would drown struggling figures in the water, and he had to go beyond the bridge before he could turn to help in the rescue. Twenty fought their way out of the car and reached the surface; they were hauled onto the *Elwood* or into skiffs that by then were swarming to help. Seven in the car did not make it.

Steamboating on the Columbia River system was not as dangerous as in other parts of the country, yet, when two steamboats ran the same route for different owners, it was a race all the way and never mind the safety valve. Either steamboats in the Pacific Northwest had exceptionally good engineers or were exceptionally strong, for no steamer blew up while racing. Ordinarily steamers only raced on the heavily travelled routes or, sometimes, on the less patronized runs when two boats happened to find themselves alongside, a reach of the river ahead, and a narrow channel beyond. Then the wheels would spin and both boats would start out at their best clip. Steamboats belonging to the same company sometimes spurted for short runs, mainly for the excitement of it, as the owner normally discouraged speeding, not out of consideration for the passengers but for safety of the boat and especially the economy of operation. A steamer running fast seemed to toss cordwood out the stack as fast as the firemen could heave the chunks toward the fire door; and as wood was not cheap, the purser aboard suffered when he felt the pace quicken—his operating costs would go up, though his receipts would not.

The favorite race courses were between Portland and the Cascades and between Portland and Astoria, the latter stretch being particularly attractive, for it was a wide, deep stream with plenty of room for straight running and no tricky cutting of corners at the bends. After the little *Columbia* first made the run in a spanking twenty-four hours, boats worked to cut the time. The *Lot Whitcomb* did it in ten hours, and after that the time was whittled down as later boats went into service. Once Astoria became the terminal of the seashore resort run and crowds began to swarm the steamers on holidays and weekends, speed became a premium as an attraction, with passengers betting on good runs. The *Emma Hayward* in her great days streaked up and down the river, showing what a steamboat could do when it tried, and later steamers upheld her reputation. The heyday of speed came with the building of the big boats in the 1880's—*Telephone, T. J. Potter, Bailey Gatzert*. When they swung out of the dock at Portland, threshed spray as their wheels reversed, and started down the river, they were worth watching; long, lean, clean-lined, tall stacks throwing a pennant of smoke, a banner with the boat's name on the jackstaff, and the national ensign at the king-post or stern, they cut the water away on either side, leaving long arrowheads of waves making toward the shore and a straight wake of froth behind. The *T. J. Potter* was probably the finest sight to watch, with her fancy pierced side wheelhouses, but the stern-wheel *Bailey Gatzert* had fine unbroken decks and a sturdy pilot house. Both of them could clip the time under five hours on the run to Astoria, yet neither could match the record of the *Telephone*. Running down from Portland on July 2, 1884, and for the last forty miles bucking a nasty wind from the sea that threw a choppy swell across the river, the big stern-wheeler made a time that would not be equalled by any rival in regular service. Down the river *Telephone* shot, docking at Astoria in four hours, thirty-four minutes and thirty seconds. On the upriver trip no boat did that well, althou˜h they were able to run to Portland in about five hours.

Steamboat captains hated to be passed on the river. Let another boat draw abreast, and the captain had to make his decision. Usually he felt that it was sheer effrontery displayed by an ungracious rival; promptly he would bellow through the speaking tube for more steam, and the race would start. On the straightaways, when the two speeding boats were on parallel courses, everything was fine, the passengers crowding the rails and cheering for whichever boat they happened to be aboard—for the passengers felt chagrined too if they saw another boat pass their own. At the bends, where the channel curved, the boats had to come close together, and at crossings, places where the channel shifted from one shore to the other, both racers had to be well piloted to pick up every advantage. Closer and even closer the two boats would come toward each other; the captains would fling open the windows in the pilot houses, or, if they were temperamental, would prance out on the roof of the texas and shout threats. One boat would knock off the other's guards; the second would wash down the decks of the first with the splash of the wheel. When it seemed inevitable that the two boats would crash, lock guards, and smash things generally, the passengers would head pell mell for the other side of the boat in an earnest effort to get out of the way. Generally, the pilots would spin a spoke or two of their wheels and the boats would squeeze past, but proud was the pilot who could neatly flick the guard of his boat against that of the other and bring away a bit of the rail or buffer, as a sort of trophy of the chase.

When the *T. J. Potter* came back from Puget Sound with a gilded broom fastened to her stack, emblematic of her victories there, it was a challenge no rival boat could afford to let pass. And great was the sorrow of the staunch and regular passengers of the *T. J. Potter* when, after rebuilding, her hull had lost the lines and grace that gave her speed so that practically any towboat on the river could keep up with her. Still, it was the *Telephone* that remained supreme; even the sleek propellers like *Georgiana* could not pace her. Though the *Telephone* had been rebuilt, she kept her speed, and she aged gracefully. In her last years she went down to San Francisco to be a ferryboat, although a single-ender and hence at a disadvantage in working in and out of slips, but that never bothered her. She would back out of her slip, sweep in an arc, reverse her wheel, and be away, leaving the pack of double-enders behind her wondering what in the world this eccentric ferryboat had in mind. The *Telephone* would be in her slip across the bay before her rivals had rounded Yerba Buena Island.

Racing became so troublesome that Portland, in desperation, passed speed laws for the river. Steamboats had been racing all the way to their docks and then on leaving, all the way down the river, kicking up rolling troughs that swept ashore to slap the piling and moored ships, sometimes hard enough to break hawsers. To check the trouble, a city ordinance forbade steamboats to travel over eight miles an hour through the congested strip of the river where the wharves were located; downstream, beyond Albina, a steamboat could go no more than twelve miles an hour until it passed the city limits near St. Johns. From there on, each steamer was on its own, according to the discretion and firm resolution of its captain. That the racing did not stop, however, with the simple passing of the ordinance was to be expected; when boats were in a good position, they just had to have their fling.

In November 1905 three boats, the *Charles R. Spencer, Dalles City,* and *Telegraph,* bound variously to Astoria and The Dalles, pulled away from their docks at the same time; immediately each captain ordered full speed and set out down the river at the best pace his engines could muster. Promptly, because the three formed a tight group, they sent out heavy bow waves that smashed against the docks lining the narrow channel. At one the British steamship *Agincourt* lay idly moored and taking it easy when suddenly she rolled and bucked. Her stern hawser snapped, the gangway to the dock splintered and dropped away, the railing of the bridge crashed against the dock wall; then the ship rolled slowly to the swell while her furious captain danced a war dance emphatic and shook his fists at the departing steamboats. But he was not through—no, he marched ashore, filed a complaint and had those three captains haled into court where they were ordered to deposit $50 apiece bail, charged with violating the city speed limits.

Even then racing did not end, though it changed a good deal, for in April 1920 two of the fine white passenger propellers on the Astoria run raced all the way down the river. The *Astorian* and the *Georgiana* gave competing service to the mouth of the Columbia after the big stern-wheelers had been retired. *Georgiana* won the downriver race, running the 110 miles from Portland to Astoria in five hours and forty-five minutes from dock to dock, but *Astorian* was not far behind, lagging by only three minutes. They had not prepared for the race, and they made all their regular landings, *Astorian* stopping twice and *Georgiana* five times—at Cathlamet, Pillar Rock, Eureka, Skamokawa and Brookfield. At Astoria the two boats hastily unloaded cargo, tossed aboard freight for upriver points and at about two o'clock in the afternoon started back, the *Astorian* slipping from her dock a few minutes ahead. Once more each boat made its necessary stops, although the backers of the *Georgiana* wailed that the *Astorian* again made only two landings and passed up her usual stop at the oil dock below Portland, while the *Georgiana* made nine stops and in addition took fuel oil at Linnton on the home stretch. The *Astorian* was technically the winner, with her upriver time of six hours and ten minutes, but the fight over which steamer was the faster went on for years when steamboatmen got together. The Harkins Transportation Company claimed the *Georgiana* was unfairly beaten and was still queen of the river. Meanwhile the two steamers continued to leave together at seven in the morning, and anyone who took them to Astoria was sure of a race.

No one would expect excitement on the run up from Bandon on the Coquille, a narrow, winding stream, with hardly enough room in it for one steamboat. But there were two steamboats, owned by rival captains, and the going was lively, if a bit confusing. "Steamboating on the Coquille," mentioned the Portland *Oregonian* in 1915, "appears to have more rivalry, ginger and kindred activity woven into it than on any waters within the jurisdiction of the Federal government." That was a masterpiece of understatement. Paddling between Bandon and the upriver towns of Coquille and Myrtle Point were the steamers *Charm* and *Telegraph* (not the Columbia *Telegraph*), and these two vessels had, admittedly, collided, but why, where, and how remained a matter of discussion. The captain of the *Charm* had a detailed account ready. It was at 2:16 p.m. on March 13, he said, while he was running from Bandon and was half a mile below Cedar Point. Close behind him came the *Telegraph* showing all inclinations and considerable determination to run down the hapless *Charm,* which whistled four times. To this, the *Telegraph* gave no answer except to go ahead at full speed. Naturally, the conditions being what they were, the *Telegraph* rammed the *Charm* and sent her limping to the beach to avoid sinking, her port bulwarks damaged and her fender strake ripped away from stem to stern.

Nonsense, retorted the captain of the *Telegraph,* replying in a formal statement. It was at 2:23 p.m. at a point two miles below Coquille, and when the *Charm* came in sight the *Telegraph* was at a landing. Just as the *Telegraph* pulled into the stream the *Charm* came alongside and attempted to cross the bow of the *Telegraph,* contrary to all rules of the road. As the *Charm* crowded in the *Telegraph* was pushed against a boom that forced it to skid into the *Charm* and damaging her somewhat when *Telegraph* backed off. Which was all very complicated. Riding steamboats on the Coquille was evidently exciting, and when there were no races and no collisions to while away the time, passengers could always reach out and pick flowers from the banks.

Now and then steamboats would smash each other's woodwork, but that was all in a spirit of good, clean rivalry and no real harm came of such boyish pranks. A steamboat had more trouble dodging ships than it did other steamboats, probably because one stern-wheeler's pilot could fairly well predict what another's would do. Regularly the stern-wheelers were run down by ships; thus, in November, 1907, the steamer *F. B. Jones* was minding her own business on a night run in the Columbia when the steamship *Asuncion* hit her. The big ship came off with only some paint marred, but the *F. B. Jones* sank and had to be raised. In 1930 the barge *Swan,* a big two-decker built in 1916 and towed from place to place as a floating dance hall and amusement boat, provided some of the gaiety for the celebration of the opening of the Longview-Rainier bridge over the Columbia. On her way back to Portland the *Swan* was rammed by the lumber steamer *Davenport* and sank, carrying down seven passengers who were trapped in her. Then back in 1881 the *Clatsop Chief,* a towboat working around Astoria, had a scow in tow when the big steamship *Oregon,* the passenger liner that hit the *Clan Mackenzie,* ploughed into the little stern-wheeler and cut her in two, sinking her immediately and capsizing the scow. The *Clatsop Chief* had no doors opening from her sides to the engine room, and her engineer had to escape by groping along a steampipe until he reached a gangway up which he could rise to the surface. There is little wonder that a steamboat begins to look battered after it has been working a few years.

Even in the boneyard a steamboat was not free from the danger of being molested by ocean-going vessels. In 1894 the *Willamette Chief* was drowsing away on the mudbank at Portland along with some hulks and waiting for the scrapper to finish her off. She had lived a full life since her first runs in the wheat trade to Astoria. After those days, she did some towing on the river, occasional jobbing, and for a time before the railroad bridge was completed, she worked in transfer service between the railroad terminals on the east bank of the Willamette and the main part of Portland on the west bank. Inclines with tracks had been built down to the water's edge, and down them were let freight cars that rolled onto rails fitted to the deck of the steamer. Once aboard, the cars were fastened, and the *Willamette Chief,* in lowly ferry service, carried them across the river. But even that work was over, and the old *Chief* lay abandoned, her white paint fading and peeling.

Across the river and little upstream from the boneyard were the railroad yards and docks at Albina, crowded with cars. By the bank rose the tall coal tipples where the colliers from Puget Sound unloaded their supplies for the O.R.&N. locomotives—for, though the company's river boats still burned wood and continued to burn it until 1905, locomotives of the company had been burning coal since 1883. Next to the tall wooden tipples was the railroad wheat dock, a long tindery wooden structure. In the river a wheat ship moored at the dock reared its tall masts and spidery rigging above the coal tipples and the buildings of the town. Coal is tricky stuff to handle, and without warning a fire broke out in the tipple and soon was roaring out of control, sending clouds of black smoke high. Crews rushed to the dock to cut adrift the wheat ship, threatened by the fire, and just as the hawsers parted, the tipple collapsed, sheeting the whole dock in flames. Promptly the tarred rigging of the ship caught fire, and slowly, floating free in the river, the burning vessel drifted with the wind, crossing the channel and grounding alongside the abandoned *Willamette Chief*. At the first shower of sparks the *Chief* blasted into fire, and in a few minutes she was a goner. Somehow it was a decent finish though; the *Willamette Chief*, overlooked in the excitement of the main fire on the docks, was spared the indignity of making a spectacle of herself at cremation as had the *S. G. Reed*.

Chapter 10

...AND HIGH WATER

THE *Lot Whitcomb* hardly started to run before she drove herself aground on the Clackamas Rapids and perched there conspicuously for a week until she could be floated off, and thereby the *Lot* established a tradition. The *Carrie Ladd,* built in 1858, the stern-wheeler that set the design for the characteristic Columbia steamer, was a good boat and could fight off competition nicely, but on one trip down from the Cascades she discovered an uncharted rock near Cape Horn, hit it and sank. Fortunately, she sank slowly, and as she went down her passengers went up until they were crowded onto her roof where they huddled until the *Mountain Buck* came by and picked them up. The *Hassalo* struck another rock years later, but she roosted, and the *Dalles City* had to take off the passengers, dropping the deck passengers at Vancouver and taking the first class on to Portland. Above the Cascades there were rocks, too, as the *Daisy Ainsworth* discovered in 1876. Making an extra run at night from The Dalles with a load of cattle, the boat came in toward what Captain Spelling thought was the light at Cascades wharf. Too late he saw that the wharf light was off to his right and that he had been aiming at a lamp shining through a window; he swung his wheel hard to starboard, but the boat did not respond soon enough and cut herself in two on a rock. Spelling and the crew got ashore, but the cattle drowned.

Beyond Celilo in 1874 the *Yakima* was making a regular run down from Wallula. A passenger aboard tried to find something to read in order to pass the rather dull time, but failed; at Umatilla he went ashore to scout for a book or some newspapers and failed again, so that he had to reconcile himself to watching the monotonous hills along the river. Near John Day Rapids, probably the worst a steamer had to pass going downstream, he was standing idly on deck, watching the boat head for a break in the white water, when he heard a dull sound "like tearing a piece of flannel," and felt the boat jar and hesitate.

"We've stuck," said the mate, calmly. Slowly the water inched up along the settling hull. "Will she sink?" asked the passenger, watching over the guard. "She's bound to sink," the mate cheered him. In the pilot house, the captain kept his wheel steady, guiding the sluggish boat toward the bank. Water lapped over the guards, and in a couple of minutes the regular gasp of the escape pipes stopped and the wheel fell idle—the furnaces were out. Up the companionway came the crew to escape the water, and in the meantime the boat glided with ominous quiet toward shore. At last she struck, and the passengers rushed to clamber over the side, only the coolness of the mate preventing a panic. Firm on the rocks the *Yakima* twisted and wedged, while her timbers splintered and the wrenched cabin dropped out glass from doors and windows. Finally, the captain ordered out the skiff and sent his women passengers ashore. Then he got a gangplank rigged and started his crew moving off baggage and light freight. Fairly soon Indians arrived in canoes to fish sacks of flour from the water, but the steamer remained firm, the sacked wheat in her hold acting like lead. While the shipwrecked ate crackers and cheese and salvaged the stock of the bar, one man located a horse and rode to Celilo for help. When night came, men gathered sagebrush for fires around which the timid huddled in blankets; the braver went back aboard the wreck to sleep. Sometime the next afternoon the *Owyhee* came up and got them, but not before the passengers erected a cairn and a signboard: "Kenney's Landing." Mr. Kenney, thus honored, had jumped overboard as soon as the *Yakima* touched the bank, drenching himself but yelling that he was going ahead to help moor the boat. Those who did not believe his motive seemed to be in the majority, and the rest, who would have jumped, had the deep sagacity not to admit it.

But these have been the casual, the ordinary wrecks. All along the Columbia and Willamette were excellent chances for spectacular smashes and runs, and there were plenty of takers. Broken by falls

and cascades, the rivers presented to steamboatmen barriers to be
avoided, but occasionally boats deliberately or accidentally rode
them. The first was the *Portland* that went over the Falls at Oregon
City in 1856, although she had not the slightest intention to try it.
Captain Jamieson was bringing her down from Canemah to the
basin in order to discharge some freight when it happened. Aboard
in addition to the captain were only a deckhand and a fireman who
was tending the engine. The river was high and Jamieson, who had
not reckoned on the pull of the Falls when he started to skirt them
into the basin, let the boat drift out from slack water. Suddenly he
felt a sickening pull to port. He rang for full speed, but the boilers
had too little steam for the engine to do more than turn the wheel.
On the bank Captain George Pease, a white-water steamboatman
himself, saw what was happening, threw a line, and yelled for the
men on the boat to jump for it. The fireman immediately dived in
and caught the line and was hauled to safety by Pease, but Captain
Jamieson and the deckhand hesistated an instant too long. When
they jumped they were swept over the Falls and drowned. The
Portland drifted to the edge, tilted down, and plunged, burying
herself in the spume and eddy below, where she came apart, her
cabin drifting ashore near Portland and her pilot house as far as
the mouth of the Willamette.

Four years later another boat made the plunge deliberately—her
captain taking her over in order to get her onto the lower river. She
was the *St. Claire,* a small steamboat of little account, built for the
Yamhill trade but never quite able to get any of it. Captain Taylor
waited until December 1861, when the water was at its peak with
one of the greatest floods in years pouring over the Falls and spreading out on the lowlands beyond to put four feet of water over the
banks at Oregon City. When Captain Taylor fired up the *St. Claire*
for the run, actually there were no falls—the river was so high that
there was only a rapid where the long drop had been. Into it Taylor
sent the steamer, coolly heading her into the drop and catching the
swirl below just right so that after a dousing and a few quick circles,
the *St. Claire* shook herself and kept going, riding the crest of the
flood. Taylor proved it could be done, and steamboatmen admitted
it, but none of them cared to follow his example.

At Upper Cascades Thompson and Coe in 1858 built a stern-
wheeler they called, with uncanny foresight, the *Venture.* When
they finished her, they took forty passengers aboard for a trial trip

and set out, but they neglected to have enough steam up and like the *Portland*, the *Venture* lacked power to keep out of the current. Before anyone could do anything, she began shooting down the Cascades, stern first. She made it beautifully, too, although she scared everyone into fits (one jumped overboard and drowned), and finally ran onto a rock below the rapids where she stuck until the rising river floated her off. In the meantime a small schooner sailed up and took off everyone aboard.

After the *Venture* had done it, other boats followed, with better luck; until the locks were put into operation at the Cascades, the only way to get a steamer from the middle to lower river was to make it shoot the rapids. In 1881 when the O. R. & N. railroad was being completed and need for steamboats on the upper river declined, a whole series of them passed, one by one, through the Cascades. Among them, the big *R. R. Thompson* provided the best show on June 3. She left The Dalles early in the morning and reached the Cascades in just two hours and one minute, an average of twenty-three miles an hour, not bad for a steamboat. Then, under full power, and with Captain McNulty at the helm, she went into the rapids, driving down the twisting six mile channel in less than seven minutes. When the *Mountain Queen* came through a few days later, there were crowds waiting, and a passenger train on the portage railroad started with her so that everyone could watch the run. Unfortunately, the spectators did not see much, for although the *Mountain Queen's* time was a slow eleven minutes, the train was a good three hundred yards behind by the time the boat reached lower landing. Later, in 1888, the *Hassalo* ran the Cascades during low water when the channel was narrower and the rocks more dangerous; in spite of that, Captain Troup got her through in seven minutes, only twenty seconds short of the record set by the *R. R. Thompson*.

At Celilo are a series of narrow rocky gorges and rapids, headed by Tumwater Falls, yet steamboats ran even them. The *Umatilla* was the first to make the run and by 1881, nine or ten steamboats, one of them the *Harvest Queen,* had gone through. The *Harvest Queen* probably had the liveliest trip through the Dalles, so that a little thing like the Cascades did not faze her. Captain Troup took her over the Tumwater, leaving the upper landing on the fourth of February. Hardly had she plunged over the brink when she came up and knocked away both rudders and part of her wheel. On the next swerve she broke a part of her starboard engine and went out of control so that she slewed into a rock, knocked a hole in her hull and filled two compartments. She glanced off, shot across to a reef, and smashed away her bow and nosing. Troup ordered the anchor dropped, but the rush of the current parted the chain. Fortunately, the crew rigged a kedge which held until the engineer could get the engine running on pillow blocks; with it working, she limped ashore for more patching and then, a week later, Troup steamed out with her again and took her through both big and little Dalles with hardly any damage.

Somehow, though, all the runs of steamboats through rapids and over falls seem calm and trivial whenever the *Shoshone* and the *Norma* are remembered. Both of them had been built out on the edge of nowhere and had a hell of a time getting somewhere. Captain Ainsworth in Portland hated to see the *Shoshone* rot away uselessly on the upper Snake and ordered her brought down the river to the Columbia. On the first try her captain gave up at Lime Point and said that the Copper Ledge Falls could not be run. For another season the *Shoshone* weathered by the bank, two caretakers aboard to nurse her. Then in March 1870 Ainsworth sent Captain Sebastian Miller and Chief Engineer Dan Buchanan to bring her down or wreck her trying. Bas Miller was the man for the job; he had been through the explosion of the *Elk* and was convinced nothing after that could bother him. The two men landed at Umatilla and started by buckboard over the Blue Mountains. When roads gave out, they used sleds; when the snow failed, they rode horseback; when the horses gave out, they walked, and got to the steamer in mid-April. Miller signed on his crew—the two caretakers and a spare who happened to be in the neighborhood. Then they overhauled the engines completely and checked everything. The mountain pine used in the *Shoshone* had become brittle and the seams had opened, but with no time to caulk them and nothing to caulk them with, Buchanan rigged hoses and pumped water over the boat until the planking swelled. While they worked, the river slowly rose until Miller felt the time had come to make a try. Downstream only a couple of hundred yards the falls roared and boiled. In the hold of the steamer Buchanan placed lighted candles that would permit him to detect leaks instantly. Lighting candles in the hold of a steamboat is not a good way to endear oneself to underwriters, but the chances that the *Shoshone* would burn before she

In 1878 the *S. G. Reed* was the last word in elegance when she joined the O. S. N. fleet.

The *Telephone* coming into Astoria.

The engine room of the *S. G. Reed*.

On Board Steamer T. J. Potter.

W. E. INMAN.
Master

FRIDAY
AUGUST 14, 1908

Luncheon

Soup
Fulton Market Clam Chowder   Consomme Royal

Salad
Cold Slaw

Sliced Tomatoes   Radishes   Young Onions   Chow Chow

Fish
Baked Halibut, au Gratin

Entrees
Blanquette of Lamb, Petit Pois   Timbale of Spaghetti a la Napolitaine
Apple Fritters, Brandy Sauce

Cold Meats
Prime Ribs of Beef   Veal   Lamb   Boiled Ham

Vegetables
Crushed Turnips   Escalloped Tomatoes
Hashed Brown Potatoes   Baked Potatoes

Dessert
                    Cabinet Pudding
Apple Pie   Assorted Fruits   Cherry Pie

American Cheese   Edam Cheese

Coffee   Tea   Milk

You were served this in the dining room of the *T. J. Potter.*
University of Oregon

The dining room of the *T. J. Potter.*
Wilson Collection

smashed were only even anyway. At last Miller rang for the engines and the crew cast off the lines. He planned to drift down the river, running the engines in reverse to build pressure on the rudders to give him steering control when he had to turn quickly.

Things started badly. Miller failed to guess the power of an eddy just above the falls so that before he could get the boat in hand she had swept around three times in the whirlpool; in the engine room already Buchanan and his fireman wondered whether they had shown vast wisdom in coming at all. But Miller straightened the *Shoshone* to the falls, felt the bow ride out over the verge, tilt and then plunge, leaving the wheel free and spinning in the air while Buchanan's comments came profanely up the speaking tube from the engine room. At the bottom of the first drop the wheel dipped again, and the part that had been weathering all year promptly broke off, letting the steamer crash into rocks that wiped off eight feet of her bow. Down in the engine room things were becoming complicated. As the boat danced and bucked, the cabin set up a caterwauling as it strained and creaked, and the signal gong clanged crazily until Buchanan had no idea whether Miller was signalling or not. Then, to add to the trouble, when the boat hit the rocks, the weight on the safety valve sprang free and steam shrieked until Buchanan could get the weight back on the rod and close the valve.

After all that, Miller landed. The crew put in a full day repairing the wheel and wondering why they came, while Buchanan looked over the hull and had some satisfaction to find that his smashed bow timbers were above the waterline. On the third day they started again, passed through a few dizzy rapids and eddys, and stopped for lunch and fuel—which they got by cutting down trees that grew by the bank. That afternoon the *Shoshone* went on, hit some more rapids and shipped water that poured into the boiler deck to chase the fireman out of the hold. Here the canyon of the Snake narrows and the walls rise for thousands of feet above the river; in the cleft the roar of the water drowned out every noise the boat made, even to the creaking and splintering of the cabin as it twisted when the boat reared and dipped. By early evening Miller tied up the boat again and the crew set to patching the wheel, making buckets out of any plank they could find; there was no shortage—a good many had worked loose here and there on the steamer. They got under way again on the twenty-third of April, four days out, and were making a good start until Captain Miller stopped for more fuel.

Then, while they were cutting down trees, a log rolled on him and knocked him out until the next day. So it continued, until on the twenty-sixth they passed the Salmon River and stopped benighted at the mouth of the Grande Ronde. From there it was easy; on the twenty-seventh Miller piloted the *Shoshone* over Wild Goose Rapids and two hours later hove in sight of Lewiston. Promptly the tension fell away, and Miller yelled down his speaking tube to the sweating Buchanan, "Say, Buck, I expect if this company wanted a couple of men to take a steamboat through hell, they would send for you and me." Probably he was right, and if his imagery was strong, he was being overly modest. Charon ferried back and forth across the Styx in a flatboat he shoved along with a pole. The Snake above Lewiston, by comparison, was something special and could make the Styx blush any day.

At Lewiston Miller and his crew tied up and went ashore, looking for the O. S. N. agent. There was the *Shoshone,* safe if not sound; she looked frayed some, here and there, her house wracked, her bow staved in, her wheel a patchwork of makeshift. She had been about given up because on her first encounter with the rock, her jackstaff had been snapped off and beat her down the river to be fished out at Umatilla. "Poor old Bas," everyone said, viewing the relic. But poor old Bas had other work to do, for Ainsworth had some more steamboats to send through some more outskirts of hell, or specifically through Cabinet Rapids into Lake Pend Oreille, and Miller was elected to do the job. He did it.

The *Shoshone?* Oh, she was taken down the Snake and the Columbia, run through the falls at Celilo (nothing to it after the Snake), used on the middle river as a cattle boat, and sent on down through the Cascades to Portland with Ainsworth himself at the helm. There she was sold to the Willamette River Transportation Company which hauled her on skids around the Falls at Oregon City in order to run her on the upper stretches. She stayed there a year, and at last, ironically, hit a rock opposite staid Salem and sank in the fall of 1874. Finally, in January of the next year, the rising river floated the hulk free and deposited it on the bank downstream at Lincoln. There a farmer took the cabin and made a chicken house of it.

The *Shoshone* had no rivals for the honor of running the Snake River Canyon until 1895 when the *Norma,* another hopeful built for business on the upper Snake, came down. Captain Gray, who brought her through, profited by Miller's experience and was ready for the rocks at the foot of Copper Ledge Falls; he built an extra bulkhead forward and filled the hull with cordwood to absorb the shock he knew was coming. Sure enough, she struck, but the bulkhead held and the boat glanced away, to continue down the gorge with little trouble, at a pace a whole lot faster than anybody aboard particularly enjoyed, especially when they were shooting through winding Hell Canyon where the river runs between the rock walls and the mist from the whitecaps hangs over the water. But the *Norma* made it with only a few dents here and there and carried wheat from Lewiston to Celilo until 1915.

There were a few steamers who tried to go in the other direction, but the Snake was too much for them. The *Imnaha* was one; she was built in 1903 to run above Lewiston and on one of her first trips she jammed at Wild Goose Rapids and went to pieces. No one has gone all the way up the Snake Canyon, although a few of the hardier sort of adventurers have gone down it in small boats since the *Norma*. Still, people live along the river above Lewiston, and no roads wind down the canyon walls to give them outlet. To them the river is the highway, even if it is a rough one, and to them a boat regularly fights its way with mail and groceries and passengers.

Kyle McGrady runs the boat and does it on schedule at that. With his thirty-four foot *Idaho* or his newer sixty-foot *Florence,* both sturdy power boats with heavy framing built to take a battering, he works his way up the river from Lewiston and against the roughest the current can offer to get as far as the lower reaches of Hell Canyon, stopping to leave mail and packages at isolated ledges that serve as landings. Going up the river is slow work, but with luck and decent water the trip can be made in a day; coming down takes only a few hours. The *Idaho* is the work-boat, able to fight her way through any kind of water. She is as unlovely as she is tough, but the *Florence* is pretty, full of glass and fine fixings to accommodate tourists that want adventure without having their clothes dampened by spray. When they ride with McGrady, they get the adventure.

By way of contrast, consider the elegant stern-wheeler *Mud Hen.* She was built on the Coquille River for use on Beaver Slough, and her dimensions were governed by her route. Hence the *Mud Hen* was thirty-two feet long, with a beam of six feet and no appreciable draft at all. Her problem was not white water, for Beaver Slough is a quiet, winding creek arched over its whole length by interlaced trees. Along this stream scraped the *Mud Hen,* often with as much as a foot of water between either guard and the bank. The steamer did not land—it just stopped for patrons to step ashore. Standard equipment for its captain and engineer—the whole crew—was rubber boots, because at night the beavers got busy building dams, and the next day the captain would have to stop the boat every few hundred yards, step over the side, wade up the stream, and kick a dam out of the way. Then he would climb back aboard, and the boat would start again its patient run until it came to another dam. Passengers had to look lively, too, if they expected to dodge the overhanging tree branches and keep their hats and hair from being snatched off and left behind. The Coquille was not a white-water stream, but its steamboats had their troubles.

Now and then the Columbia or Willamette can become down-right perverse. Sometimes one flooded, sometimes the other; sometimes both did, and when that happened Portlanders looked around for the nearest rowboat. In 1861 a whopping flood gathered in the upper Willamette and came roaring down, bringing barns, houses, and trees with it; the whole town of Champoeg came along, all but a couple of sheds that were on a ridge and avoided being washed away. At Salem, the *Onward* sailed onto the town's streets instead of hiding itself under a high bank. At Portland the water climbed over the banks and wandered through the muddy streets. Again in 1894 the water rose in the Willamette, poured over the Falls, swept past the city and then came back, for the Columbia was full and built up a backwater. That time the water rose above Front Street to First and beyond, and people went around in skiffs from flatboat to flatboat, anchored in front of flooded stores. The unfinished Union Station was a brick island in water four feet deep that reached far across the old Guild's Lake and toward the hills; the railroad to Goble disappeared under the flood, cutting off train service to Seattle. In order to keep the trains moving, the Northern Pacific ran its big ferry *Tacoma* from Kelso up to Portland instead of shuttling it across the river from Kalama to Goble. So while the flood lasted, the *Tacoma* every morning squeezed her way through the open draws to tie up at the public levee above Jefferson Street. In the afternoon she would start back, catch the drag of the current, and finally get past the bridges, no easy job because the *Tacoma* was 334 feet long, with a beam of 42 feet, and on the double tracks along her deck a whole passenger train could be placed.

Everywhere was water. In the Columbia Gorge, the railroad washed out, stopping all communication; the O.R.&N. had abandoned its river service only a year before, bringing down the last of its boats, and now there was considerable wailing. To get mail and passengers through, the company decided to send the *Harvest Queen* to run all the way to The Dalles. She had come down through the Cascades, but boatmen were skeptical that she could go back up. The *Queen* steamed for the Cascades and tried hard, but at the end of the first day she dropped back to a landing to wait for another chance. On the second try, with her engines straining, the *Harvest Queen* worked inch by inch up the Cascades until she was in sight of slack water above the upper landing. Then, just as she was about to make it, she swerved into a rock and stuck fast, with four feet of water in her hold. When she had been bailed out and freed, her captain took her back to Portland, admitting the attempt to be hopeless, and the plan to run her from the Cascades to The Dalles to meet the *D. S. Baker* and thus restore the old service during the flood had to be abandoned.

The Columbia Gorge could always be counted upon to provide the unexpected in the way of harassments for steamboatmen. "You cannot tell," said a steamboat captain on the Columbia, "what the weather will be any winter." Or, he might have added, any other time. The river winds between the mountains placidly blue between green walls, sometimes; at others, the water is darklingly gray, flecked with white from the whipping wind that roars back and forth through the Gorge. "Predictions don't predict" is an old saying about Oregon weather, and in the Gorge it was right.

In 1904 the stern-wheeler *Charles R. Spencer,* a big, fast boat, was on the run between Portland and The Dalles. At The Dalles she unloaded her freight on July 11 and tied up for the night, ready to make her usual pleasant trip down the river in the morning. Before daylight wind started to sweep up the river and was growing steadily more violent when the boat left her dock. She immediately caught the wind head-on and began fighting for headway. The White Salmon ferry cut across ahead of her, veering far out of her course and beating back and forth to make her landing. Aboard the *Spencer* thirty passengers huddled in the cabin, not caring to brave the gale that whipped along the decks. At Lyle she ran into something new: high swells that came rolling up the river like a tidal bore, water gathered by the wind and driven back against the current. In her chains and through the deck stanchions the wind howled and whistled, and the whole boat plunged and bucked, her bow pounding into each swell with a shuddering jolt. Then her chains parted and the hull promptly hogged so much that a main steam line broke, filling the boat with clouds of steam that rolled up from the engine room. In the pilot house Captain Johnson set a course for the Oregon shore, moving diagonally across the river to prevent having the swells swamp his wrenched and crippled boat, and slowly, fighting the wind all the way, while the bow and wheel sagged, threatening to split the cabin, he guided her to shallow water where he could launch his small boats. In them he sent his passengers ashore to wait while the purser found a farmer's team and drove to Rowena to telegraph for help. The up-bound boat, the *Dalles City,* came by about then and tried to stop but dared not venture into the shallows as she was herself being driven by the wind so much that she had to keep moving. The passengers were finally gathered up by a train and taken on to Portland while the gale continued, blowing itself out after the second day. When the water calmed, the *Charles R. Spencer* limped on its way, had its hog-chains renewed and tightened, and in a week was back on the run as if nothing had happened.

Sometimes the trouble was ice. The rivers now and then would be sheeted over and the boats would cluster at the bank with men hacking at the ice pushing against their sides in an attempt to keep the hulls from being crushed. In 1862 a storm struck Portland on the first of January, covering the country with snow and ice that lasted two months until a thaw broke the blockade. In the meantime, steamboats remained almost completely idle. When the railroads came, Portland felt that the days of the blockades were over, but they were not, for snow drifted in the Gorge year after year, stopping all traffic on the lines. During December of 1884 a storm suddenly moved west down the Columbia from inland, leaving the river between The Dalles and the Gorge frozen over and bringing snow that, caught by the wind, quickly began to drift. Two days later, just after midnight, the regular westbound express train left The Dalles for Portland, its way being cleared by an engine and snowplow running just ahead. Near Viento, at the head of the Gorge, an avalanche of wet, sticky snow nearly buried the plow and blocked the line ahead. Still the snow drifted, threatening to bury the train; to prevent it, Conductor Lyons had the engineer back the coaches onto a low trestle that would probably remain above the drifts, and then Lyons started out to walk to the nearest telegraph station, four miles. There he wired for help and food, then went back to his train. By morning the passengers could see nothing but falling snow, and the prospects of release were slim—the track behind had been drifted over as soon as the train had passed. All day they waited, keeping warm by burning wood from the tender, but getting hungrier all the time. At last men on snowshoes packed in food from relief trains that fought their way from both directions, but there was no chance to get the passengers out. Another day came and went, and another, until on the fourth day the storm slackened and the passengers were taken out. When trains stalled in the snow, and they did more than once, a steamer worked as near as it could, and its crew would break a path through the brush and snow to the coaches. Then down it the passengers could stumble to the bank and onto the relief boat, leaving the train to be hauled away when the plows could reach it.

In January 1886 unfortunately both the railroad and the river closed, snow drifting into the railway cuts, and ice extending from bank to bank on the river. Heroic methods to open the way had to be found. In Portland just then the O.R.&N. had its brand-new white elephant, the huge iron side-wheeler *Olympian,* one of Villard's more expensive good ideas. Built on Chesapeake Bay, the *Olympian* and her near-sister *Alaskan* followed designs popular on Long Island Sound and in the Chesapeake rather than designs tried and found suitable to the Pacific Northwest. At the moment her design did not matter, but her iron hull did. Wooden steamers tore their planking to ribbons when they rammed into floating ice, but an iron one would not, so the *Olympian* was sent up to open a way through the ice to the Cascades. She could crunch through floating ice without much trouble, except for an occasional smashed bucket on her wheel; and when she came to sheet ice, her captain would back her off and then send her forward at full speed until her bow would ride up on the ice, smashing it by sheer weight. The idea worked, and the *Olympian* reached the Cascades and began to bring down waiting mail and passengers; as soon as the emergency passed, the wooden steamers went back to work, for the *Olympian* cost too much to operate.

The twin side-wheelers had been built primarily for service on the Sound. The *Olympian* was rated at 1400 tons and was 270 feet long with a 40 foot beam. When light, her draft was over eight feet, making her unfit for most waters around Oregon, except the lower Columbia to Astoria. Everything about her was the latest. Her grand saloon, reaching the length of the main cabin, was 200 feet long, with mahogany furniture, upholstered in plush, resting on Wilton velvet carpet. Off the saloon opened fifty staterooms, each fitted with all the latest in polished mirrors and washstands; some cabins had brass bedsteads instead of the conventional berths. Incandescent electric lights shone in every part of the boat. From her dining saloon, seating 130 passengers, her fancy chandeliers and her ebony trimmed grand staircase to her wide guards and arching paddleboxes she looked elegant and expensive, and she was.

Boats might come to grief on the river occasionally, but the mouth of the Columbia took its regular toll, from the time of the *Peacock* which left her name on the spit where she grounded in 1841 to the *Ohio* in 1936, foundering in a gale. Fog, winds, treacherous currents, and uncertain piloting all combined to send ships smashing onto the beach. In April 1879 the big paddler *Great Republic,* running as an opposition boat to the regular line, came up from San Francisco with 846 passengers on board. It was midnight when she came opposite the mouth of the river, the sky clear and bright, the sea calm. Rather than wait for daylight, the *Great Republic* took aboard its pilot and headed into the mouth, moving slowly through smooth water, her head set toward Sand Island. The captain, peering through the dark, saw the island ahead and called to the pilot who said they needed to run closer to it before turning away, but the current was strong and before the pilot could get the big ship veered onto a new course, he felt her slide onto the sand. It was high tide then, and the next day's tide failed to lift her free; meanwhile the captain had sent his passengers ashore in the tug boats that came out from Astoria to help. Slowly the *Great Republic* settled into the sand, the next tide began to break over her, and gradually she went to pieces.

From the mouth of the Columbia to the farthest branches of its tributaries, water sometimes rolled white, wind roared, or snow drifted, and hardy was the boat that rode the river. In spite of the chances for damage a great majority of steamers lasted a long time and finally ended their days in some muddy boneyard waiting to be dismantled. The steamboat, like the native, took only a short time to get used to the climate.

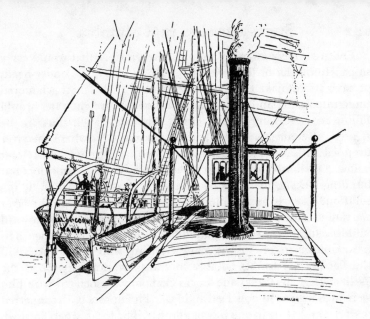

Chapter 11

OPEN RIVER

AFTER a generation or two, the people who lived along the Columbia and Willamette finally became convinced that there was nothing they could do about the weather, but that certain other natural phenomena they could tinker with and perhaps improve. The rivers needed some altering here and there to put more water where more water ought to be by moving aside minor obstructions—and a town itself sometimes raised money and did its own job of blasting and dredging. Oregon City cut a channel of sorts through the Clackamas Rapids after it found that boats at low water often had to turn back at Milwaukie. Portland, too, had trouble with the channel: Swan Island divided the waters annoyingly and sent out a sand bar to ground unwary ships, and below the city some of the sloughs meandered uncertainly toward the Columbia. To raise funds for river improvement Portland citizens named a committee which, unlike many committees, set about its work so well that shortly it had collected over nine thousand dollars. Then another committee took over the spending of the money, surely a more congenial task at any time.

The great desire was for an open river, a river that would carry ships without let or lighterage from its mouth to the upper heads of navigation; make the rivers unbroken in their length, clamored the enthusiastic, and the millennium of low freight rates would follow inevitably, probably within Thursday week. First to be cleared, of course, were the Falls at Oregon City where the river dropped into a horseshoe-shaped trough, a little over forty feet below. Obviously, removing the falls was an impossibility, but building locks to lift boats by a series of water steps would be the solution. As early as 1858, long before the commerce on the river warranted costly projects, steamboatmen made gestures toward building locks at the Falls, and talk went on until 1868 when Bernard Goldsmith, one of the many Germans who became active in the Pacific Northwest, notably in transportation, organized the Willamette Falls Canal and Locks Company. Associated with him were such men as Joseph Teal and D. P. Thompson, both connected with steamboating in one way or another. The locks, when finished, would break the monopoly of the People's Transportation Company which had control of the basin on the Oregon City side. The locks would be far safer, for although only two boats had gone over the Falls, one intentionally, the chance of accident persisted.

To help the locks along, the state legislature in 1868 granted a small subsidy and clapped on an impossible time limit. Doubly handicapped, the Locks Company could do nothing but issue an optimistic prospectus that predicted as many as 60,000 tons of freight and 20,000 passengers would pass through the portage in a year—a prediction only a few hundred per cent an overstatement. The legislature, convinced, increased the aid in 1870 to $200,000 in state bonds, limited the toll to half a dollar a ton for freight and ten cents a head for passengers, retained the right to purchase the locks in ten years, and claimed ten per cent of the net profits. The last term was easily handled; as the company never made any profits, net or gross, the state did not have to worry about any income. As soon as the state aid became sure and ample, the company went to work cutting its canal around the Falls on the west bank; to meet the threat, the People's Transportation Company furiously got franchises and set crews hacking another canal on the east bank. The Locks Company continued, pecking at the hard rock and nibbling along not rapidly but constantly, and viewed with slightly concealed distaste by Ben Holladay. When the ditch was ready, masons and carpenters put in the ponderous wooden locks, and by the late fall of 1872 the job was finished. On January 1, 1873, the company had to open its locks in order to receive state aid, but when the time came, Holladay had tied up all the steamboats. Finally, to perform the ceremony, the Locks Company secured in Portland the otherwise undistinguished steamboat *Maria Wilkins* and sent her through the locks with a load of distinguished officials. Jacob Kamm was there and naturally so were Colonel Teal and Mr. Goldsmith, prime movers of the project. Harvey Scott was along representing the Press, and Governor Grover dignity and the State. Congratulations passed back and forth along with oratory, and libations and other refreshments were handy and plentiful. It was a big day.

Somehow, when it was all over, the locks opened the river but not so well as had been expected, and before long the Locks Company itself became a monopoly and the object of wrath. Its big steamers—*Governor Grover, Willamette Chief,* and *Beaver*—carried freight; then, almost as if a sinister shadow were cast over the bright light of enterprise, the Oregon Steam Navigation Company became owners.

On the Columbia the Oregon Steam Navigation Company was well satisfied with its portage railways, thank you. Its own freight moved freely, and at a profit, and other companies could take their chances; of course, the trains did have an uncanny way of not arriving at the landing at a convenient time for rival boats, but no one could prove it was deliberate. Other companies might try, but they were prejudiced. The Army Engineers surveyed the Cascades in 1875 and recommended construction of a canal around the upper stretch of white water, and in the next year Congress appropriated $90,000 to start work. Although work did start, progress appeared more in the reports than at the canal, and more and more money had to be added to the sum to keep the project alive. For ten years the ditch grew slowly. The building of the railroad along the south bank in 1884 largely removed the pressing need for a canal anyway; freight and passengers which the O. S. N. had once carried on boats now went through on the O. R. & N. train. The O. R. & N. found it had a surplus of boats on the upper river and sent them one by one through the Cascades to new jobs below. By 1893 that left the upper river almost without steamers, and shippers had a choice—the railroad or nothing. They could no longer choose between two services of the same company. Great was the cry and impressive the reverberations while the wheat men of the high country demanded competition by steamboat. They shook Congress into action, and in 1893 it granted an appropriation of $1,239,653 which permitted completion of the canal, and in November 1896 it opened, with both the O. R. & N. and Regulator Line boats on hand to pass through.

The canal itself was about 3,000 feet long and passed around the upper Cascades where the river was practically unnavigable. At the lower end was a lock of two chambers, each a little over 460 feet long, which gave a lift ranging from 24 feet at low water to 14 feet at high water. The cut ran through rock, and the canal had heavy masonry walls with a controlling width of 90 feet and a depth of 8 feet, enough to handle easily any boat that might come to the river. Altogether, the Cascade Locks were impressive and became one of the sights no tourist missed. Near the railway station which bore the name, the O. R. & N. cleared out the brush in a grove of trees and made a picnic ground for groups and parties, where, in the shade, the people gathered in crowds, some coming in special excursion trains on the railway, others by special boats, to spend the day and to watch an occasional steamer pass through the canal and rise or fall in the lock. At last steamboats moved without interruption from Portland to The Dalles without having to unload at the portage and turn back.

At the same time work went on at the Cascades, the Army Engineers were improving the mouth of the Columbia, so long the despair of ships entering the river. The river, at low tide, meandered through channels cut in shifting sand, and a pilot coming through deep water one day was not sure that he would find it there the next. Ship after ship went on the shoals, wedged, and then broke up under the pounding of waves. Two problems faced the engineers: to find a way to make the channel deep enough at low tide to permit ships of ordinary draft to enter, and to keep the channel open once it had been dredged.

Colonel Eads faced the same problems at the mouth of the Mississippi. On first glance there seemed to be little similarity between the clear Columbia and the muddy Mississippi endlessly dumping its silt into the Gulf, but the effect was the same, however, because the ocean kept pushing sand up toward the mouth of the Columbia and building bars that the outflowing river had to cut through. Surveys in 1878 showed that an application of the methods Eads had used just below New Orleans would be effective, and in 1884 the first appropriation was passed for construction. The money lasted only a few months, yet the work finished showed that the idea was right. Simply, the river mouth was to be controlled between two dikes or jetties of stone; one would strike out from the north shore and the other from Clatsop Spit. Between the two the water of the Columbia would have to rush seaward, and in its movement it would constantly scour its own channel through the sand and maintain the proper depth. Finally in 1888 sufficient funds were appropriated to push the work rapidly.

Along the sands of Clatsop Spit, a tangle of railway tracks crawled from a wharf to the jetty itself, and on the tracks engines and cars shuttled back and forth. First, pile drivers pounded timbers into the sands to form trestles; then on the trestles, railroad track went in as the work moved out to sea. Engines pushed strings of cars loaded with rock to be dumped into the water. Gradually, as more and more rock went into the sea beside the trestle, it packed and emerged as a long, solid ridge or dam against which the waves piled sand to make the whole thing an extension of the spit itself. Where the bottom seemed unstable, trainloads of brush or small trees with their branches left on would be dumped to form a mat that held the rock in place until the waves did their work of scooping sand.

Behind the jetty and in the quiet waters of Young's Bay other work went on. The rock, so liberally sent into the water, came from more than a hundred miles up the river and had to be brought down on barges. For hauling them, the Engineers built a stern-wheeler, the *Cascades*, a big boat, long and slim, ordinary except for her pilot house with its rounded front. Built in 1882 when the work was first being projected, she handled in barges all the materials, and that included half a million feet of piling and 900,000 tons of rock in the first years of building. She pushed what the barges carried, and the barges—there were about a dozen of them—looked like steamboat hulls with a flush deck and small house at the rear with the steering wheel open to the deck. On the trips the *Cascades* would take one barge directly ahead, lash one to either side of it and back a little bit so that their sterns were alongside the steamer's foredeck; outside them would be another pair, the five forming a V and at the same time giving their host plenty of control in the channel. Back and forth on the job the *Cascades* shuttled for years, for the jetties took a long time to finish and then had to have constant attention.

Forced between the jetties, the Columbia stopped wandering along the bar looking for a place it could cut to reach the sea; now it flowed steadily, gouging out its channel through what had been the bar until a shipmaster was sure he could find thirty feet of water. Later, after 1905 when larger steamships had drafts of well over twenty feet, the channel had to be deepened again, and the old *Cascades* hauled more rock. The jetties grew from the first thousand feet built in 1884 until the south jetty reached out seven miles from its beginnings at Fort Stevens, and toward it from Cape Disappointment the north jetty stretched four and one-half miles and gathered behind itself a shoal that enlarged Peacock Spit.

The Willamette was a notoriously tricky stream for steamboats with its bars and rocky reefs and its annual accretion of logs and snags brought down by high water and left lying about where they could reach out and spike steamboats that went by them. By 1871 the Engineers were set to work clearing the channel to Eugene from Portland so that steamboats might expect six feet of water to Oregon City and at least two and one-half feet all the way up to Eugene. By sweating profusely and using lots of powder and dynamite, gangs were able to keep the river up to expectations, although traffic hardly warranted their labors. In 1904 attempts to keep a channel open to Eugene to any standard depth finally were given up, and strident was the wailing of the Eugeneans at the news. Later Corvallis was the head of a maintained depth and only snagging continued to Harrisburg.

Part of the Willamette work included the maintenance of the Yamhill where, to provide for proper steamboating, a four-foot channel had to be opened for boats going up to Dayton for wheat. The Engineers in 1900 built near Lafayette a single lock 40 feet wide and 210 feet long which permitted a boat to be lifted 16 feet and proceed upstream in slack and comparatively deep water. It was a pleasant lock where the tender could grow gray in solitude, undisturbed in his meditations, because only an occasional steamboat came along to wake him up. At the beginning there was practically no traffic on the Yamhill, and what there was steadily declined until, in 1921, only one lone ton of freight went through the locks, travelling in solitary grandeur. In addition, about 2,100 tons of rafted logs went down the river, along with 26 passengers that year. For a time, no tonnage at all passed through the locks, but eventually logging companies made use of the river, and by 1941 business had picked up sharply. In that year 99,000 tons of logs in tow of small tugs went down the Yamhill through the locks, and in

1943 the tonnage rose to 101,981, to fall slightly with the end of the war to a mere 79,895 in 1946.

Steamboating above the Cascades had disappeared for a time after the O. R. & N. removed its boats in 1892, but before long a new company, the Dalles, Portland and Astoria Navigation Company, put the *Regulator* and *Dalles City* into service and became known as the Regulator Line. Both boats were fitted for freight and passengers and together revived the river trade so well that the O. R. & N. countered by building in 1899 at Portland a new stern-wheeler, *Hassalo,* third of the name. She was a fine boat, 186 feet long with a slim beam of 30 feet, and loaded she drew only $5\frac{1}{2}$ feet. When everything was ready, her owners made test runs with her on the quiet water of Willamette Slough and gasped as she clipped off 26 miles an hour, a speed great enough to let her run to Astoria in four hours. Her engines were horizontal, each with a high and low pressure cylinder with a 98-inch stroke. The two engines were operated by a single control so that one engineer could handle both easily and without aid, even in starting them. Altogether, the *Hassalo* was the best boat yet to go on the river.

Just as her engines and machinery were the very latest, so were her fittings, especially her dining room, pantry, and kitchen, for the *Hassalo* was to be an elegant floating hotel. Nothing was lacking: the dining room had small tables for privacy, and the lounges offered fine leather seats, something like those in Pullman cars, ranged along the sides so that passengers could watch the scenery of the river and still loll in comfort without braving the wind on deck. She ran both the Astoria and the Cascades routes, but her reputation came from the way she swept back and forth between The Dalles and Portland, and she kept the *Telephone* and *T. J. Potter* busy defending their reputations against her claim to be the fastest riverboat in the world. On the Cascades route she could push the *Bailey Gatzert* of the Columbia River and Puget Sound Navigation Company to the limit when they sprinted.

The Columbia River & Puget Sound Navigation Company was Scott's line, Scott of the *Ohio* who had done it again with his propeller *Flyer* and his stern-wheelers *Telephone* and *Bailey Gatzert,* each identified by a wide band of white on their stacks that marked them as boats of the White Collar Line. One of Scott's steamers left Portland for The Dalles every morning, except Sunday, at 7 o'clock. The White Collar Line merged with the Dalles, Portland and

Astoria Navigation Company in 1903, and about then real competition broke out. Captain Hosford had the *Ione* at work, and Captain E. W. Spencer put his steamer *Charles R. Spencer* onto the run at the same time. The *Ione* was an informal boat that did not worry about racing or trivialities like schedules. She started out on her run and meandered back and forth across the Columbia, stopping at any landing for anything. If the churning was not quite finished, a farmer said so, and the boat waited; if a farm wife wanted to go down to Camas for shopping, or a lady at Camas wanted to go to Portland on a buying spree, the *Ione* took her. She was a friendly boat that never put on airs. The big *Bailey Gatzert* might sweep grandly by her, rocking her in its wake, but the *Ione* did not mind. Rather the *Ione* habitues crowded the rail and waved while the *Ione* whistled and continued nosing along the bank from landing to landing. The *Charles R. Spencer,* on the other hand, was a fast boat and would give the Regulator Line a run for its money by making a round trip between Portland and The Dalles daily. All the very best fixings were on the *Spencer,* too; an awning spread over the upper foredeck and under it were seats for 200 passengers. A new whistle she tried out made the Portland water front stuff its ears with cotton while the tottery old piling under the docks trembled dangerously—the *Spencer's* whistle might not have been melodious but she sure was loud; other boatmen trembled at its hoot and the trees by the riverbank huddled shivering before its blast.

Above The Dalles the river lay idle, though a rising clamor for river improvements came from the wheat growers of the Inland Empire, encouraged by the formation in Portland of the Open River Association in 1904. The barrier of Celilo must be removed, was its cry; the monopoly of the railroad must be broken; a canal must be built instantly. A boat railway, proposed in the 1890's, with its cradles or its boat-elevators, now would not serve, although money had been appropriated to build one and by some miracle not spent. Group after group rallied to the cry for an Open River. The Portland Chamber of Commerce, viewing the sudden rise of ports on Puget Sound, especially upstart Seattle, joined in the campaign to save the Inland Empire from economic disaster—and from Seattle. So the next move was to organize the Open River Navigation Company to put its own boats on the river above Celilo, connect with the State Portage Railway there and with the *Charles R. Spencer* below.

In 1906 the Open River Navigation Company started to run a small stern-wheeler, the *Relief*, that could carry 120 tons of wheat but never could muster power enough to climb Umatilla Rapids and had to be content with cargo gathered below there. The second boat, *Mountain Gem*, was better, and with arrangements made to connect also with the boats of the Regulator Line, the Open River group was in a position to give real competition to the railroad. As the Regulator Line had passed into the ownership of James J. Hill of the Great Northern, Northern Pacific, and the Spokane, Portland and Seattle Railway, no doubt the Regulator Line was quite happy to cause trouble for Edward Harriman's Union Pacific, now the direct owner of the railway along the river. Then the Open River company put in service its third boat, the *J. N. Teal*, named for the most active exponent of the open river idea, but it burned at once and had to be rebuilt completely. Not until 1908 was it ready, when with two other boats, the *Inland Empire* and the *Twin Cities*, built for Columbia and Snake River services, the company had an ample fleet. On the Snake the *Norma, Spokane, Lewiston,* the twin-stacked *J. M. Hannaford,* and the *Joseph Kellogg* were running. The Columbia was seeing steamboating as it had not since the days of the Oregon Steam Navigation Company.

In the meantime, the Celilo Canal surveys were finished and work got under way. The canal opened into the river just above Celilo Falls and not far below the head was the first lock. The ditch crowded closely between the river and the high cliffs, paralleling very closely the Portage Railway and O. R. & N. tracks. At Ten Mile Rapids a second lock broke the canal, and at Five Mile Rapids was a third; from there the canal went straight to the foot of Big Eddy, passing through the last lock before returning to the river. Over-all the canal was about eight miles long and circled past most of the rapids, although below Big Eddy there was still rough water at Three Mile Rapids, but not enough to cause a boat too much trouble. Scattered along the canal were turnouts where boats moving in opposite directions might pass. Since the canal is only sixty-five feet wide at the bottom, it is too narrow to permit boats to pass each other and, as towboatmen discovered, not wide enough for easy handling of barges which become difficult to control in the narrow ditch, especially when a wind whips over the river.

Still, the Celilo Canal was big enough and deep enough—eight feet—for any steamboat that might conceivably need to use it. On

April 28, 1915 the *J. N. Teal* and the *Inland Empire* passed through it upriver, and again a couple of days later the *Undine,* from Portland, which came for the festivities arranged at the canal's opening but first went on up the river. When the *Undine* came back down it had aboard in addition to its load of notables from Portland, another batch from the Inland Empire (Portland's Inland Empire, according to the Portland Chamber of Commerce) all in a sweat to whoop and hurrah at the opening and most of them with speeches and statements neatly typed for any occasion. On May 5, trains came up from The Dalles with more people and the steamers of the Open River Navigation Company arrived, also with delegations. When the ceremony got under way, the Honorable Joseph N. Teal—like father, like son—made a speech, noting that the shackles were broken, the river was free at last, free of tolls. Then, as he crept toward his conclusion, his fancy soared off into the fine free spaces of rhetoric:

Our faces are still set to the future, and we must never falter or tire until from the mountains to the sea our great river is free as the air we breathe, and the land it waters and serves is giving forth in abundance all the fruits of the soil—until this country becomes indeed an empire, not only of productiveness, but of the highest type of American citizenship.

Having delivered the oration, Teal boarded the *Undine* to go down the river with the other dignified celebrants who transferred at Portland to the *Georgiana* bound for Astoria. There, aboard a tug they passed out onto the open ocean; they had traveled from their Inland Empire to the sea by toll-free waterway.

Mr. Teal did not go beyond Portland; he had another speech to make, this time at Oregon City. There the movement for an open river had been active also. The Willamette locks which passed from owner to owner, never making any profit, to be sure, but still representing a monopoly, were now being operated by the Portland Railway, Light and Power Company, into whose hands they had finally come. The demand had grown for public rather than private ownership until the Portland company sold the locks to the federal government on April 26, 1915, and on May 6, 1915 they were dedicated and formally opened. At the dedication Joseph N. Teal spoke, as his father had spoken at their original opening, forty-two years before. Now the younger Teal said, "The Willamette and its great sister, the Columbia, sound the tocsin of freedom together, and for the first time since they began to flow to the sea, commerce can move over them without paying a toll because of some obstruction to navigation."

Commerce did not seem to take immediate advantage of its opportunity on the Willamette. The main freight was barges of cordwood going down the river to be burned in the furnaces and cook stoves of Portland homes. Approximately 6,000 passengers a year went through the locks, most of them on boats of the Oregon City Transportation Company which was running its *Grahamona, Pomona* and *Oregona* as far as Corvallis.

Hardly had the Celilo Canal opened before steamboating on the Columbia seemed to collapse; excursion runs to The Dalles out of Portland kept lively, but above Celilo somehow the enthusiasm died out. The Open River Navigation Company, founded with such high ideals, having found that there was too great a difference between promises and prospects of cargo and the amount of freight actually brought down to the landings, quietly sold its fleet to another company. Only the *Twin Cities* remained in service above Celilo, and the Regulator Line held a virtual monopoly below The Dalles. Then The Dalles-Columbia Line put the *State of Washington* to work and brought down the *Twin Cities* to run on a weekly trip between Portland and Pasco. Shortly this service disappeared, too, leaving only the Regulator Line boats to The Dalles, the local *Ione* and *Tahoma* to Cascades and occasionally beyond, and the Union Pacific steamers at Lewiston.

Steamboating struggled to survive, but after 1919 the new locks at Celilo lay virtually idle until barge traffic began to develop. Below The Dalles one by one the steamers dropped out of the trade; the opening of automobile highways removed the tourists from the excursion boats, and the building of the Spokane, Portland and Seattle Railway along the north bank took the traffic from the formerly isolated landings. A last gasp had been the plan to run the steamer *Nespelem* up to Wallula; she would pick up her freight in Portland and go without stop to Celilo, and then touch at places like Blalock, Rufus, Umatilla, Wallula, and at the landings transfer the freight to motor trucks for delivery to Walla Walla and other inland towns. Captain Graham had planned something of the same system when he organized his Inland Empire Boat and Truck Line in 1920. For thirty-three years his line, the Oregon City Transportation Company, had been active on the Willamette, but now he announced withdrawal from there and transfer of the fleet's best boat, the *Grahamona,* to the Columbia. To prepare her for the job, she was hauled out, had new keelsons added, her guards sponsoned, and her furnaces fitted for coal burning (she had been a wood-burner, like all Willamette boats of the line) because fuel oil would be too expensive on the new run, at least until it had been developed.

Another idea for speeding river freight was tried when the fast *Olympian,* formerly the crack boat *Telegraph,* went onto the route from Portland to The Dalles, going up one day and returning the next. She had space for 300 passengers, 120 of them riding comfortably in the usual Pullman seats ranged along the walls of the lounge and 100 more in seats placed on deck. But her system for handling freight was the sign of a recognition that the automobile was here to stay as a force in transportation. Freight was loaded on two-ton motor trucks which were driven directly onto the boat's freight deck; at the other terminal the trucks were driven up the ramp and continued on their way, offering door-to-door service. But not enough doors opened to it. In 1923 the last stern-wheel packet gave up the run to The Dalles.

The ending of steamboat runs did not mean the end of traffic on the river or the demand for improved waterways. In 1932 the Army Engineers completed a survey of the entire Columbia River system for possible development of its use in irrigation, navigation, and, now a new interest, power. The Engineers pointed out that boats of various types were in fact blocked only at Kettle Falls, although the channel needed much maintenance and could be improved by a series of dams located at the several rapids, dams that would have many purposes: to maintain even flow throughout the year, to permit slack-water navigation, to furnish water for irrigation districts, and to generate electricity. Work began in 1933 on a power and navigation dam at Bradford Island, below the Cascades and conveniently within Multnomah County in Oregon, from whence would come the labor needed. After five years of work the Bonneville Dam was finished in 1938. The structure is in three parts: across the main channel a spillway dam regulates the height of water in the reservoir or pool behind it; across the chute between Bradford Island and the Oregon shore is a powerhouse with its penstocks; and adjoining the powerhouse there lies against the bank a navigation lock large enough to handle seagoing vessels of about 8,000 tons. The lock itself is 76 feet wide and 500 feet long, cut into the rock of the channel and given height by concrete walls. Its lower

mitre gates are huge steel leaves 102 feet tall, for a vessel is raised
over 50 feet in a single lift.

When the dam began to back water behind it, the Cascades, so
long a barrier and trouble spot to steamboats, slowly quieted and
fell silent as they were buried beneath still water; the edge of the
slack water moved inch by inch up the river while the dam filled,
reached the old Cascade Locks and drowned them except for an
outline of masonry. At last the rolling river stood quiet all the way
to the foot of Big Eddy. Above there Tumwater Falls and the rapids
still brawled and thundered. Now The Dalles, that had been a river
port since the roaring days of the Idaho rush, had hopes that it
would be an ocean port, especially when the *Charles L. Wheeler,*
not a stern-wheeler but a big, rather ugly ocean freighter, came in
between the jetties, moved up the river to the Bonneville Dam, was
lifted slowly to the level of the pool, and continued on to the new
port dock at The Dalles.

Here was a river with slack-water navigation waiting to be used,
and the barges used it; the advantages of the stern-wheeler with its
light draft and its ease of handling in rough water no longer
equalled the efficiency and economy of the propeller, the low, unlovely tugboat coughing its way along with a covey of barges.

Not the slack water, good for steamboats, made the dams primarily important, but the rushing water, pouring through the penstocks and spinning turbines which ran electric generators. Power
and irrigation replaced the old cry for the open river, so that when,
in April 1947, first work began on another great dam on the Columbia, its navigation lock, to be like the one at Bonneville, hardly
received notice, yet the McNary Dam, blocking the river at Umatilla
Rapids, would back the water to Pasco and make the river an easy
highway for tugs and barges. Perhaps some day there would be other
dams with navigation locks beyond, maybe on the Snake, too. At
least, Joseph Teal, father and son, can rest easy—the river, from the
sea to the Snake will be open, even if the only stern-wheeler above
Camas is the old *Georgie Burton,* drowsing over her past in dignified
retirement at The Dalles while the twin-stacked diesel tugs move
by with their laden barges.

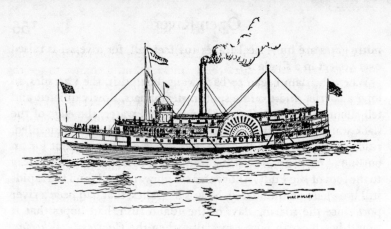

Chapter 12
BY THE SEA

WHEN MAY COMES to the Oregon country, the rains sweeten and subside and suddenly the countryside burgeons into brighter green; then the folks long to go on pilgrimages, to seek strange strands and unknown shrines in the time of the picnic, the excursion, and the vacation. When May came to England, good Queen Elizabeth, along with her court, assorted lute players, and servants with hampers, would board a barge on the Thames and go a-Maying with Corinna. So it was in Oregon—when Spring came, the people went down to the riverbank, hailed a steamboat and went excursioning some place. Perhaps it was the frontier urge driving them on; perhaps it was the scent of springtime and an earnest desire that came with it to do nothing, accompanied by a lot of other people.

Excursions were got up for any occasion or event, and sometimes for none at all. If a river town had a baseball team, the whole shebang crowded onto a steamboat and went to the next landing for a game, fetching along a band to help out. If a political rally had a torchlight procession scheduled, steamboats brought mobs of partisans with a band, to join in. When springtime came, the Sunday school had to have a picnic, and what could be nicer than a ride on the river on a steamboat? Or some captain, having no cargo waiting, ordered posters advertising a grand excursion aboard his splendid steamer, hired a band, and collected fares from the crowds that

[154]

clambered up the landing stage ready for the trip. Anything would do to gather a crowd. Strawberry picking and a chance to see the new Cascades tramway filled the *Lot Whitcomb* in 1851—at $10 a head or, significantly, $15 a couple. The stern-wheeler *Westport,* built in 1878, spent most of ten years carrying hunters to shooting grounds along the lower Columbia, especially when the ducks were flying. When the locks were under construction at Oregon City, a steamboat load of sightseers came up from Portland to watch a series of powder blasts set off in the excavation; later, steamers ran to Canemah with crowds bound for the amusement park on the bluffs above the Falls.

A pleasure trip on the river, whether it be a mere jaunt of a few hours or a journey to a resort, was always the same. The crowd started arriving early, but the last ones aboard normally had to scramble before the boat pulled too far away from the landing. On the foredeck the band tuned up and belabored airs hitherto familiar; in the parlor the ladies gathered, and on the decks people strolled, their ease disturbed by children racing excitedly back and forth and swinging happily from the hog-chains. The bartender was kept busy, and the steward and cooks got meals ready for those who wanted to eat in the dining room. Most people, however, brought baskets of lunch, and the families gathered in shady spots on deck to bring out their sandwiches, cakes, pies, and inevitable heavy potato salads. The boat sloshed casually along, the band blared, the children screamed and ran, and the sun beat down. When evening came, the children finally fell silent or into complaining whines, while the young couples waited for the moon to rise. The band, exhausted, relaxed and left the river undisturbed. Finally the excursion was over, the boat docked, the people went wearily ashore, and the crew walked decks that crunched with egg shells. A regular outing came each year when hundreds rode steamboats on the Willamette to a huge camp meeting on the riverbank a little above Salem. There, under arbors, preaching and gossiping lasted a week, and it was darkly rumored that all who attended did not do so to escape worldly pleasure. The steamboatmen asked no questions: they hauled cargoes of sinners seeking salvation, and hauled back the regenerate without noticing much difference. Once aboard the steamer the camp meeting crowd acted like all others.

These were the occasional excursions, run for special occasions. Two routes, however, came to be regular excursion runs and devel-

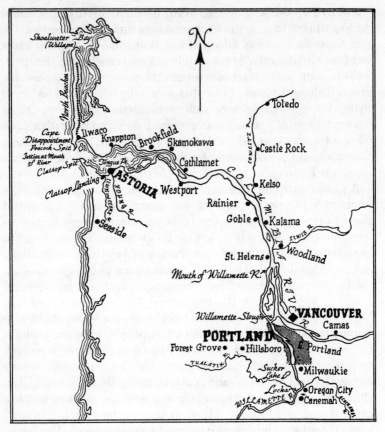

THE SEASHORE ROUTE

oped boats and services that catered primarily to pleasure seekers.
To the Cascades went sightseers wanting to look at the Columbia
Gorge and do it in one day; to Astoria went those who wanted to
spend time at the seashore. The Cascades run became a short trip for
tourists; the Astoria run became a fast transfer route between the
city and the resorts for those who were in a hurry. Both routes had
attracted pleasure riders from the beginning, but the Astoria line
was the first to become primarily an excursion trip, since more
vacationists used it.

Astoria itself offered little to the excursionist. A town built on
stilts out over the tide flats and living mainly on fishing, some sea
trade, and lumbering, Astoria remained for many years markedly

ugly, so that its strongest partisans talked about its setting, with the forested hills rising behind it and the broad bay before it, or its quaintness with the wooden streets, and tactfully said nothing about the town itself. One did not, it seemed, stop at Astoria, except to change boats and go somewhere else. And he went to the shore, either north or south.

South from the Columbia stretch the Clatsop Plains, fronted by the ocean and wide, clean beaches, and backed by quiet woods and the wandering Lewis and Clark River that parallels the coast for miles, sometimes coming within sound of the breakers not more than two or three miles to the west. The country was ideal for camping, and by the 1860's many Portlanders were able to take time away from their work in the crowded city—as they thought the place had become—for a holiday at the shore. In summer whole families migrated to the beach where father unpacked the tent and started assembling it while mother got the younger children out of earshot. Soon a colony of tents fringed the beach on the margin between the sand and the cool woods; from rough stone fireplaces rose pungent smoke, spiced by the smell of burning bacon, for the ladies were not sure of the techniques of cookery in the open, and the men, left to the art, paid no attention to occasional spots of char and ash that blighted the products of their skill. In the mornings and afternoons the people picnicked, strolled on the beach, wandered in the woods, or hunted and fished in the back country. Hardier ones draped themselves in yards of clinging cloth and braved the surf itself. It was a time of pleasure and of ease.

To bring down the vacationists with their plunder, the Oregon Steam Navigation Company quickly began running special boats for their benefit. In July 1862 the *Jennie Clark* started service, going down the river from Portland once a week. A round-trip fare cost $15, but no one complained. Clatsop Beach would rival Newport and Long Branch, and the Clatsop Beach crowd could afford the costs. When the *Jennie Clark* came down the river, she made no landing at Astoria—boats on the ordinary workaday runs stopped there—but turned into Youngs Bay and threaded up the Lewis and Clark River to Fort Clatsop. There her passengers could hire horses or carriages for the short trip through the forest to the beach, or, if they wished, they could walk—it was not too far.

In time, as the few in 1862 became the hundreds in 1870, the vacationist did not have to take along his own tent. He could stop at a

hotel that was, in fact, the residence of a family of French half-
breeds. There he ate French cooking, lived in a building "decidedly
of a bygone order of architecture," and generally felt free from the
niceties of city society. "Perhaps it is the very lack of conventional
luxury," wrote one visitor, "which makes the place popular." Perhaps it was. Shortly, the writer added, someone would take advantage of the chance to open a real hotel so that Clatsop Beach would
become a real resort.

Shortly someone did—Ben Holladay, always overflowing with
good ideas. In 1873 he built the Seaside House, a rambling hotel
that was gaudy and elegant the way the people of that day wanted
things to be. In it, Holladay held his usual lavish blowouts, enter-
taining the very best and most useful people, feeding them fine
food, and putting good wine within reach. Around the hotel, built
on the shore some distance below the old Clatsop Beach and reached
by stage, a settlement slowly grew, with its saloons and other places
to catch the eye and the coin of the tourist. So rapidly did the beach
colony mushroom that by 1876 the steamboat *Bonita* tried to run as
a night boat to Seaside, leaving Portland in the evening after dinner
and reaching Clatsop Landing early in the morning. Not enough
people felt the need for such haste, and the *Bonita,* after a few trips
gave up, but the idea was sound, and the Astoria night boat soon
became an institution on the river. Often the night boat was comfortable but too slow for the day run; the big *R. R. Thompson*
became one and served faithfully. So in her later years did the *Emma
Hayward,* but the night boats never received the great popular affection and tradition of the fast day boats.

The night boat left Portland late enough so that a businessman
could have dinner, gather up his family, take the boat, and be at
the beach by mid-morning the next day; he could spend a day at the
shore, settle his family, and be back at the office again the second
morning. Later, as Portland grew and the beach rush increased, a
boat left the city dock shortly after noon on summer Saturdays and
raced down the river to reach Astoria in late afternoon so that its
passengers could be at Seaside by evening and get in a weekend at
the beach. Of course, all trips were not so innocent—businessmen
going down to the shore for a jolly weekend with the family. On the
night boat gentlemen did not promiscuously hail other gentlemen
by name or later mention having seen each other. Like the Fall
River Line out of New York, the Astoria night boat inestimably

advanced the cause of romance, lasting and otherwise, around Portland.

As time went on, the casual informality of the Clatsop beaches disappeared. Cottages displaced tents, and the Seaside House imposed a kind of society on the shore. Promenaders still paced the hard sand and poked at shells; men still hunted and fished in the woods and streams behind the beach; bathers still timidly tried the surf, but the old informal parties around the fires at evening, the old storytelling, the old neighborliness disappeared. Behavior proper to the resorts of the East became proper at Seaside. Social distinctions marked out lines, for by the middle Eighties, mobs of people swarmed down the river. Practically everybody in Portland could spend a week at the beach, and all chose Seaside. Larger boats had to go on the route to carry them, and the large boats were not able to go up the Lewis and Clark River but stopped at Astoria. From there smaller shuttle boats like the *General Canby* ran to the old landing.

On the north shore, beyond Cape Disappointment, a long tongue of sand, wooded and cool, but some said windy, stretched up to enclose Shoalwater Bay, or after a later spell of civic renovation tinkered with the name, Willapa Harbor. Though a couple of hopeful towns were laid out opposite Astoria, Shoalwater Bay became mainly a settlement of oyster-fishermen. A few vacationists to escape the crowds went across to the north beaches, carried in the little propeller *U. S. Grant* which busied itself at all sorts of tasks: towing, carrying mail to the towns on the bay, running up to Clatsop Landing, handling business between the forts at the mouth of the river, and giving service to Ilwaco, the town at the base of the peninsula.

Above Ilwaco the Methodists opened a camp ground far from the contaminations of the ungodly at Clatsop, and to Ilwaco went the genteel, the middle-class families searching for a place of their own. Soon Ilwaco began to rival Clatsop, even though the confirmed Clatsopolites sniffed disdainfully. Before long both beaches were to be invaded by even larger crowds.

In 1889 a narrow gauge railroad began running trains from Ilwaco across the neck of the peninsula and within a year it extended all the way to Nahcotta; at Ilwaco the trains met the steamer from Astoria or eventually, Portland. But Baker Bay, fronting Ilwaco, is shallow, and only at high tide could a large steamboat reach the dock with its passengers, and the railroad accepted the inevitable—its timetable fit the tides. Just in time for high tide at Ilwaco, a pompous little train rattled in from Nahcotta and waited at the wharf; then, from across the bay would come the steamer, a neat side-wheeler such as the *Ocean Wave,* and tie up at the dock. Passengers rushed ashore to get good seats in the narrow coaches, while freight and baggage from the boat was tumbled on the dock. Quickly, before an ebbing tide could ground it, the boat hurried off, and the train whistled shrilly and clattered away with its load of passengers. The Ilwaco Railway and Navigation Company was at least distinctive in its timetable, so distinctive, indeed, that the time-table became one of its best advertised features.

With the growth of the shore resorts in the late Sixties, the Oregon Steam Navigation Company began to look with interest at the Astoria run, hitherto neglected in favor of the more prosperous Cascades and upper river route to the mines, especially when the mining boom slacked off. In 1871 the first of a fleet of big, fine boats took to the river, flying the pennant of the O.S.N., the *Emma Hayward,* fitted with good cabins and comfortable parlors; until supplanted by larger vessels built to carry increasing crowds, she ran the route, aided now and then by the less elegant *Dixie Thompson.* About a decade later came the gaudy *S. G. Reed,* a masterpiece of machinery and ornamental gingerbread. The new steamer, built to match the *Wide West* and *R. R. Thompson* and intended for the lower river run, was fitted expressly for passenger service. She was tall and elegant and, like her sisters, flaunted her name on an elaborate cornice around her pilot house. During her lifetime she was a pleasure boat, and finally in 1894 when she was burned for her metal, she furnished a spectacle—a river excursion boat brought down a crowd from Portland to see her destroyed. Then in 1888 the memorable boats began to come to the route and compete for the business, boats noted for their speed, their lavish fittings, their comfort. U. B. Scott, successful in his Willamette River ventures, turned to the lower Columbia in that year and put the *Telephone* on the river, a long, sleek stern-wheeler that could not be beaten in any race. But the crack boat was the *T. J. Potter.*

Already the *Wide West,* built for the Cascades run, had in her ten years become a legend of luxury, and the *T. J. Potter* carried on the tradition. A hull, designed with fine lines for speed and fitted for big side wheels, took shape at the shipway at Portland. Then on the hull the upper works of the old *Wide West* were placed intact, altered only enough to allow for the side wheels—for the *Wide West* was a stern-wheeler. Inside, the cabins were newly decorated and furnished even grander than before to tempt travellers. From the lower deck swept a grand staircase, rising to a landing where it divided to reach the upper saloon. At the head of the stairs hung a mirror, the largest in the whole Northwest. In the saloon was a grand piano, ornately carved and gorgeous in a case of bird's-eye maple. In the dining room smaller tables seating families took the place of the long common table of earlier boats. Dark wood paneling and beams ornamented the room and set off the linen and silver, and the meals, too, were memorable. Broad decks extended fore and aft for casual promenades and comfortable watch of the passing river. Gaudiest of all were the paddle boxes; from a carved lunette spread a fan of tracery and fretsaw work that made the boxes look like patterns of white lace. No other boat in the West had such magnificent paddle boxes, and few in the East competed for ornateness of the design. A single, tall stack rose forward of the wheels, and from a large texas towered a tall pilot house. Altogether, the *T. J. Potter* was a handsome boat to watch as she swept back and forth on the river.

Rumor said the *Potter* was modeled after the Hudson River boat *Daniel Drew* or *Daisy Drew*—the sources vary—but she showed her own individuality of design. There were no heavy hog trusses arching over her hurricane deck, no stolid bulk from boilers on the guards, nothing but grace and prettiness. And the *T. J. Potter* was a river boat, nothing else. When the O.R.&N. tried to use her on Puget Sound, she rebelled. Let the slightest sea be running when she set out from Seattle to Tacoma, and the *Potter* promptly started to roll, lifting ponderously first one wheel out of the water and then the other. In her cabins the passengers, unused to such antics on the forty-mile run, felt the rise and sickening fall and soon lost interest in the trip, the boat, themselves. Only dizziness seemed to be in the world, and a regret at the most recent meal. A few shennanigans like those, and her owners took her back to the Columbia where for thirty years she worked the summer run down the river as nicely and as smoothly as you please.

Riding the *Potter* was an occasion. At one o'clock every summer Saturday when she pulled away from Ash Street, she had aboard a crowd that recognized her dignity and elegance, for the very, very best people of Portland took her when they went down to the shore.

They knew her cooks were excellent, her meals worth remembering, her cabins as tastefully and ostentatiously fitted as the parlor of any fine home in Portland. And her bar—its mirror, its glass, its skilled and tactful bartender—outshone any other bar in the whole country. The best brandy, whiskey, wines, the best cigars, the best mixed drinks and cocktails came across the towel-wiped mahogany of the *T. J. Potter.*

Even after her first hull wore out and a new one took its place, the boat kept its reputation. The old *Potter* could push the *Telephone* in a race, but the new *Potter* could not; a change in hull lines slowed her down. She was in a way less pretty, too; the domed pilot house looked too much like a cheap ornament, and the paddle boxes, their fan of plain piercings, lost their old charm. But the crowds still took the *Potter;* it was something to be done. Everyone rode her to Astoria or on to the Ilwaco dock to connect with the narrow gauge that had been bought by her owners, the O.R.&N.

The *Potter* was too dignified to race frequently, although, of couse, now and then she would outsprint another boat. She nearly raced once, and rivermen argued what might have happened long after it did not happen at all. On a sultry, Saturday afternoon in August, 1895, the *T. J. Potter* waited at her dock, her wheels idling, her stack showing a streamer of smoke; passengers came aboard early and clustered along the rail watching the *Telephone,* scheduled to pull out at one o'clock at the same time that the *Potter* left. It would be a race all the way down the river, everyone knew; on the boiler deck firemen stacked bolts of wood, carefully selected and set aside long before for just such an occasion. The engineer waited for the speaking tube to whistle at him and the pilot to give the order. On the *Telephone* the same things were happening, and its passengers crowded the rail to watch the *T. J. Potter.* In the pilot house the minute hand of the clock moved closer and closer to the hour; imperceptibly the wheels began to turn to get the engine rhythm established for a quick start. At a few seconds before the hour, both the *Potter* and the *Telephone* whistled for an open draw.

Downstream, the tender on the Burnside bridge dropped his barrier and swung his span open, ready for the race. Almost at once the *Telephone's* wheel threshed the water and the boat shot into the stream. The *Potter's* pilot leaned toward the speaking tube—no confounded rival was going to jump the gun on him and get away with it.

A mud clerk rushed into the pilot house from below. "Hold the boat—the Major's going to Astoria!" he yelled. And that ended it. When Major O'Neill spoke, the crew obeyed, for Major O'Neill was receiver for the Oregon Railway and Navigation Company and brooked no racing of his boats. With studied calm the Major came aboard, just late enough for the pilot to see the stern of the *Telephone* disappear beyond the draw, and the Major strolled the deck where the pilot could see him and would not be tempted to steal a sprint or two. The *T. J. Potter* went down the river that day in sober dignity. At least, reflected the chagrined crew, all bets were off.

When winter came, the *Potter* went off the day run to Astoria and became the night boat, but even then she was crowded, and on more than one night, people slept in deck chairs or, not finding any not already staked out and claimed, rolled in a blanket on the deck and hoped that the rain would not drive too hard.

In 1916 the old boat was condemned as unfit for passenger service and hauled off the run; after that, she served now and then as a barracks boat for construction crews and strikebreakers, and finally, in 1925, she was dragged from the boneyard, the roosting pigeons in her cabins were shooed off, and a towboat came alongside to take her down to a mud flat on Youngs Bay, where she was burned for her metal. Ten years later her ribs and keel were still lying in the mud. Maybe they are still there.

Her rivals on the run for a time had been the iron side-wheelers *Alaskan* and *Olympian,* but they never caught on and were too expensive to operate anyway. Though the O.R.&N. ran other boats on the route, none seemed to catch the affections as did the *T. J. Potter.*

Seaside kept growing, as did the Ilwaco beaches. More and more they became mob resorts, with cheap concessions and all the trappings of amusement parks; each spring the amusement rides and shows were shipped down the river, each fall, again dismantled, they came back to Portland. Then came 1905—the year Portland splurged and held its Lewis and Clark Exposition. The Oregon country had seen crowds of people coming overland before, but nothing like the thousands that poured in now to see the sights. That year the Astoria boats barely handled the crowds, and more and more steamers went into service. When the railroad from Astoria finally got to Goble, joined the Northern Pacific, and became the Spokane, Portland and Seattle, much of the seaside traffic promptly moved by rail, not because it was much faster, for the trains made the trip in only an hour less time, but because the railroad said modestly of itself that it was modern, that steamboats were slow and old-fashioned.

Tourists seemed not to agree. After all, if it is scenery that is wanted, it is much handier to a riverboat's open deck than it is to a closed coach. San Francisco held its exposition in 1915 and another horde of sightseers took in Portland on the trip. They wanted to see the country and they did—on the riverboats. But they neglected Astoria. It was true that the boats ran full, but the old excitement and glory had gone. Even the stern-wheelers were vanishing, although the *Undine* was busy.

The new boat on the Astoria run was not a stern-wheeler at all but a graceful little propeller, *Georgiana*. Named for Mrs. H. L. Pittock, the *Georgiana* slid down the ways from Supple's boat-yard at Portland on June 20, 1914. She had a straight stem and rounded stern that gave her a chubbiness of line, but otherwise she was trim and graceful, with a raked mast and single funnel. Built solely for the passenger trade, with freight space deliberately small, the *Georgiana* had the compact neatness and fine fittings of a private yacht. Passengers came aboard on the enclosed main deck where there were smoking and lounge rooms, each equipped with Pullman-type seats by wide windows to give a clear view of the scenery. Her galley and dining room were small but carefully arranged, for with her speed and traffic she would not have to supply meals to more than those who especially wanted to be served. On the top deck was the pilot house, fitted with the best and newest equipment, including something new on riverboats, an engine-room telegraph like that of an ocean liner, supplanting the wheezing speaking tubes, the bell pulls, and the gongs.

Afloat, the *Georgiana* caught the eye and held it; below the waterline her hull was bright red, but everything above was white, funnel and all. When she went into service, Captain Hosford, her master, was proud of the ship the Harkins Transportation Line had given him. The *Georgiana* drew crowds and kept alongside the best of the paddlers; moreover she outlasted them all on the run. When the railroad ended the passenger trade to Astoria, the *Georgiana* shifted to freight, stopping at all the landings along the lower Columbia—a string of them that depended on steamboats, little places and big: St. Helen's, Kalama, Goble, Rainier, Buck's, La Du,

One of the late stern-wheelers on the Willamette River
was the newer *Beaver*.

On Arrow Lakes, the old *Minto* still runs faithfully for
her owners, the Canadian Pacific.

C. Bradford Mitchell

Trim and pretty, the *Lake Bonneville* (ex-*Georgiana*) ran
the Columbia River for a quarter of a century.

W. J. Gould Collection

Ferry *Tacoma* carried Northern Pacific trains between Goble and
Kalama until the railroad between Portland, Vancouver and Kalama
was finished.

The *T. J. Potter*, leaving Portland, passes the *Harvest Queen*.
Wilson Collection

Coffin Rock, Fluhrer's, Stella, Midway, Nisqually, Eureka, Cathlamet, Skamokawa, Brookfield, Pillar Rock, Altoona. Then the highway cut along the shore, and automobiles raced along it, taking the
rest of the traffic from the boats. But the *Georgiana* kept working,
finally going down the river one day and coming back the next,
alternating with the motor vessel *L. O. Hosford,* named for the first
captain of the old boat. During the hard times of the 1930's the
Georgiana kept on the job when other lines quit and when the railroad itself sharply cut service to Astoria; ironically, the *Georgiana*
in a way profited by the times—her low rates (fare to Astoria was
one dollar) got riders who could not afford the bus or train. At last,
in 1939, the *Georgiana* gave up; there simply was not enough traffic
on the lower river to warrant any sort of steamer's running in local
service. But there was Bonneville Dam, and everyone was interested
in it. So the *Georgiana* went to the dock, received another coat of
white paint and a new name, *Lake Bonneville,* and tried to revive
the run to Cascades. After a season of that the *Lake Bonneville* was
tied up at a dock. Today her white paint is peeling, her stack has
spots of rust, and her glory is gone, but somehow, idly floating alongside the dock among brightly-sailed fishing boats, she still has a
jaunty flair about her, as if she were about to toot her brass whistle
and head out into the river.

The Cascades run that the *Lake Bonneville* tried to revive was
once a great excursion route. Since the time of *Fashion* and *Belle,*
steamers ran from Portland to Cascades, and during the roaring
days of the O.S.N. the biggest and best of the line went up to the
portage railroad with loads of passengers and freight. Then, when
the locks opened, the run extended to The Dalles, but just about
then the tourist began to arrive. The day of glory for the old Umatilla House had passed; travellers went up the river to The Dalles
and came right back down, and a good boat could make the round
trip in a day. New boats, fine and fast, began hauling the sightseers
and, incidentally, carrying freight. The *Charles R. Spencer* was one
of them, the *Hassalo* another. And there was the *Bailey Gatzert.*

Mention steamboating to an Oregonian whose memories go back
thirty years, and he promptly says, "I rode a steamboat once—the
Bailey Gatzert." He may have forgotten the *T. J. Potter* of the
O.R.&N., or the *Lurline* and the *Undine* of the Harkins Line, or
the Regulator boats, but he remembers the *Bailey Gatzert.* To him,
steamboating meant the *Gatzert* and nothing else. Probably there

is reason for the legend, because the boat was planned deliberately to be the finest, most elegant steamer in the Pacific Northwest.

A firm at Seattle built her and named her for one of its members, but almost before she took to the water, she was purchased by the Columbia River and Puget Sound Navigation Company, the line organized by the U. B. Scott who operated the *Telephone* and other big boats on the lower Columbia and the swift *Flyer* on the Seattle run. For a short time the new boat ran out of Seattle and built up a great reputation, especially when the *Greyhound* came onto the Sound from the Columbia and began to boast about its speed, flaunting an effigy of a greyhound on her pilot house and, more insulting, carrying a broom lashed to her masthead. Naturally, the *Greyhound* and the *Bailey Gatzert* raced, with side bets up. After the race, it was the *Bailey Gatzert* that had a greyhound on her pilot house and a broom at her masthead. But the *T. J. Potter* ran away from her, and that settled that, and the effigy and the broom moved again.

The *Gatzert* was taken to the Columbia River in 1892 and used mainly as a spare boat for a few years, until she took over the Cascades run to The Dalles, flying the flag of the Dalles, Portland and Astoria Navigation Company, and on that route she made her reputation. With large public rooms, wide decks, and comfortable cabins, the *Bailey Gatzert* was easy to ride. She was fast, too—as she proved one day in June 1914. She left The Dalles at 3:10 in the afternoon and headed down the river, out to make time, and at 9:03 that evening she touched Alder Street Dock in Portland. On the way she had stopped at landings four times and lost nearly an hour locking through at Cascades, so that in actual running time she had used only a few minutes over five hours running the 115 twisting miles down the river. It was not a race, except that passengers aboard wanted to be in Portland early enough that night to see the electrical parade which was to be an especially spectacular part of that year's Rose Festival.

On the opening day of the Festival a few days earlier all sorts of craft—yachts, work boats, gasoline tugs, and steamboats, each decorated with roses and evergreens and each trying for the prize offered the best decorated vessel—had held their own parade on the river. On board the *Bailey Gatzert,* acting as royal barge for the day, the Queen of the Rose Festival, a girl from a railroad freight office, reviewed the passing fleet and awarded the prizes to *N. R. Lang,* the winner, and *Ruth,* the runner-up. As each boat came abreast the *Gatzert,* it saluted and added to the capophony of whistling, from the brassy bleat of the hooters on the tugs to the deep, hollow whoom of the steamers. In the parade were the stern-wheelers of the Oregon City Transportation Company and the stern wheel harbor towboats *C. Minsinger, Joseph Kellogg, Diamond O,* and *Hustler.*

The whole river was a show in itself, and something always caught the interest of a passenger. Down around Astoria he gasped to see horses plodding through the water, far from land, hauling fish nets through the shoals. One year he saw a river full of seals, so many that they crowded up to the Cascades; from the steamer decks a regular fusillade was kept up, and from hunters in rowboats, to kill the creatures before they ruined the fishing. There were fish-wheels, too, spidery wheels mounted on barges or by the banks, endlessly turning with the current and scooping up salmon to be dumped into boxes for the canneries. And there was always the scenery as the boat went from the broad river near its mouth, past the head-lands opposite the Cowlitz, past Coffin Rock, and on up into the Gorge where towers, and spires, and straight black cliffs rose sheer from the river, where spindles of water fell white down them to mist away into the green bases, where the water roiled over the rocks, and where beyond rose the snow-topped peaks of Hood, Adams, and St. Helens. Sightseers wanted to look at their scenery in those primitive times, not have it pointed out to them by a roadside sign that, with luck, they could read as they roared past. On the steamboats they had the chance; from the decks they could watch the river roll before them as if they were standing in front of a bright panorama.

So many people took the boats that schedules of sightseeing runs, supplementing the regular runs, became part of the shipping news of the Portland papers. In the summer of 1905, when the Exposition was drawing its crowds, the *Bailey Gatzert* ran twice a day to Cascade Locks, leaving at 8:30 in the morning and 5:30 in the afternoon. She charged $1.50 for the trip and served meals aboard. Competing with her was the *Undine,* which left at 8:30 each morning and again at 6:00 in the evening, with an added attraction—a stop at historic Vancouver Barracks. Downriver to Astoria went the *Lurline,* starting at seven in the morning and taking in all the historic spots along the lower river. In 1915 the *Bailey Gatzert* still ran excursions to the Cascade Locks, but made only one leisurely run each day, pulling out from Alder Street Dock at nine in the morning and returning at 5:30 in the afternoon. Also, the *Georgiana* was making her trips to Astoria. For those who did not want to spend a full day on the river, the *America* went down to St. Helens in the afternoon, taking its passengers along Willamette Slough, and transferring them to the *Georgiana* when it came back and stopped at St. Helens. And the *Grahamona* ran three times a day to Oregon City.

Even after the sightseers deserted the river, other pleasure seekers turned to it, sometimes not venturing beyond the banks, being content to spend their time on amusement rides at Oaks Park and Faloma. Or they could get the pleasure aboard the big barge *Swan*, built in 1916. She was a squarish, rather clumsy craft, looking like a steamboat shorn of bow and stern and pilot house, but she held the crowds, up to 500 at a time. Both of her decks were fitted out as dance halls, and on a platform halfway between them a band blared ragtime or jazz, or in her last years, swing, according to the tastes of the dancers. Behind a puffing tug she made her cruises, idling along the river usually in the moonlight, or, the moon not being handy, at least after dark when romance and sentiment best flourish.

The excursion boats contributed to the life of the people in their own way. They gave no service to the scattered landings, carried few passengers on business, contributed little to transportation and development of the Columbia; but they gave glamour and excitement, quiet pleasure and escape. The plodding *Modoc* and *Ione* and *Oregona* at their daily chores were merely parts of business, but the parade of big white boats that carried the crowds meant excitement. A great fleet they were, and their names take oldsters back nostalgically—the *Emma Hayward* and the *S. G. Reed,* the *Alaskan* and the *Olympian,* the *T. J. Potter* and the *Ocean Wave,* the *Hassalo* and the *Bailey Gatzert,* the *Telegraph* and the *Telephone,* and trailing along behind, the ugly duckling that became a *Swan*.

Chapter 13
EAST SIDE, WEST SIDE

PORTLAND is the Paradox of the Pacific. It is the largest city on the Columbia River, but is actually on the tributary Willamette. The seaport for the wheat and commerce of the whole river system, it is a hundred miles inland up the river. It takes pride in its staid, self-righteous New England conscience that has been precariously imposed on its little-mentioned Southern go-it-easy temperament, and both are troubled by occasional bursts of frontier exuberance and growth. Its name is not its own but came out of a gamble. It can be unsentimental about landmarks but goes into a month-long spell of civic ecstasy when its roses bloom. Names like Sullivan's Gulch and Ardenwald, Mock's Bottom and Murray-mead, and fine flashes of romanticism borrowed from Scott—Ivanhoe, Waverly, Killingsworth—abound in the city. Lacking Lowells to speak to its Cabots, its people talk freely to God, especially editorially about the weather. The salmon aristocracy and the shipyard workers find after a few years a common bond of suspicion directed toward strangers so that the city grows protestingly and reluctantly. Its business district is on the west side where the streets are narrow, and its residences are spread over miles of the east side where the streets are wide. The city parks take in everything from poison oak to an extinct volcano. And through its center runs the river that makes it two cities.

[169]

Portland has always been a river town and probably always will be, and much of its peculiar quality comes from the presence of the winding Willamette with its wharves and shipyards, its narrow bridges, and its constant changing life. From the time that Portlanders chipped in to buy the *Gold Hunter* and fought Astoria and St. Helens to get the terminal of the Pacific Mail steamers, the city has depended on the river to be its highway to the world. Geography seemed to be against it: St. Helens had deeper water, Milwaukie had a good building site, Oregon City had water power, and Astoria had the sea. But Portland had a grim determination and a canyon that led back through a low pass to the Tualatin farms. When the new town looked over its assets, it found only the canyon handy, but it found also that Astoria was too far away from other settlements, that Oregon City was cut off by the Clackamas Rapids, that St. Helens had no back country, and that Milwaukie was pinched between Portland and Oregon City. Whereupon Portland started to grow, and its growth was nicely regulated by the rivers.

Not the long steamboat runs index its progress but the short ones, and very soon after steamboating began, Portland became the center for a series of lines up and down the rivers. Between Portland and Oregon City steamboats shuttled like commuter ferries between a city and a suburb. In the first year that steamers ran on the Columbia and Willamette, the strip from Portland to the Falls became infested with boats, all competing for the trade between those places. As it is doubtful whether the two towns together could muster over a couple of thousand inhabitants, pickings for the steamers were slim, and the fight raged furiously between the little propellers *Eagle, Blackhawk,* and *Major Redding,* which were joined the next year by the *Allan,* the *Washington,* and the pioneer *Columbia.* From that time the route was established, and eventually it settled down to some order when the *Alert* and the *Senator* (until it blew up) gave twice daily service. Most boats used had to be small and light draft to pass the Clackamas Rapids, and later steamers like *Elmore* and *Elwood* provided the type, with the Oregon City Transportation Company's larger but specially built *Pomona* and *Grahamona* continuing the trips well into the 1900's. After the locks at Oregon City opened, boats for points beyond the Falls began their runs at Portland, but even then the shuttle boats kept running, so that in the 1890's the *City of Sellwood* started what was frankly a suburban service between the city and nearby hopeful Sellwood.

In the other direction, down the river, several short runs started from Portland. Of course, the big, through lines with their spectacular, fine boats, provided the show along the water front when the *Emma Hayward, T. J. Potter* and the *Telegraph* were working the Astoria route, and the *Wilson G. Hunt, Wide West,* or *Bailey Gatzert* ran to Cascades and The Dalles. As they pulled in or out, plumes of steam and clouds of smoke rising above the wharves, and their chime whistles moaning, people stopped to watch, but the little boats plodding on their daily tasks splashed by and got no attention at all. The little boats on the short routes were more useful than picturesque as they carried their loads of groceries and farm products and their passengers faithfully to make Portland the trade center it became.

Every small settlement had its landing at which only the peddler boats, the stubby little traders ever stopped. The great white packets swept by disdainfully, a passing spectacle of romance each day, while the small stern-wheeler, edging its way up to the bank and putting its landing stage ashore, brought a daily connection with the world. At the town landings loungers may have gaped in awe at the big boats, but, in spite of their sneers, they felt affection for the little ones, their daily friends that came in with the mail and newspapers, and freight, and milk cans. Steamboats that wandered up and down Willamette Slough were of that sort, casual, informal boats, and so were those, like the *Ione,* that worked up beyond Vancouver.

The local run between Portland and Vancouver, one of the first to start, wavered uncertainly; it never quite became a commuter line, nor quite a farmer's route. By 1855 the *Eagle* was making the trips daily, getting away from Vancouver at half past eight in the morning and reaching Portland at noon, starting back at three, and tying up at home by six in the evening. But the *Eagle* soared freely from one route to another and soon spread its wings elsewhere, leaving the route unserved. Then in 1858 at Milwaukie was built the *Vancouver,* a side-wheeler designed for the run to Portland from Vancouver. She was only 84 feet long, but aboard her Captain James Troup got the experience that gave him mastery of the river. On the Vancouver route traffic was local and small boats could handle it; moreover, many of the big steamers on the Cascades run stopped at the town too. That the steamboats had to run first down the Columbia and then up the Willamette, around two sides of a triangle, slowed the time to two hours, but nothing could be done about it until 1888 when the Portland and Vancouver Railway was finished. Starting at the east landing of the Stark Street Ferry, the railway headed almost due north to the Columbia River and connected with its own ferryboat *Vancouver* which crossed directly to the Washington side. Promptly, passengers took to using this third side of the triangle, and the Vancouver steamboat route dropped in importance to become merely a hauler of freight.

Downstream from Portland the Cowlitz run for a time came to rival that of the Cascades in business, but never in spectacle—it passed through no grand scenery and served no booming gold rush. The Cowlitz route at best was a connecting link in a through service, and in the last years was just a farmer's convenience. Between Portland and the Puget Sound settlements passengers could choose their routes: either the long way around by river, sea and Sound, or the short, but infinitely less comfortable route by river, land and Sound. From Portland the traveller rode by steamboat to the Cowlitz River and as far up that stream as the stage of water allowed, sometimes clear to Toledo. At low water, he had to change at the mouth to a rowboat or Indian canoe to be carried upstream, but in any case eventually he had to go ashore and take a stage coach that then jounced him overland to Olympia. There he could recover and take another boat on up to Seattle, Victoria, or the Fraser River.

When the Northern Pacific Railroad completed its line from Tacoma to the Columbia River at Kalama, a town located a few miles up the river from the mouth of the Cowlitz, steamboats continued to handle all passengers and freight from Kalama to Portland. Though traffic rivalled that on the Cascades run, less powerful and elegant steamers could be used, smaller boats like the *Rescue* and others that developed no tradition, because the big Astoria boats stopped at Kalama to make connections. Then along the south bank from Portland the Northern Pacific built a railroad to Goble, opposite Kalama, and ran through trains, ferrying them across the river on the huge, cumbersome iron-hulled ferry *Tacoma* that carried on her deck two lines of track, enough for an entire passenger train. When the *Tacoma* began running in 1883, the passenger and freight steamboats dropped out of use, although steamers for local service along the Cowlitz River kept running.

For the Cowlitz there eventually developed a very shallow draft type of boat able to squirm along on practically no water at all.

One of the first was the *City of Quincy,* followed in 1895 by the *Chester,* designed and built by Joseph Supple at his boatyard in Portland and containing all the characteristics found in other shallow-drafts later built in the Pacific Northwest. The *Chester's* hull had little, if any, dead rise, a short rake astern, and a very full forward to give the greatest bearing surface possible, so that in the water the boat floated like a shingle on a pond. The hull was flexible, supported by hog-chains and planked with cedar, and it had to be. Sandbars meant nothing to the *Chester.* When she came to a place where there was less water than she drew, the steamboat merely slid its broad flat hull up onto the bar, spun her wheel and sucked out the sand so that she could inch her way across. After a trip or two the *Chester* had to be hauled out and new planking put on her ribs—the sand having literally worn away the bottom of the boat. The steamer had other odd habits in operation. The Cowlitz in its upper stretches is not only shallow but narrow as well, and the *Chester* did not worry about heading into a wharf or levee. When she came abreast of a landing, she just stopped, and farmers casually drove their teams and wagons into the river beside the boat. There was no danger that the horses would be swept away; the water came no higher than their fetlocks. When too little freight to be handled in a wagon had to be moved, a deckhand merely took off his shoes, rolled up his pants a couple of inches, stepped overside, and waded ashore with the parcel. On board the *Chester* steamboating became charmingly informal; it was something like working in a rambling warehouse that really rambled. Up and down the Cowlitz the *Chester* ran, connecting at Kelso with larger boats and giving the people along the river means for reaching the outside; not until 1910 did the *Chester* withdraw for a season and then only because the river fell so low that a channel a foot deep could not be maintained. Finally, in 1917 the boat gave up completely.

Portland's riverfront was busy. The wheat ships, the ocean traders, the coastwise liners, and the lumber tramps brought the world to the shores, and in and out among the ships went the sternwheelers, all sizes and descriptions: big ones on the main river routes, smaller ones to the nearby towns, tramp and jobbing steamers, tugboats and ferries. The river from the Public Levee at Jefferson Street on down past Albina and toward St. Johns was lined with wharves, some big, some little, and most aging ungracefully as the years went on. At Ash Street many of the river boats landed, and others tied up at Alder Street. Ocean liners moored at the Ainsworth Dock below Couch Street or across the river at the Oregon & California Railroad Dock. Wheat ships collected in the lower river where the O.S.N. had maintained its boneyard for derelict steamboats and where later the O.R.&N. tied up its old steamers. Back and forth shuttled the ferries from landings at Stark Street, at Burnside, and up near Madison. The riverfront was ugly, a succession of wooden gables facing the stream and covering warehouses that rose from spindling, uncertain piling; glaring signs sprawled across the gables, and beyond the docks rose the shoddy backs of brick buildings along Front Street. The main docks were double-deckers, built to accommodate the vagaries of the river; when the river was low, steamboats loaded and unloaded at the lower level, when it was high, they tied up at the second floor. Occasionally, especially after 1910, old piling rotted and a wharf, by then often disused, would lean creakingly forward and settle into the river.

When a steamer arrived, it would work its way up to the dock, open wide doors on its lower deck, and take aboard landing stages so that its passengers and freight could be unloaded. In the street before the dock, drays jammed, sometimes lined up for blocks waiting to leave or pick up freight, and in the midst of the tangle the hotel omnibuses stood expectant—a driver on the box and a runner at the curb. Rather than rushing out to grab the bag of a passenger, the runners merely cried their hotels in a peculiar, almost musical chant that startled people who were used to the raucous shouts of runners in the Eastern states. Over it all rose the steamboat whistles, everything from deep booming chimes to high pitched yowls from the jobbing steamers and tugs. At least one steamer had a calliope whistle on which tunes were played to warn of its coming. A river town, Portland centered its activity as close to the waterfront as it could; on Front and First streets were the main banks like the ornate Ladd and Bush Building, the main hotels like the St. Charles, the New Market Theatre, the Skidmore Fountain, the office buildings; farther back, after 1890, towered the Oregonian building, leading the procession of business back from the Willamette.

To the river the city looked for business and activity and now and then for help. The summer of 1873 was dry, and early in the morning of August 2, a fire started in a furniture store on First Street near Taylor. Promptly the fire bells clanged, and the volunteers turned out, sleepily, to drag their hose carts and pumpers to the fire.

By the time they arrived, a shaft of flame, fed by paint and oil, roared over the roof, and the firemen recognized that the best they could do was to prevent its spread. More alarms sounded until the whole city woke up, and in fifteen minutes the fire mushroomed over the block, seizing the Metropolis and the Multnomah hotels. A breeze that blew down from the hills sent it roaring toward the river and the north and threw out side fires toward Second Street. Portland called for help. The telegraph brought word to Salem where the volunteers loaded their carts on flat cars, lashed them in place, and climbed aboard as an engine coupled on to take the train down to Portland. On the river, steamboats tied up by warehouses while firemen, boatmen, and volunteers in general hustled goods from the docks onto the decks of the boats. Back and forth across the river the steamboats went, hauling loads of salvage. The Lick House and the Kellogg caught and burned, threatening the nearby St. Charles. The train from Salem made the fifty miles in an hour and a quarter, and its reinforcements snatched off their carts, dragged them down to the ferry and hurried them across the river. They took over the fight at the St. Charles and ran a hose line to the roof to keep it wet down. From windows they spread blankets along the side of the building facing the fire and doused them constantly. Then the Kellogg Building collapsed, sending out floods of sparks and flame, but the Salem crew saved the St. Charles, then unrivalled for luxury on the Pacific Coast, although the fire caught up with the engine of Columbia No. 3 on the waterfront and burned it.

George Kellogg had brought the *Oneatta* from Yaquina Bay and was using her on the Vancouver run when he got word of the fire. Promptly he took aboard the Vancouver volunteer department and headed down the river, giving his steamer every ounce of steam her boilers would allow and making Portland in less time than any steamboat had made before. What the time was, no one knew exactly; everybody was too busy to keep records. All day the fire raged and the volunteers fought it; when night came eight blocks along the waterfront had been swept away and inland everything to Second Street had burned. While the crews worked, incendiarists, their minds twisted peculiarly, set other fires apart from the main one (and probably had started it, too), but the firemen got them out. What finally stopped the flames was the fire of the year before which had burned a strip that had not been rebuilt and set a barrier that could not be crossed. All day the steamboats worked, their pumps filling the firemen's hoses, and their decks carrying everything that could be dragged out of the buildings close to the river. As Portland that night looked over its damage it could be thankful that the loss was not greater, that so much had been saved and taken across the river.

Portlanders were proud of the steamboats and liked to roll their names over their tongues. They were good names, sometimes imaginative, sometimes literal, but always with associations that brought memories. Naming steamboats was always a personal matter, and yet owners had curious ways of repeating patterns. Some names recurred monotonously: *Portland, Columbia, Enterprise.* Many were named for girls: *Eliza Anderson, Daisy Ainsworth, Mary, Claire, Jean.* Some were named for men: *A. A. McCully, John H. Couch, Joseph Kellogg, Frederick K. Billings.* Virtues attributed to boats were common, some for speed like *Telegraph, Despatch, Antelope, Gazelle,* and some for noble purposes like *Relief, Rescue, Regulator.* Practically every place in the region had a boat named for it, from *Astorian* and *Canemah* to *Asotin* and *Spokane,* and some had two or three. Then there were the irrepressibly irreverent who saddled their steamboats with names hardly dignified like *Mud Hen* and *Skedaddle,* or *Shoo-Fly* and its inevitable sequel *Don't Bother Me,* or *No Wonder,* the last as bad a pun as was ever launched, for she was a rebuilding of an older *Wonder.* In contrast were the unromantically literal names like *O. & C. R. R. Ferry No. 1, Veto No. 2,* and *Stark Street Ferry No. 7.* And there were classic names drawn from the golden ages, names like *Echo* and *Iris, Calliope* and *Undine, Ceres* and *Pomona.* There were Spanish names like *Manzanillo* and Indian names like *Kiyus,* names of States, and names of occupations, names of animals (a whole zoo of them, a Noah's Ark), names of countries. names of everything. While the settlers put names on the land, they reserved some of their pets for names on the river.

Small boys knew all the names of boats and would reel them off by the yard on almost no provocation; they could recognize the whistles, too, and tell whether it was the *Undine* coming in to the wharf or the Stark Street ferry arguing over right of way with a towboat, or the *Grahamona* calling for the draw at Morrison Street.

Something of the glory departed from the river when bridges spanned it. One by one they appeared, the spindly tall trusses at Morrison Street in 1887, the boxy Howe trusses of the double-decked railroad bridge in 1888, the Burnside Bridge in 1893, just something more to clutter the river and make steamboatmen unhappy. The bridges supplanted the ferries. Some had been oddities like those that tried to haul themselves back and forth by winding a cable over a steam-driven drum aboard the boat. After a few trips, they usually let the cable go and took on side wheels. A river ferry is not a beautiful boat—flat, stubby, with its stack and wheelhouse centered, its long, narrow cabins on the guards, its open deck; almost no one, even with practice, can muster nostalgia for them, but boats like the *W. S. Mason,* or *City of Vancouver,* or *Lionel R. Webster* served their purpose. There is a good deal more romance in a big ferry like the *Tacoma* or in a flat-bottomed scow that swings across the stream on the power of the current than there is in a squatty little steam river ferryboat.

It is hard, too, for most people to find the stern-wheel towboat romantic or to lament its passing, but a confirmed steamboatman can, and should; the towboat, lowly and plodding in its social position among the stern-wheel steamers, gave life to the river and kept old boats busy and happy long after their tinsel tarnished, their carpets wore out, and their last passenger had gone ashore. More than one veteran steamer of a major route, stripped of its fancy fixings, ended its days shoving steamships up and down the river between Astoria and Portland.

The difference between a stern-wheel towboat and a passenger boat on the Columbia is not immediately apparent, for both have the lines characteristic to the waterways of the Pacific Northwest. Both have a shallow hull about five times longer than its beam and curving to a sharp prow. Normally the dead rise is slight so that the decks are almost flat. The lower or freight deck is enclosed from the wheel well forward, with wide side doors on the guards which extend out slightly from the hull. Above the freight deck, which houses both the boilers and engines, is a cabin deck with a wide central hall, rounded glassed-in saloons forward and aft, and railed decks all around. Above on the hurricane deck is a small texas, sometimes also glassed-in and rounded forward (but that elegance appeared only on the largest packets), and finally, perched high on the texas is the pilot house with its cornice of fretwork. Some pilot houses were elaborately rounded or domed, but most were content to be utilitarian, a glass box well forward from where the pilot could watch the water. Back of the pilot house is a single, tall stack, banded near the top, but without any elaborate cut-out design at the cap. Amidships rise the king post and, on larger boats, four or more hog posts supporting hog-chains form trusses to keep the hull in alignment. And at the rear is the wheel, almost invariably encased in an elaborately designed box ever since it had appeared on the *Cascades* in 1870. The boxed wheel on passenger boats had a definite virtue—it kept spray from the rear of the boat and permitted open observation decks all the way around the cabin. Finally, on a painted scroll across the rear of the box or wheelhouse was the name of the boat and its home port, and the name appeared again on the prow and on elaborately lettered boards on three sides of the pilot house.

Any stern-wheeler could be used for a towboat, but the *J. Ordway,* built in 1876, had no other purpose except to haul booms of logs on the river. Log hauling always required steamers and still does, and special methods had to be developed for towing logs. First they are collected in booms—that is, they are gathered between heavy logs that have been chained together in two strings; then, when the boom is ready, the rear is enclosed either by bringing the bindings together or by lashings to form a raft shaped something like a steamboat hull in outline. From the towboat a line, fastened to a winch, passes through a swivelled block on the king post and is secured to the fore end of the boom, and if more than one boom has to be moved, the line extends back from boom to boom. So that the boat may have a chance to maintain steerage way, its king post is mounted just abaft of amidship on the centerline. To insure control of the boat, auxiliary or "monkey" rudders are mounted on the fantail astern the wheel and are, when the boat is not in motion, out of the water. But let a twenty-foot wheel begin to turn, and its buckets, twenty-four or more feet long, spinning at up to thirty revolutions a minute and dipping nearly three feet, promptly kick up a surge of water that the rudders can grip.

Such a boat was the *Gamecock,* built in 1910. When she started upriver with a tow, she provided a whole procession. First came the steamer herself, and then a thousand feet astern, on the cable, her first section or boom, itself up to five hundred feet long; behind it, another thousand feet, would trail a second section, and behind it a third, until from the jackstaff of the *Gamecock* to the end of her tow would be nearly a mile. The long tows are no longer common, but still some snorting little gasoline or diesel boat will go past with its boom trailing behind it seemingly indefinitely. Log booms are always trailed, but log rafts, cradled and bound for trips down the coast, are pushed to the mouth of the river.

Rafting from the Columbia to California began in 1894, after an unsuccessful attempt to send one from Coos Bay in 1892. The rafts were more or less alike: in a heavy cradle or frame the logs were placed and bound together with heavy chains until ten thousand or more logs were tied into a solid cigar-shaped raft. Then the cradle was released and the whole raft floated, drawing as much as twenty feet of water but having not more than seven feet of free-board. The 1894 try, put together at Stella, forty miles up the river from Astoria, failed when a gale loosened the chains and let the entire thing go to pieces, but in 1895 another raft was patiently assembled and bound in a way to prevent its loosening and drop-ping out stray logs. Then the *Relief* took the clumsy thing down the river and turned her over to the collier *Mineola* which, not meeting any troublesome winds, succeeded in getting it into San Francisco Bay after only five days. When a raft is being handled at sea, it is trailed on a cable; in the river it is pushed and is treated like any ordinary ship.

Barges and ships in the Columbia are pushed along, the towboat going alongside or to the quarter where it can get a good grip for maneuvering the tow against the current. For a time the big stern-wheeler *Claire* had a blunt foredeck, or "buffalo," fitted with buf-fers so that she could shove a barge or scow along directly ahead, but eventually the deck was cut back to the usual width of the guards. Out of the towing method grew a curious structural detail found on Columbia River stern-wheel towboats. Extending out on both sides of the pilot house are narrow platforms, or flying bridges, to permit the captain to get a close watch of his tow when coming alongside or moving on the river. On most of the steamers the flying bridge was an afterthought, something built later and looking it, but not on the *Jean.*

Certainly not on the *Jean,* for when she was launched in 1938 for the Western Transportation Company she had all the latest gadgets practical river men could think of. Built to be a towboat, she has no wasted space and nothing aboard that is unnecessary, and every-thing handy that is. Her hull is steel, slightly over 140 feet long, and rather broad of beam, a full 40 feet. Her hold in the usual shallow hull is less than eight feet and she floats on rather than ploughs through the water. Above the hull her superstructure is also steel, nicely smoothed and rounded, with none of the angularity of the older boats. In fact, from the bow, she looks like a regular steamship that has somehow unaccountably lost its freeboard, for her cabin is streamlined forward, and her pilot house, rising high above it, is part of the structure, not a sort of crackerbox afterthought—and her flying bridges give her a peculiar effect of breadth and weight. In her engine room are cross-compound engines, drawing steam from oil-burning boilers. But the most unusual thing in her construction is her wheel, although as she goes by on the river few would notice anything strange. At the stern is the conventional box with a fantail and rudders, but under the box is not one wheel but what amounts to two. Or, to express it in language that may be clearer to the layman though horrifying to a steamboatman, she is a side-wheeler with both wheels astern. That is, the broad stern wheel is divided, and each half is separately driven and controlled so that one part can go forward and the other astern at the same time.

It would seem that one might check the other, but they do not, and the *Jean* has some peculiar abilities in maneuvering around tight places. Set one wheel turning forward and the other astern, twitch the rudder, and the towboat turns nicely in her length without going forward at all. Or turn the rudder hard over, and the *Jean* begins to crab sideways directly abeam. It is not every steamboat that can go forward and back and then sideways, too; the *Jean*, with her accomplishments, is a mighty handy steamer when the channel is swift and the moorage tight.

As the *Jean* goes about her work, few Portlanders give her a second glance, unless it be malignant because she gets to a drawbridge and holds up traffic while she goes through. Some watching her might say that not many like her were around any more, and they would be right. The decline in stern-wheelers started in the middle 1920's when steamboat building stopped and scrapping began. By 1940 less than a dozen survived, and today only five still live. Scattered up and down the river are relics of them: the *N. R. Lang*, stripped of engines, serves as a floating workshop for her owners, and the *Pomona* is another workshop farther up the Willamette. On the Vancouver shore *The Dalles* lies partly submerged, her engines dismantled. The *Annie Comings* became a houseboat for small craft after she served her time in the Navy. The *Stranger* did war duty, too, her hulk being used as a housing unit at Salem, until she settled onto the bank. The *Lewiston* is in Alaska, on the

Below the Falls at Oregon City, a stern-wheeler pushes a
heavy barge to the mills.

The *Umatilla*, showing her monkey-rudders on the fantail,
moves slowly through the Celilo Canal.

Western Transportation Company

With her twin wheels, twin stacks, and trim steel superstructure,
the *Jean* is one of the latest in river towboats.

Yukon; so is the *Northwestern,* on the Kuskokwim River at Bethel. And on the Columbia and Willamette rivers, still working are the survivors of the once great fleet. The *Henderson,* forty-five years old, is hard at it for the Shaver Transportation Company. The big *Claire* and the new *Jean* handle the towing and tonnage for the Western Transportation Company, moving 400,000 tons of freight each year; every day they leave Portland to run between Oregon City and West Linn on the Willamette and Camas on the Columbia, their loads largely paper products and materials from the mills. There is the *Portland,* too, the long slim towboat operated by the Port of Portland Commission, and soon another will take her place. And there is the *Georgie Burton* . . .

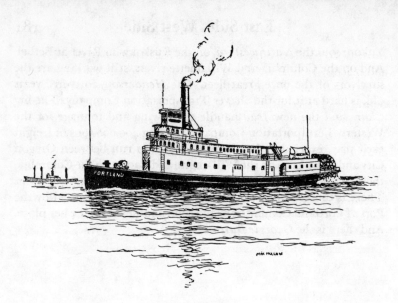

Chapter 14

THE WHEELS TURN SLOWLY

THURSDAY MORNING, March 20, 1947, opened gray. A fog clung close to the water all along the Columbia and the Willamette. At her dock in Portland, the *Georgie Burton* had steam up and her crew aboard, ready for the day's run. Inside and out she was clean, her house gleaming in white, and her hog-frames and king post black; even her stack shone in new paint. Slowly she slipped into the river and turned downstream. Now and then her whistle boomed three blasts as she made her way along the channel, and on the banks people turned to watch her pass. For forty-one years the *Georgie Burton* had been going about the rivers as she carried freight and did towing jobs, but this was an occasion—the *Georgie Burton* was on her last trip.

Back in 1906 she had been launched on the very day that San Francisco was shaken down and then burned by an earthquake and fire, but even the best friends of the boat denied a connection. She had been given the maiden name of Mrs. H. L. Pittock, whose husband combined the jobs of publishing the *Oregonian* and directing, among other things, a steamboat company. It was a good name, and it was a good boat that bore it. Moreover, the new *Georgie*

Burton had good ancestry, because into it had gone part of the house and machinery of the *Albany,* built back in 1896, and the *Albany* in turn had inherited a good share of the usable parts of the *N. S. Bentley*—was a rebuilding of it in fact—and the *N. S. Bentley* had been launched in 1886 for the Oregon Development Company.

At Vancouver the *Georgie Burton* tied up at a wharf to take aboard a special crew of the old timers, men who loved the river and the steamers and were helping retire the boat in real style. Judge Fred Wilson was there; son of a steamboat captain, Judge Wilson inherited an affection for steamers that passed beyond a hobby into a consuming purpose. Aboard the *Burton,* Judge Wilson knew his place and acted as purser. Men from the boats themselves took tricks at the wheel as the steamer went on up the river: Captain Winslow, Captain Fidler—seventeen years aboard the *Burton* as her commander—Captain McClintock, Captain Monical, all veterans on the river. And there were newspapermen aboard, of course, to cover the story and be in on the party. All along the river, people stood on the banks to watch her; school children turned out to see the steamer go by—later, in their "social living" classes their teachers would ruin the memory by hitching it to a "significant" unit of some sort or another. On up the Columbia the *Georgie Burton* sloshed along while the fog thinned and the sky brightened. She passed familiar places, the sights passengers watched for and remembered, like Cape Horn and Multnomah Falls. She reached the lower Cascades and entered the tall lock of Bonneville Dam. Slowly the lock filled and the *Georgie Burton* slid out into the slack water beyond, riding over what had been the awesome Cascades, now nothing more than a quiet pool. Off the starboard bow a line of masonry near the bank was all that remained above water of the Cascade Locks. A captain pointed out where the *Regulator* hung herself on a rock, and another one remembered the *Fashion.* Here was where *Hassalo* went nearly a mile a minute through the rapids. Beyond the point, to port, the Upper Cascades and its reconstructed blockhouse, and a little farther the spot where the Indians came down to the river. Near Hood River, where the gorge widens, the *Spencer* had broken her back in the gale, and the big twin-stackers *Oneonta* and *Iris* had brought a touch of Upper Mississippi to the Columbia.

The *Georgie Burton* kept going, as she always did when she set out on a run. Always the *Georgie* had been a dependable boat, not subject to temperament and ailments. When her companions had trouble, she went out to help them along. The *Patricia,* a diesel tow-boat, broke down one time, and the *Georgie* fetched her in. The big *Chief* got her propellers all tangled with the river bottom once and broke her shafts; the *Georgie Burton* went out, took over the *Chief's* tow, went up the river with it, then came back and picked up the *Chief* and brought her to port. The *Georgie Burton* asked no favors; she had towed her 400 million feet of logs without a murmur or a major breakdown, had pushed hog-fuel barges uncomplainingly, fueled hundreds of ships during wartime, towed tons of paper from the Camas and Oregon City mills, and in her spare time helped the Port Commission's *Portland* with the docking and moving of ships in the harbor. The *Georgie* might now and then whack off a few of her wheel buckets on something in the river, but they were easy to fix while a tow was being loaded. She was a working girl if there ever was one. This trip was easy, just another run, a little longer than usual maybe, but just another run.

Finally the *Georgie Burton* passed The Dalles, where the whole town turned out to watch, and went on to edge into the pool at the foot of Celilo Canal. There the voyage ended, the boat was at her last berth. Not quite the last, to be exact; shortly she would be drifted down to The Dalles, slid into a cradle, and towed up onto the land, to become a marine museum, a relic of the great days on the river, when The Dalles was a roaring river town and the big boats came and went. It was fitting that a steamboat should be preserved and that it should be at The Dalles. Diesel towboats might shove barges back and forth on the river, handling tonnage greater than anything Ainsworth and the O.S.N. had even vaguely conceived, but the diesel towboat, compact and unemotionally utilitarian, somehow lacked the glamour and the glory of the white cabins, the tall stacks, and the flashing wheels of the steamboat. Still,—who knows?—sometime a diesel towboat, her days of usefulness over, and her type disappearing, may be hauled up beside the *Burton.*

The Oregon country needed reminders of the times when steamboats opened it and moved its goods. At Champoeg are a number of the name-boards of the old boats and other relics, and at Portland a sentimental steamboatman has kept some mementoes of the boats that he watched dismantled, but no entire steamer was preserved, not until L. Rex Gault, the President of the Western Transportation Company, owner of the *Georgie Burton,* got together with

Judge Wilson and his cronies ("enthusiasts" is a nicer, newer word) and arranged to give the boat to The Dalles. It was a good gesture, and an appropriate one.

The day of the stern-wheeler was over—or almost over. When the *Georgie Burton* went up the river that March morning, she passed a shipyard where the wrights busied themselves with welding torches at assembling a new steel hull, strangely unlike the hundreds of hulls that Portland shipyards turned out during both World Wars. This one was long and thin and very shallow, and from its transom heavy frames extended back to a fantail. This was another stern-wheeler being built.

The Port of Portland Commission had a towboat, the *Portland*, built in 1919, but it needed a replacement; the old boat had put in a quarter of a century of hard work and was aging and worn. The *Portland* was a stern-wheeler, long and lean, with a short cabin on top of the freight deck, and a texas and pilot house at the front of it. At the end of the closed freight deck was an uncovered stern wheel, one of the few on the river. But stern-wheelers were old-fashioned, and the new boat, to be another *Portland*, probably would be a sleek stout diesel.

Promptly the harbor pilots complained, and at an open hearing they voiced their laments and objections while the exponents of diesels replied, but, when it was all over, the pilots had won: the new boat would be a steam stern-wheeler, not a diesel propeller. It might be old-fashioned, but it was what the pilots wanted, and what they said they had to have if they were to meet conditions around Portland harbor.

Not only the type of tow being moved on the Columbia and Willamette rivers, but the part of the river being used also governs the kind of operations followed. On the lower river below Portland single-screw diesel or steam towboats are commonest, for the river is deep and easy to navigate; on the river above Vancouver the channel narrows, and a diesel there usually has twin stacks abreast so that its pilot can look both forward and aft in checking his marks. A stern-wheeler had no particular advantages over a screw-driven towboat, except possibly that it has no blades to foul, and as new boats were built, they tended after 1920 to be conventional though rather shallow and broad-hulled screw steamers. The *Shaver*, built in 1908, was an ordinary stern-wheel towboat, and she stayed that way until 1927 when her owners, the Shaver Transportation Com-

pany, rebuilt her. It is common enough for a stern-wheeler to be
rebuilt; most of them were at one time or another, but with the
Shaver, things turned out differently from usual. Her stern wheel,
fantail, and cylinder timbers were removed, and her engines replaced by a pair of diesels set amidships. Then into the hull were
built semi-tunnel twin-screw mounts, propellers fitted onto them,
and the boat, in appearance generally unchanged except for the
missing stern wheel, went back to work. The idea was sound, and
shortly stern-wheelers on the Mississippi were rebuilt in the same
way, and new tunnel-screw towboats there followed the design of
the *Shaver.*

To the pilots an ideal harbor towboat had to have certain qualities
and abilities. The river at Portland is narrow and subject to sharp
rises during freshets, to strange currents, and sharp gusty winds that
make handling ships a peculiarly tricky job. In the narrow channel
when a steamship is turned, the steamer's hull with its deep draft
serves almost as a swinging lock gate, backing up the whole force of
the river against the ship while it is broadside to the current. To
keep a ship under control and not let it get away so that it starts
caroming off wharves and ships as it goes down the river, a towboat
has to have plenty of power and leverage. That means the towboat
has to be long, very long, and to have a sure grip on the water. It
must be able to respond to every call by the pilot, must be able to go
forward or to back quickly, must be able to hold the ship steady.
A wide paddle wheel at the stern, biting three feet into the water,
with ample buckets, will do all that and will act either as a brake or
as a lever to shove a ship ahead. A stern-wheeler with high-pressure
engines, working separately, will give the sort of power a pilot likes
to feel under him.

Next, the pilot must be high enough and far enough forward to
see his tow and the river. On a stern-wheeler the tall pilot house is
atop three decks, and yet the boat is not top-heavy. The pilot must
be able to see in all directions, and on a stern-wheeler that can be
achieved by narrowing and shortening the cabin so that the vision is
not obstructed when the pilot looks down alongside or astern. A
pilot wants to feel that he has a solid platform under him, a platform that he can move about easily and shove hard against something at the same time.

And so the new *Portland* was designed. Its hull is rather flat,
probably not much over nine feet in depth of hold, and it is full

forward, to eliminate buffer guards. It is long, nearly 190 feet from stem to transom, and 30 more feet to the fantail, so that the boat is 219 feet over all. It is fairly broad of beam, 42 feet. It has two high-pressure single-expansion steam engines that develop up to 2,000 horsepower. In the cabin are quarters for the crew. Its wheel is covered, and on the fantail are those ingeniously contrived monkey rudders, developed on the Columbia River boats as real help to the pilot in tight maneuvering. Some might complain that Portland was being "back-woodsy" in building a stern-wheeler in the year 1947, but the pilots know best—after all, they have experience behind their arguments, and they feel the responsibility a pilot has when he is moving a huge ship in a crowded harbor among traffic and through narrow bridge draws.

When the designs were finished and bids called, shipbuilders all over the United States wanted to look over the plans, but the work had to be done in Portland. The Northwest Marine Iron Works got the contract and, using the side-launching ways of the Gunderson Brothers' Engineering Corporation, laid the keel in February 1947. The new boat, to cost $472,000 when finished, is all-steel, with a welded hull and house; parts of it were fabricated and assembled and then hoisted into place, a construction device perfected in the Portland shipyards during the mass-production years of World War II.

By Spring the boat took form and on May 18 it was launched, a whole battalion of dignitaries on hand to help do the job right and proper. From the ways the new *Portland* went to the Port's drydock for fitting, where her boilers were finished, her engines installed, her machinery put in order, her cabins completed. In the Fall she was put into service, replacing the earlier *Portland* and taking over her duties. She is worth stopping to watch, for her long, low hull with its big wheel astern and its pile of cabins and pilot house forward, her tall stack, her sturdy shoulders, show real power and carry on the old tradition. The *Georgie Burton* left the river to good hands, and the new *Portland* is welcomed by the dwindling group of stern-wheel veterans. Even the streamlined *Jean* can be impressed by the stranger on the river. The wheels would still be turning.

STEAMERS OF THE COLUMBIA RIVER SYSTEM

Listed are the steamboats driven by paddles operated on the Columbia River System and on the coastal rivers and inland lakes of Oregon, and in addition, the screw-propelled steamers used on the rivers before 1860 or referred to in the text.

Key to Symbols:

A—abandoned	R—rebuilt
B—burned	S—in service
D—dismantled	T—transferred
N—renamed	W—wrecked

A minus sign before the date of disposition indicates that the vessel was out of existence or registry by that year. A minus sign before date of building indicates that the boat arrived that year on the Columbia, date of building unknown.

NAME	TYPE	WHERE BUILT	DATE	TONS	LENGTH	DISPO-SITION
A. A. McCully	Stern	Portland, Ore.	1877	498	148	B 1886
Aberdeen	Stern	Okanagan Ldg., B.C.	1893	...	146	....
Active	Stern	Canemah, Ore.	1865	260	122	D 1872
Advance (gas)	Stern	Portland	1903	11	70	— 1907
Ainsworth	Stern	Ainsworth, B.C.	1891	...	...	....
Alaskan (iron)	Side	Chester, Pa.	1883	1718	276	W 1889
Albany	Stern	Canemah	1868	328	127	W 1875
Albany	Stern	Portland	1896	431	151	R 1906 to *Georgie Burton* ex-*N. S. Bentley*
Alberta	Stern	Bonner's Ferry, Ida.	1895	...	140	.... ex-*State of Idaho*
Albina (ferry)	Side	Portland	1875	78	...	— 1880
Albina (ferry)	Side	Portland	1880	85	85	— 1898
Albina No. 2 (ferry)	Side	Portland	1883	205	107	— 1900
Alert	Stern	Oswego, Ore.	1865	341	135	— 1878
Alert	Stern	Bandon, Ore.	1890	96	69	W 1919
Alexander (gas)	Stern	Astoria, Ore.	1907	13	39	R 1918 to screw
Alexander Griggs	Stern	Wenatchee, Wn.	1903	...	111	W 1905
Alice	Stern	Canemah	1871	457	150	D 1888
Alice V (ferry)	Side	Salem, Ore.	1890	41	66	— 1896
Alida	Side	Seattle, Wn.	1870	114	107	— 1892
Alkali	Side	Alkali, Ore.	1884	24	61	— 1900
Allan (iron)	Screw	......	−1852	10	...	— 1856
Almota	Stern	Celilo, Ore.	1876	502	157	D 1901
Alpha	Screw	Wallowa Lake, Ore.	1888	...	...	....
Altona	Stern	Portland	1890	201	120	R 1899
Altona	Stern	Portland	1899	329	123	T 1907 to Alaska
Alviso	Stern	Sausalito, Calif.	1895	197	115	T 1910 to California

NAME	TYPE	WHERE BUILT	DATE	TONS	LENGTH	DISPO-SITION
America	Screw	Portland	1912	125	105	S
Anita	Stern	McMinnville, Ore.	1894	...	103	D 1894
Ann	Stern	Umatilla, Ore.	1868	83	78	W 1869
						ex-*Lewiston*
Annerly	Stern	Jennings, Mont.	1892	128	93	— 1899
Annie	Stern	Portland	1897	157	103	D 1899
Annie Comings	Stern	Portland	1903	452	150	W 1907
						ex-*Wm. M. Hoag*
						R 1909
Annie Comings	Stern	Vancouver, Wn.	1909	464	152	D 1941
Annie Faxon	Stern	Celilo, Ore.	1877	709	165	R 1887
Annie Faxon	Stern	Texas Ferry, Wn.	1887	514	165	W 1893
Annie Stewart	Stern	San Francisco, Cal.	1864	316	155	T 1881
						to Puget Sound
Artisan (gas)	Stern	Portland	1911	15	40	R 1922
						to screw
Asotin	Stern	Celilo	1915	...	140	— 1920
Astorian	Stern	Portland	1890	361	142	A 1908
						ex-*Clara Parker*
Astorian	Screw	Dockton, Wn.	1911	255	127	W 1923
						ex-*Nisqually*
B. H. Smith, Jr.	Stern	Portland	1900	91	109	A 1931
						ex-*Metlako*
Baby	Stern	Eugene, Ore.	1894	...	30	D 1895
Bailey Gatzert	Stern	Ballard, Wn.	1890	500	177	R 1907
Bailey Gatzert	Stern	Portland	1907	878	194	A 1926
Barry-K	Stern	Portland	1923	581	160	T 1942
						to Alaska ex-*Lewiston*
Beaver	Side	London, Eng.	1834	187	101	W 1888
Beaver	Stern	Portland	1873	282	125	W 1879
Beaver	Stern	Portland	1906	421	152	A 1935
						ex-*Glenola*
Belle [of Oregon City] (iron)	Side	Oregon City, Ore.	1853	54	96	D 1869
Bertha (gas, ferry)	Stern	Wallula, Wn.	1915	15	50	A 1925
Bessie	Stern	Castle Rock, Wn.	1884	...	67	D 1885
Bismark	Stern	Woodland, Wn.	1892	191	104	W 1898
Blackhawk (iron)	Screw	......	—1851	...	40	D 1852
Bonanza	Stern	Portland	1875	651	152	W 1888
Bonita	Stern	Portland	1875	527	155	W 1892
Bonita	Stern	Portland	1900	198	109	N 1902
						to *Metlako*
Bonnington (steel)	Stern	Nakusp, B.C.	1911	1700	203	D 1946
Brewster Ferry (gas)	Side	Brewster, Wn.	1926	22	52	W 1942
Bridgeport	Stern	Pateros, Wn.	1917	438	122	A 1942
C. Minsinger	Stern	Portland	1909	179	122	A 1940
C. J. Brenham	Stern	Noyo River, Cal.	1869	133	102	— 1895
C. R. P. A. (gas)	Stern	Astoria, Ore.	1918	30	57	R 1927
						to screw
Cabinet	Stern	Cabinet Rapids, Mont.	1866	...	113	D 1876
Calliope	Stern	Corvallis, Ore.	1870	143	100	D 1887

NAME	TYPE	WHERE BUILT	DATE	TONS	LENGTH	DISPO-SITION
Camano	Stern	Wenatchee, Wn.	1898	59	90	W 1904
Canby	Stern	Keno, Ore.	1904	48	67	— 1912
Canemah	Side	Canemah	1851	88	135	— 1857
Capital City	Stern	Port Blakeley, Wn.	1898	552	150	A 1919
						ex-*Dalton*
Capt. Al James (steel, diesel)	Screw	Pasco, Wn.	1940	162	81	S
Carolina (S.S.)	Screw	Philadelphia, Pa.	1849	545	150	T 1854
Carrie	Stern	Rainier, Ore.	1867	110	82	D 1876
						ex-*Rainier*
Carrie Ladd	Stern	Oregon City	1858	...	126	D 1864
Carrie Norton	Stern	Canemah	1878	13	...	— 1880
Cascade	Stern	Utsalady, Wn.	1864	401	155	D 1870
Cascades	Stern	Portland	1882	451	160	R 1912
Cascades	Stern	Portland	1912	407	160	B 1943
Cascadilla	Stern	Columbus, Wn.	1862	...	106	D 1866
Catherine	Stern	Portland	1923	95	112	— 1941
Champion	Stern	Oregon City	1875	634	157	W 1891
Charles Bureau	Stern	Okonagon, Wn.	1908	99	80	A 1919
Charles L. Wheeler, Jr. (S.S.)	Screw	Portland	1918	2205	289	S
Charles R. Spencer	Stern	Portland	1901	474	284	N 1911
						to *Monarch*
Chelan	Stern	Wenatchee, Wn.	1902	244	125	B 1915
Celilo	Screw	Celilo, Ore.	1863	37	59	— 1898
Chester	Stern	Portland	1897	130	101	A 1919
Chief (steel, diesel)	Screw	Slidell, La.	1932	143	99	S
						ex-*Jennie Barbour*
City of Ellensburgh	Stern	Pasco, Wn.	1888	213	119	D 1905
City of Eugene	Stern	Eugene, Ore.	1894	339	130	— 1918
City of Frankfort	Stern	Portland	1889	...	124	R 1891
						ex-*Traveler*
City of Frankfort	Stern	Clatskanie, Ore.	1891	184	125	N 1895
						to *H. C. Grady*
City of Klamath	Stern	Klamath Lake, Ore.	1884	...	...	....
City of Quincy	Stern	Portland	1878	195	109	T 1882
						to Puget Sound
City of Salem	Stern	Portland	1875	457	157	D 1895
City of Sellwood	Screw	Willamette, Ore.	1883	28	70	R 1889
						to *City of Astoria*
City of Vancouver (ferry)	Side	St. Johns, Ore.	1909	460	142	T 1918
						to Puget Sound
						N—*City of Tacoma*
Claggett (gas, ferry)	Side	Independence, Ore.	1926	24	61	A 1947
Claire	Stern	Portland	1918	563	157	S
Clara Parker	Stern	Astoria	1881	258	107	R 1890
						to *Astorian*
Clatsop Chief	Stern	Skipanon, Ore.	1875	...	58	W 1881
Clatsop Chief	Stern	Portland	1881	102	74	A 1889
Cleona (gas, ferry)	Side	Hood River, Ore.	1921	10	56	A 1926
Cleveland	Side	Portland	1879	47	61	— 1887

NAME	TYPE	WHERE BUILT	DATE	TONS	LENGTH	DISPO-SITION
Coeur D'Alene	Stern	Coeur D'Alene, Ida.	1883	...	...	D 1892
Colonel Wright	Stern	Deschutes, Ore.	1858	...	110	D 1865
Columbia (S.S.)	Side	New York	1850	777	193	T 1862 to China
Columbia	Side	Astoria	1850	75	90	D 1852
Columbia (S.S.)	Screw	Chester, Pa.	1880	2721	309	— 1895
Columbia	Stern	Little Dalles, Wn.	1891	529	153	B 1894
Columbia	Stern	Rufus, Ore.	1902	84	77	R 1906 to Relief
Columbia	Stern	Wenatchee, Wn.	1905	341	131	B 1915
Columbia	Stern	Northport, Wn.	1907	69	61	B 1911
Columbus (ferry)	Side	Columbus, Wn.	1880	...	...	— 1895
Companion (gas)	Stern	Astoria	1905	14	45	R 1939 to screw
Coos	Side	Empire City, Ore.	1874	53	58	— 1898
Corvallis	Stern	Portland	1877	...	100	W 1896
Cowlitz	Stern	Tualatin River, Ore.	1857	41	76	R 1868 to Wenat.; ex-Swan
Cowlitz	Stern	Portland	1917	99	109	W 1931
D. S. Baker	Stern	Celilo	1879	710	165	D 1901
Daisy	Side	Albina, Ore.	1886	25	60	— 1895
Daisy Ainsworth	Stern	The Dalles, Ore.	1873	673	177	W 1876
Daisy Andrus (ferry)	Side	Portland	1883	121	102	— 1895
Dalles	Side	Cascades, Wn.	1862	...	70	A 1868
Dalles City	Stern	Portland	1891	402	142	R 1909
Dalles City	Stern	Portland	1910	345	151	N 1920 to Diamond O
Dalton	Stern	Port Blakeley, Wn.	1898	552	150	N 1901 to Capital City
Dayton	Stern	Canemah	1868	202	117	D 1881
Delrio	Stern	Wenatchee, Wn.	1915	189	80	A 1922
Dewdrop	Stern	Astoria	1881	110	80	D 1887
Diamond O	Stern	Portland	1887	316	143	A 1919 ex-Fannie
Diamond O	Stern	Portland	1910	345	151	— 1935 ex-Dalles City
Dispatch	Stern	Bandon	1890	24	52	— 1904
Dispatch	Stern	Parkersburg, Ore.	1903	250	111	R 1922 to John Wildi
Dixie Thompson	Stern	Portland	1871	443	155	D 1893
Don't Bother Me	Side	Bird's Island, Ore.	1873	74	74	D 1880
Dora	Stern	Randolph, Ore.	1910	47	64	A 1927
Douglas (gas)	Stern	Wenatchee, Wn.	1914	12	41	A 1924
E. D. Baker	Stern	Vancouver, Wn.	1862	...	116	A 1863
E. N. Cooke	Stern	Portland	1871	416	150	W 1890
Eagle (iron)	Screw	Philadelphia	—1851	20	...	D 1871
Echo	Stern	Canemah	1865	273	122	D 1873
Echo	Stern	Coquille, Ore.	1901	76	66	— 1911
Egalite	Stern	Woodland, Wn.	1891	120	76	D 1896
Elathine (ferry)	Stern	Hover, Wn.	1920	29	56	....
Eleanor (gas, ferry)	Stern	Burbank, Wn.	1916	20	56	A 1924

NAME	TYPE	WHERE BUILT	DATE	TONS	LENGTH	DISPO-SITION
Elenore	Stern	Portland	1895	493	160	— 1896
Eliza Anderson	Side	Portland	1858	276	197	T 1859
						to Puget Sound
Eliza Ladd (ferry)	Stern	Portland	1875	118	...	D 1885
Elk	Stern	Canemah	1857	60	...	— 1861
Ellen	Stern	Pasco, Wn.	1915	45	63	— 1920
Elmore	Stern	Portland	1895	493	160	A 1917
Elsie May (gas, ferry)	Stern	Wallula, Wn.	1899	32	40	R 1907
Elsie May (gas, ferry)	Stern	Wallula, Wn.	1907	26	54	— 1915
Elwood	Stern	Portland	1891	510	154	T 1898
						to Alaska
Emily M	Stern	Brownsville, Ore.	1898	12	32	T 1900
						to Alaska
Emma Hayward	Stern	Portland	1871	613	177	D 1900
Enterprise	Stern	Canemah	1855	...	115	T 1858
						to Fraser River
Enterprise	Stern	Canemah	1863	194	120	D 1875
Enterprise	Stern	Gardiner, Ore.	1870	247	...	W 1873
Enterprise	Stern	Astoria	1883	94	81	D—1892
Enterprise	Stern	Portland	1890	137	106	R 1902
Enterprise	Stern	Portland	1902	333	115	A 1916
Enterprise	Stern	Wenatchee, Wn.	1903	129	86	W 1915
Etna	Stern	Portland	1906	13	60	— 1919
Eugene	Stern	Portland	1894	350	140	D 1906
Eva	Stern	Portland	1894	130	90	— 1918
Express	Stern	Oregon City	1854	69	111	D 1863
F. B. Jones	Stern	Portland	1901	303	143	A 1937
F. M. Smith	Stern	Portland	1895	295	125	T 1901
						to Calif.; ex-*H. C. Grady*
Fannie	Stern	Portland	1887	316	142	R 1906
						to *Diamond O*
Fannie Patton	Stern	Canemah	1865	297	132	D 1880
Fannie Troup	Stern	Portland	1864	229	124	W 1874
Fashion	Side	Vancouver, Wn.	1853	...	80	D 1861
						ex-*James P. Flint*
Fay No. 4 (gas)	Stern	North Bend, Ore.	1912	179	136	T 1913
						to California
Fenix	Side	Canemah	1852	...	93	N 1854
						to *Franklin*
						ex-*Shoalwater*
Fire-Fly	Screw	San Francisco?	—1853	...	...	W 1854
Fleetwood	Screw	Portland	1881	135	111	T 1888
						to Puget Sound
Florence (steel, gas)	Screw	Clarkston, Wn.	1939	13	60	S
Forty-Nine	Stern	Ft. Colville, Wn.	1865	219	114	— 1877
Franklin	Side	Canemah	1854	49	93	R 1856
						to *Minnie Holmes*
						ex-*Fenix*
Frederick K. Billings	Stern	Celilo	1881	401	199	R 1885
Frederick K. Billings	Stern	Pasco, Wn.	1889	749	200	W 1900
G. K. Wentworth	Stern	Portland	1905	325	145	A 1925

NAME	TYPE	WHERE BUILT	DATE	TONS	LENGTH	DISPO-SITION
G. M. Walker	Stern	Portland	1897	154	85	N 1913
						to *Woodland*
G. W. Shaver	Stern	Portland	1889	313	140	N 1902
						to *Glenola*
Gamecock	Stern	Portland	1898	772	178	R 1910
Gamecock	Stern	Portland	1910	464	160	A 1938
Gazelle	Side	Canemah	1854	...	145	W 1854
Gazelle	Stern	Portland	1876	157	92	T 1884
						to Puget Sound
Gazelle (gas)	Side	Portland	1905	13	50	A 1929
Gen. J. W. Jacobs	Side	Portland	1908	319	126	— 1931
Gen. Jeff C. Davis	Side	Victoria, B.C.	1898	227	120	— 1931
						ex-British S.S. *Dochesnay*
General Canby	Side?	South Bend, Wn.	1875	89	85	T 1894
						to Puget Sound
Geo. W. Bates	Stern	Portland	1902	99	108	— 1935
						ex-*Paloma*
George E. Starr	Side	Seattle, Wn.	1880	473	148	A 1921
Georgiana	Screw	Portland	1914	261	135	N 1939
						to *Lake Bonneville*
Georgie Burton	Stern	Vancouver, Wn.	1906	382	154	R 1923
						ex-*Albany*
Georgie Burton	Stern	Portland	1923	520	154	A 1947
Georgie Oakes	Stern	Coeur D'Alene, Ida.	1892	...	150	....
Gerome	Stern	Wenatchee, Wn.	1902	109	81	W 1905
Glenola	Stern	Portland	1889	313	140	R 1905
						to *Beaver*
						ex-*G. W. Shaver*
Gold Gatherer	Stern	Whiskey Bottom, Ida.	1890	40	66	— 1904
Gold Hunter	Side	New York	1849	510	172	T 1851
						became *Active*
Goliah	Side	New York	1849	235	155	— 1898
Gov. Newell	Stern	Portland	1883	206	112	D 1900
Governor Grover	Stern	Portland	1873	404	120	D 1880
Governor West (gas, ferry)	Stern	Maryhill, Wn.	1915	23	63	N 1925
						to screw
Grahamona	Stern	Portland	1912	443	150	N 1920
						to *Northwestern*
Great Republic	Side	New York	1867	3882	360	W 1879
Grey Eagle	Stern	Newburg, Ore.	1894	218	111	R 1907
Grey Eagle	Stern	Portland	1907	151	110	A 1930
Greyhound	Stern	Portland	1890	180	139	T 1890
						to Puget Sound
Greyhound	Stern	Kelso, Wn.	1920	81	65	— 1935
Gwendoline	Stern	Golden, B.C.	1894	...	...	....
Gypsy	Stern	Portland	1895	213	101	W 1900
H. C. Grady	Stern	Portland	1895	295	125	N 1898
						to *F. M. Smith*
						ex-*City of Frankfort*
Harvest Moon	Stern	New Era, Ore.	1889	68	82	D 1897
Harvest Queen	Stern	Celilo	1878	846	200	D 1899

NAME	TYPE	WHERE BUILT	DATE	TONS	LENGTH	DISPOSITION
Harvest Queen	Stern	Portland	1900	585	187	A 1927
Hassalo	Stern	The Dalles, Ore.	1880	462	160	D 1898
Hassalo	Stern	Portland	1899	561	181	A 1927
Hassaloe	Stern	Cascades, Wn.	1857	...	135	D 1865
Hattie Belle	Stern	Portland	1892	208	110	D 1906
Hazel & Helen (gas)	Side	Astoria	1909	10	35	R 1930 to screw
Helen Hale	Stern	Kennewick, Wn.	1912	52	100	B 1913
Henderson	Stern	Portland	1912	430	159	S
Henrietta	Stern	Sucker Lake, Ore.	1869	46	54	D 1879
Henry Villard	Stern	Pend Oreille, Ida.	1881	...	150	....
Hercules	Stern	Portland	1899	560	160	— 1935
Hoosier	Side	Portland	1851	5	50	W 1853
Hoosier No. 2	Side	Canemah	—1855	...	...	R 1857
Hoosier No. 3	Side	Canemah	1857	27	...	....
Hustler	Stern	Portland	1891	204	102	R 1908
Hustler	Stern	Portland	1908	96	105	A 1936
Hydra	Stern	St. Helens, Ore.	1876	75	70	D 1882
Idaho	Side	Cascades, Wn.	1860	278	147	T 1881 to Puget Sound
Idaho (gas)	Screw	Lewiston, Ida.	1922	12	58	S
Illecillewaet	Stern	Revelstoke, B.C.	1892	...	...	....
Imnaha	Stern	Lewiston, Ida.	1903	330	124	W 1903
Independence	Side	Monticello, Wn.	1857	...	100	D 1864
Inland Chief (steel, diesel)	Screw	Seattle	1937	902	191	S
Inland Empire	Stern	Celilo	1908	416	151	N 1920 to *Service*
International	Stern?	Nelson, B.C.	1896	...	142	
Interstate	Stern	Vancouver, Wn.	1924	336	132	A 1936 ex-*Oregona*
Ione	Stern	Portland	1889	215	130	R 1911
Ione	Stern	Newport, Wn.	1908	431	129	— 1918
Ione	Stern	Vancouver, Wn.	1911	389	148	W 1937
Iris	Side	The Dalles	1863	402	162	D 1870
Isabel	Stern	Salem, Ore.	1882	217	120	W 1890
Isabel	Stern	Golden, B.C.	—1908	...	...	
Islander	Stern	Portland	1926	82	65	— 1940
J. Ordway	Stern	Portland	1876	292	131	D 1897
J. A. Munroe	Side	Astoria	1905	83	62	— 1935
J. M. Hannaford	Stern	Potlatch, Ida.	1899	746	169	D 1906
J. N. Teal	Stern	Portland	1907	513	160	A 1927
James Clinton	Stern	Canemah	1856	...	90	B 1861
James John (ferry)	Side	St. Johns, Ore.	1907	114	90	— 1916
James P. Flint	Side	Cascades, Wn.	1851	...	80	R 1853 to *Fashion*
Jean	Stern	Portland	1938	533	140	S
Jennie Clark	Stern	Milwaukie, Ore.	1855	50	115	D 1863
John Gates	Stern	Celilo	1878	673	150	D 1894
John Wildi	Stern	Parkersburg, Ore.	1903	173	112	A 1927 ex-*Dispatch*

NAME	TYPE	WHERE BUILT	DATE	TONS	LENGTH	DISPO- SITION
John F. Caples (ferry)	Side	Portland	1904	192	100	A 1927
John H. Couch	Side	Westport, Ore.	1863	255	123	D 1873
Joseph Kellogg	Stern	Portland	1881	322	128	R 1900
Joseph Kellogg	Stern	Portland	1900	462	139	N 1921
						to *Madeline*
Josie McNear	Side	San Francisco, Cal.	1865	159	109	D 1878
Julia	Stern	Port Blakeley, Wn.	1858	325	147	D 1872
Julius (gas)	Stern	Salem, Ore.	1909	48	61	— 1911
Katie Hallett	Stern	Clark Fork, Ida.	1882	...	135	D 1885
Katie Ladd	Side	Portland	1871	110	...	— 1878
Kehani	Stern	Portland	1892	118	90	R 1905
						to *Ottawa*
Kiyus	Stern	Celilo	1863	...	140	W 1866
Klickitat	Side	The Dalles	1898	118	72	— 1902
Klamath	Screw	Klamath Falls, Ore.	1905	69	75	— 1913
Kokanee	Stern	Nelson, B.C.	1896	...	143	D 1923
Kooskanook	Stern	Nelson, B.C.	1906	1008	194	D 1931
Kootenai	Stern	Little Dalles, Wn.	1885	371	139	— 1895
Kootenay	Stern	Nakusp, B.C.	1897	1117	184	D 1920
L. P. Hosford (steel, diesel)	Screw	Portland	1931	680	145	N 1938
						to *Indian*
La Center	Stern	La Center, Wn.	1912	67	65	A 1931
Lake Bonneville	Screw	Portland	1914	261	135	S
						ex-*Georgiana*
Latona	Stern	La Center, Wn.	1878	129	90	D 1892
Lena	Stern	Sauvies Island, Ore.	1884	30	45	D 1895
Leona	Stern	Portland	1901	179	105	B 1912
						ex-*McMinnville*
Leviathan	Screw	Benecia, Calif.	1858	...	...	T 1867
						to British Columbia
Lewiston	Stern	Umatilla, Ore.	1867	...	78	N 1868
						to *Ann*
Lewiston	Stern	Riparia, Wn.	1894	513	165	R 1905
Lewiston	Stern	Riparia	1905	548	166	B 1922
Lewiston	Stern	Portland	1923	581	160	N 1940
						to *Barry-K*
Liberty	Stern	Bandon, Ore.	1903	174	91	— 1918
Lionel R. Webster (ferry)	Side	Portland	1904	343	139	A 1935
Little Annie	Stern	Coquille River, Ore.	1877	86	70	— 1892
Lizzie Linn	Side?	Wallula, Wn.	1883	23	...	R 1887
Lizzie Linn	Side?	Wallula	1887	39	58	— 1892
Logger	Stern	St. Helens, Ore.	1924	447	156	A 1940
Lorelei	Stern	Lewiston, Ida.	1895	8	38	D 1898
Lot Whitcomb	Side	Milwaukie, Ore.	1850	600	160	T 1854
						to California
						N—*Annie Abernethy*
Lucia Mason	Stern	St. Helens, Ore.	1883	178	109	W 1891
Luckiamute Chief	Stern	Salem	1878	69	60	D 1879
Lurline	Stern	Portland	1878	481	158	R 1878
Lurline	Stern	Portland	1878	406	152	— 1935
Lytton	Stern	Revelstoke, B.C.	1890	125	131	— 1903

NAME	TYPE	WHERE BUILT	DATE	TONS	LENGTH	DISPO-SITION
M. F. Henderson	Stern	Portland	1901	534	159	W 1911
McMinnville	Stern	Canemah	1877	417	132	D 1881
McMinnville	Stern	Portland	1899	137	90	R 1901
						to *Leona*
Mable	Stern	Huntington, Ore.	1898	59	70	D 1899
Madeline	Stern	Portland	1900	408	139	A 1929
						ex-*Joseph Kellogg*
Major Redding	Screw	....	—1851	...	...	D 1852
Manzanillo	Stern	Portland	1881	217	110	D 1893
Margey	Stern	East Portland	1885	163	64	T 1890
						to Puget Sound
Maria	Side	Fraser River, B.C.	1858	...	100	D 1864
Maria	Stern	Portland	1887	202	115	A 1923
Maria Wilkins	Stern	Portland	1872	97	77	D 1882
Mary	Side	Cascades, Wn.	1854	...	80	D 1862
Mary Bell	Side	Portland	1869	138	102	D 1873
Mary Moody	Stern	Pend Oreille, Ida.	1866	...	...	D 1876
Mascot	Stern	Portland	1890	267	132	R 1908
Mascot	Stern	Portland	1908	299	141	B 1911
Massachusetts, U.S.S.	Screw	Boston, Mass.	1845	765	161	N 1863
						to *Farralones*
Mata C. Hover (gas)	Stern	Hover, Wn.	1906	14	61	— 1910
Mathloma	Stern	Portland	1896	...	134	— 1927
Messenger	Stern	Empire City, Ore.	1872	136	91	B—1879
Messenger	Stern	Portland	1891	126	100	B 1896
Metlako	Stern	Portland	1900	91	109	N 1925
						to *B. H. Smith, Jr.*
						ex-*Bonita*
Millicoma (gas)	Stern	Marshfield, Ore.	1909	14	55	R 1917
						to screw
Milwaukee (ferry)	Side	Portland	1880	37	50	— 1895
Minnehaha	Stern	Sucker Lake, Ore.	1866	104	71	D 1876
Minnie (gas)	Stern	Portland	1907	11	47	— 1910
Minnie Holmes	Side	Canemah	1856	...	...	D 1858
						ex-*Franklin*
Minto (steel)	Stern	Nakusp, B.C.	1898	830	162	S
Missoula	Stern	Thompson Rapids, Mont.	1866	...	93	D 1876
Modoc	Stern	Portland	1889	372	142	R 1898
Modoc	Stern	Portland	1898	480	155	T 1913
						to Puget Sound
Modoc	Stern	Klamath Lake, Ore.	1910	...	60	....
Monarch	Stern	Portland	1901	598	181	T 1914
						to California
						ex-*Charles R. Spencer*
Montesano	Stern	Astoria	1882	123	80	T 1889
						to Grays Harbor
Mountain Buck	Side	Portland	1857	...	133	D 1864
Mountain Gem	Stern	Lewiston, Ida.	1904	469	150	A 1924
Mountain Queen	Stern	The Dalles	1877	719	176	R 1889
						to *Sehome*

NAME	TYPE	WHERE BUILT	DATE	TONS	LENGTH	DISPO-SITION
Moyie (steel)	Stern	Nelson, B.C.	1898	830	162	S
Mud Hen	Stern	Coquille River, Ore.	1878	...	32	— 1892
Multnomah	Side	Oregon City	1851	...	108	D 1864
Multnomah	Stern	East Portland	1885	312	143	T 1889
						to Puget Sound
Myrtle	Stern	Myrtle Point, Ore.	1909	36	57	A 1922
Myrtle	Stern	Prosper, Ore.	1922	36	60	A 1940
N. R. Lang	Stern	Portland	1900	528	152	D 1940
						ex-*Salem*
N. S. Bentley	Stern	East Portland	1886	431	151	R 1896
						to *Albany*
Nakusp	Stern	Nakusp, B.C.	1895	1083	171	B 1897
Naomi	Stern	Wallula, Wn.	1896	9	43	— 1899
Nasookin (steel)	Stern	Nelson, B.C.	1913	1869	200	A 1947
Nellie	Stern	Salem	1879	...	50	D 1882
Nellie	Stern	Portland	1899	180	115	D 1908
Nelson	Stern	Nelson, B.C.	1891	496	134	B 1919
Nespelem	Stern	Wenatchee, Wn.	1917	349	131	N 1920
						to *Robert Young*
Nestor	Stern	Catlin, Wn.	1902	97	82	A 1929
New Tenino	Stern	Celilo	1876	42	146	D 1879
						ex-*Tenino*
New Volunteer	Stern	Newport, Ida.	1901	105	72	— 1906
New Western Queen (ferry)	Side	The Dalles	1898	120	76	D 1916
New World	Side	New York	1849	531	216	T 1868
						to Puget Sound
Newport	Stern	Newport, Wn.	1907	129	92	— 1919
Nez Perce Chief	Stern	Celilo	1863	327	126	D 1874
No Wonder	Stern	Portland	1889	269	135	A 1930
Norma	Stern	Bridgeport, Ida.	1891	488	160	A 1915
North Pacific	Side	San Francisco	1871	488	167	T 1898
						to Puget Sound
North Star	Stern	Jennings, Mont.	1894	...	...	B 1902
North Star	Stern	Wenatchee, Wn.	1902	144	100	R 1907
North Star	Stern	Wenatchee	1907	198	100	B 1915
North West	Stern	Portland	1889	324	135	T 1907
						to Alaska
Northwest	Stern	Columbus, Wn.	1877	356	124	D 1885
Northwestern	Stern	Portland	1912	433	150	T 1939
						to Alaska
						ex-*Grahamona*
O.&C.R.R. Ferry No. 1	Side	Portland	1870	658	...	— 1880
O.&C.R.R. Ferry No. 2	Side	East Portland	1879	414	122	T 1898
						to California
						became *Vallejo*
Occident	Stern	Portland	1875	587	154	D 1892
Ocean Wave	Side	Portland	1891	724	180	T 1898
						to California
Ocklahama	Stern	Portland	1876	582	152	R 1897
Ocklahama	Stern	Portland	1897	676	161	A 1930

NAME	TYPE	WHERE BUILT	DATE	TONS	LENGTH	DISPO-SITION
Ohio	Stern	Portland	1874	347	140	D 1881
Okanagon	Stern	Deschutes, Ore.	1861	278	118	D 1876
Okanogan	Stern	Wenatchee, Wn.	1907	432	137	B 1915
Olympian (iron)	Side	Wilmington, Del.	1883	1419	262	W 1906
Olympian	Stern	Everett, Wn.	1903	386	154	A 1924 ex-*Telegraph*
Oneatta	Side	Pioneer, Ore.	1872	118	82	T 1882 to California
Oneonta	Side	Celilo	1863	497	150	D 1877
Onward	Stern	Canemah	1858	120	125	— 1880
Onward	Stern	Colfax, Ore.	1867	155	98	T 1879 to Puget Sound
Oregon	Side	Fairfield, Ore.	1852	...	100	W 1854
Oregon (ferry)	Stern	Arlington, Ore.	1889	39	48	— 1918
Oregona	Stern	Portland	1904	370	132	R 1924 to *Interstate*
Orient	Stern	Portland	1875	587	154	B 1894
Oro	Stern	Wenatchee, Wn.	1896	103	84	— 1898
Orondo Ferry (gas)	Side	Orondo, Wn.	1925	21	51	— 1935
Ottawa	Stern	Portland	1905	77	89	A 1920 ex-*Kehani*
Otter	Stern	Portland	1874	118	87	T 1875 to Puget Sound
Owyhee	Stern	Celilo	1864	313	115	D 1876
Paloma	Stern	Portland	1902	185	102	N 1919 to *Geo. W. Bates*
Panama (gas, ferry)	Stern	White Salmon, Wn.	1914	15	52	T 1922 to Mexico
Patricia (steel, diesel)	Screw	Portland	1937	148	84	S
Pasco-Burbank Ferry	Stern	Pasco, Wn.	1916	37	58	A 1922
Pastime (gas)	Stern	Coquille, Ore.	1900	11	45	— 1901
Pedler	Stern	Marshfield, Ore.	1908	407	124	— 1910
Petona	Side	Portland	1853	...	81	....
Pilgrim	Stern	Portland	1893	56	72	— 1901
Pioneer	Side	Milwaukie	1866	70	98	D 1873
Plymouth (ferry)	Stern	Pasco, Wn.	1924	30	54	A 1928
Pomona	Stern	Portland	1898	365	134	R 1926
Pomona	Stern	Portland	1926	216	120	D 1940
Portland	Side	Portland	1853	...	90	W 1857
Portland	Stern	Portland	1919	801	185	S
Portland (steel)	Stern	Portland	1947	...	219	S
Portland No. 1 (ferry)	Side	Westport, Ore.	1865	107	101	— 1880
Power City (gas)	Stern	American Falls, Ida.	1910	60	65	— 1915
Powers	Stern	North Bend, Ore.	1909	99	90	A 1926
Pronto	Stern	Portland	1906	94	100	— 1935
Ptarmigan	Stern	Golden, B.C.	1908	...	...	....
Queen (gas)	Side	The Dalles	1915	49	63	A 1924
R. C. Young	Stern	Salem	1892	108	83	B 1892
R. R. Thompson	Stern	The Dalles	1878	1158	215	D 1904
Rainbow	Stern	Marshfield, Ore.	1912	75	64	A 1923

NAME	TYPE	WHERE BUILT	DATE	TONS	LENGTH	DISPOSITION
Rainier	Stern	Rainier, Ore.	1867	...	82	R 1868 to *Carrie*
Ramona	Stern	Portland	1892	176	100	R 1896
Ramona	Stern	Portland	1896	...	118	T 1898 to Alaska
Ranger	Stern	Portland	1865	199	113	B 1869
Rattler (ferry)	Side	Ainsworth, Wn.	1884	52	76	— 1904
Rebecca C	Side	South Beach, Ore.	1883	15	60	— 1898
Regulator	Stern	The Dalles	1891	434	152	R 1899
Regulator	Stern	Portland	1899	508	157	B 1906
Reliance	Stern	Canemah	1865	316	143	D 1871
Relief	Stern	Oregon City	1858	97	110	— 1865
Relief	Stern	Blalock, Ore.	1906	229	118	A 1931 ex-*Columbia*
Relief	Stern	Coquille, Ore.	1916	44	64	— 1927
Rescue	Stern	Monticello, Wn.	1864	126	95	D 1878
Resolute	Stern	Portland	1870	51	57	W 1872
Restless	Stern	Gardiner, Ore.	1876	101	71	— 1895
Revelstoke	Stern	Nakusp, B.C.	1902	309	127	B 1915
Rival	Stern	Oregon City	1860	211	111	D 1868
Robert Young	Stern	Wenatchee, Wn.	1917	349	131	A 1937 ex-*Nespelem*
Rogue River	Stern	Portland	1901	80	66	W 1902
Roosevelt (ferry)	Side	North Bend, Ore.	1921	197	96	— 1939
Rossland	Stern	Nakusp, B.C.	1897	884	183	S 1918
Rough	Stern	Ainsworth, Wn.	1907	17	53	— 1908
Rowena Lyle (gas)	Side	Rowena, Ore.	1921	14	49	— 1928
Rush (ferry)	Side	Hood River, Ore.	1889	12	40	— 1895
Rustler	Side	Portland	1882	90	79	B 1892
Ruth	Stern	San Francisco	1893	14	41	— 1907
Ruth	Stern	Golden, B.C.	1894	...	...	....
Ruth	Stern	Portland	1895	515	156	— 1920
Ruth	Stern	Newport, Wn.	1908	274	116	— 1914
S. G. Reed	Stern	Willamette, Ore.	1878	800	175	D 1894
S. T. Church	Stern	Portland	1876	555	154	D 1892
St. Claire	Side	Ray's Landing, Ore.	1859	...	80	D 1865
St. Johns (ferry)	Side	Portland	1912	370	125	A 1923
St. Paul	Stern	Trinidad, Wn.	1906	208	116	B 1915
Salem	Stern	Portland	1880	351	150	R 1900 to *N. R. Lang*
Salem Ferry Boat No. 2	Side	Salem?	—1876	38	...	— 1882
Salem No. 3	Side	Portland	1881	52	66	— 1895
Sarah Dixon	Stern	Portland	1892	369	140	R 1906
Sarah Dixon	Stern	Portland	1906	368	161	A 1935
Sarah Hoyt	Side	Oregon City	1855	...	145	N 1855 to *Senorita*
Satellite	Stern?	Empire City, Ore.	1871	105	72	— 1888
Sehome	Side	Portland	1889	692	192	T 1889 to Puget Sound ex-*Mountain Queen*
Selkirk	Stern	Wenatchee, Wn.	1899	223	111	W 1906

NAME	TYPE	WHERE BUILT	DATE	TONS	LENGTH	DISPO-SITION
Senator	Stern	Milwaukie, Ore.	1864	298	132	W 1875
Senorita	Side	Oregon City	1855	...	145	D 1859
						ex-*Sarah Hoyt*
Service	Stern	Celilo	1908	416	151	A 1930
						ex-*Inland Empire*
Shaver	Stern	Portland	1908	368	155	R 1927
Shaver (diesel)	Screw	Portland	1927	423	131	S
Shoalwater	Side	Canemah	1852	...	93	N 1853
						to *Fenix*
Shoo Fly	Stern	Canemah	1870	317	126	D 1878
Shoshone	Stern	Boise Ferry, Ida.	1866	300	136	W 1874
Shoshone	Stern	Coeur D'Alene	1908	11	54	A 1922
Skedaddle	Stern	Portland	1862	...	60	D 1869
Skookum	Stern	Aberdeen, Wn.	1904	302	112	— 1942
Slocan	Stern	Slocan Lake, B.C.	1897	...	155	D 1927
Snake River (gas, ferry)	Stern	Ainsworth, Wn.	1918	13	52	A 1941
Speilei	Stern	St. Helens, Ore.	1914	75	76	A 1940
Spieler	Stern	Ridgefield, Wn.	1906	36	61	— 1915
Spokane	Stern	Celilo	1877	673	150	R 1899
Spokane	Stern	Riparia, Wn.	1899	561	160	W 1923
Spokane	Stern	Bonner's Ferry, Ida.	1891	400	125	B 1895
Spokane	Stern	Newport, Wn.	1903	323	132	A 1922
Spray	Stern	Deschutes, Ore.	1862	235	116	D 1869
Staghorn	Stern	Portland	1898	...	178	W 1898
Stark Street Ferry	Side	Portland	1880	174	119	— 1897
Stark Street Ferry No. 7	Side	Portland	1884	299	130	— 1897
State of Idaho	Stern	Bonner's Ferry, Ida.	1893	...	140	R 1895
						to *Alberta*
State of Washington	Stern	Tacoma, Wn.	1889	605	170	W 1920
Stranger	Stern	Portland	1928	358	130	D 1940
Success	Stern	Canemah	1868	344	132	D 1877
Success (gas)	Stern	Gold Beach, Ore.	1903	14	45	— 1907
Surprise	Stern	Canemah	1857	120	130	D 1863
Swallow	Stern	Portland	1867	33	45	D 1877
Swan	Stern	Tualatin River, Ore.	1857	...	76	N 1857
						to *Cowlitz*
Swan	Stern	Gardiner, Ore.	1870	131	...	— 1880
Swan	Barge	Portland	1916	538	125	— 1940
T. J. Potter	Side	Portland	1888	659	230	R 1901
T. J. Potter	Side	Portland	1901	1017	234	A 1921
Tacoma (iron, ferry)	Side	Portland	1884	1362	334	T 1916
						to Puget Sound
Tahoma	Stern	Portland	1900	261	118	R 1910
Tahoma	Stern	Portland	1910	99	118	A 1928
Telegraph	Stern	Everett, Wn.	1903	386	154	N 1913
						to *Olympian*
Telegraph	Stern	Prosper, Ore.	1914	96	103	A 1940
Telephone	Stern	Portland	1885	386	172	B 1887
Telephone	Stern	Portland	1888	500	200	R 1903
Telephone	Stern	Portland	1903	794	202	T 1909
						to California

NAME	TYPE	WHERE BUILT	DATE	TONS	LENGTH	DISPO-SITION
Tenino	Stern	Deschutes, Ore.	1861	...	135	R 1869
Tenino	Stern	Celilo	1869	329	136	R 1876
						to *New Tenino*
The Dalles	Stern	Portland	1921	516	170	D 1940
Thomas L. Nixon	Stern	Pasco, Wn.	1888	515	159	D 1901
Three Sisters	Stern	East Portland	1886	355	141	D 1896
Toledo	Stern	Portland	1878	...	109	R 1885
Toledo	Stern	Portland	1885	226	128	W 1896
Tongue Point (gas)	Stern	Portland	1911	87	65	A 1931
Topsy	Stern	Corvallis, Ore.	1885	43	73	D 1893
Trail	Stern	Nakusp, B.C.	1896	...	165	....
Transfer (gas, ferry)	Stern	Allegany, Ore.	1907	8	28	— 1921
Transit (gas)	Stern	North Bend, Ore.	1907	14	36	— 1911
Transit (gas, ferry)	Side	Marshfield, Ore.	1908	38	60	— 1935
Traveler	Stern	Willamette, Ore.	1878	238	124	R 1889
						to *City of Frankfort*
Twin Cities	Stern	Celilo	1908	418	151	A 1931
U. S. Grant	Screw	Brooklyn, Ore.	1865	47	...	W 1873
Umatilla	Stern	Cascades, Wn.	1858	91	110	T 1858
						to Fraser River
						ex-*Venture*
Umatilla (gas, ferry)	Stern	Plymouth, Wn.	1908	14	59	A 1927
Umatilla	Stern	Celilo	1908	300	184	R 1928
Umatilla	Stern	Celilo	1928	551	160	W 1941
Uncle Sam	Stern	Corvallis, Ore.	1911	82	81	— 1915
Undine	Stern	Portland	1888	375	150	A 1922
Undine	Stern	Portland	1921	516	170	— 1935
Unio	Stern	Canemah	1861	112	96	N 1861
						to *Union*
Union	Stern	Canemah	1861	112	96	D 1869
						ex-*Unio*
Valley Queen	Stern	Independence, Ore.	1898	92	86	D 1899
Vancouver	Side	Milwaukie, Ore.	1857	41	84	R 1870
Vancouver	Stern	Vancouver, Wn.	1870	130	95	D 1885
Vancouver (ferry)	Side	Portland	1893	211	108	— 1918
Venture	Stern	Cascades, Wn.	1858	...	110	N 1858
						to *Umatilla*
Veto No. 1 (ferry)	Side	Portland	1879	75	85	B 1887
Veto No. 2 (ferry)	Side	Portland	1880	117	90	— 1892
Victoria	Stern	Independence, Ore.	1909	42	64	— 1913
Volunteer	Stern	Footner, Wn.	1900	40	51	— 1905
Vulcan	Stern	Portland	1892	327	144	A 1914
W. H. Pringle	Stern	Pasco, Wn.	1901	575	166	W 1906
W. R. Todd	Stern	Ainsworth, Wn.	1906	167	102	W 1912
W. S. Mason (ferry)	Side	Portland	1894	322	122	A 1927
Wallamet	Side	Canemah	1853	272	150	T 1854
						to California
Wallowa	Stern	Lewiston, Ida.	1904	...	125	D 1914
Wallulah (gas)	Stern	Corvallis, Ore.	1914	98	81	A 1919
Wanista (gas)	Stern	Ainsworth, Wn.	1908	34	58	A 1927
Wanista (ferry)	Stern	Kennewick, Wn.	1917	53	56	— 1926

NAME	TYPE	WHERE BUILT	DATE	TONS	LENGTH	DISPO-SITION
Wasco	Side	Cascades, Wn.	1855	...	...	— 1861
Washington (iron)	Screw	....	—1851	...	...	W 1857
Washington	Stern	Vancouver, Wn.	1881	292	142	T 1882
						to Puget Sound
Wasp	Stern?	Klamath Lake, Ore.	1914	...	50	....
Wauna	Stern	Portland	1906	149	118	A 1937
Web Foot	Stern	Celilo	1863	504	150	D 1871
Welcome	Stern	Portland	1874	327	127	T 1881
						to Puget Sound
Welcome	Stern	Coquille, Ore.	1900	30	56	W 1907
Wenat	Stern	Portland	1867	88	77	T 1878
						to Puget Sound
						ex-*Cowlitz*
Wenatchee	Stern	Wenatchee, Wn.	1899	77	79	B 1901
Weown	Stern	St. Johns, Ore.	1907	372	153	A 1938
Western Queen	Side	The Dalles	1879	94	72	— 1898
Westport	Side	Westport, Ore.	1878	204	118	B 1886
Wide West	Stern	Portland	1877	1200	218	D 1887
Wilhelmina	Stern	Lewiston, Ida.	1907	13	59	— 1910
Willamette (iron)	Screw	Wilmington, Del.	1849	450	175	T 1852
						to California
Willamette Chief	Stern	Portland	1874	587	163	R 1878
Willamette Chief	Stern	Willamette, Ore.	1878	693	163	B 1894
Willamette Squaw	Stern	Portland	1875	32	75	— 1880
Wilson G. Hunt	Side	New York	1849	437	186	T 1870
						to Puget Sound
Wm. M. Hoag	Stern	East Portland	1887	452	150	R 1903
						to *Annie Comings*
Winema	Stern	Klamath Falls, Ore.	1904	...	125	— 1925
Wonder	Stern	Portland	1877	320	121	D 1888
Woodland	Stern	Portland	1897	99	85	R 1917
						ex-*G. M. Walker*
Woodland	Stern	Portland	1917	91	81	A 1929
Yakima	Stern	Celilo	1864	455	137	W 1876
Yakima	Stern	Ainsworth, Wn.	1906	393	137	A 1924
Yamhill	....	Canemah	1851	...	...	— 1852
Yamhill	Stern	Canemah	1860	72	76	D 1863
Yukon	Stern	Rufus, Ore.	1895	33	48	— 1904

The following steamboats were built and operated on Klamath Lake between 1890 and 1910; most were stern-wheelers, but no complete data appear: *Alma, Eagle, Hobson, Hooligan, Hornet, North Star, Oregon,*

TABLE OF DISTANCES

1. *Columbia River*

	ELEVATION	MILES TO MOUTH	MILES TO PORTLAND	
Ilwaco		7	109	
Clatsop Landing			110	
Astoria		10	100	
Skamokawa		30	80	
Rainier		64	46	
Kalama		71	39	
St. Helens		82	28	
Mouth of Willamette River		98	12	
Vancouver		105	18	
Lower Cascades		144	57	Bonneville Dam, tidewater
Hood River		167	80	
The Dalles	96	188	101	
Celilo		201	114	Celilo Canal
Umatilla		292	205	
Wallula		315	228	
Mouth of Snake River	312	324	237	
Pasco		328	241	
Priest Rapids	400	396	309	

	ELEVATION	MILES TO MOUTH	MILES TO WENATCHEE	
Rock Island Rapids	544	453	7	
Wenatchee	588	465	. . .	
Brewster	728	530	65	
Mouth of Okanogan River		533	68	
Bridgeport	751	542	77	
Grand Coulee	933	590	. . .	

	ELEVATION	MILES TO MOUTH	MILES TO LITTLE DALLES	
Little Dalles	1245	733	. . .	
International Boundary	1292	749	16	
Mouth of Clark Fork		751	18	
Nelson, B.C.	1415	779	46	Mouth of Kootenay River
Lower Arrow Lake		787	54	
Upper Arrow Lake		845	112	
Nakusp, B.C.		871	137	
Arrowhead, B.C.		908	175	
Revelstoke, B.C.		937	204	
Boat Encampment	2000	1015		
Golden, B.C.		1117		
Lake Windemere		1190		
Columbia Lake	2650	1210		

[204]

2. *Willamette River*

	ELEVATION	MILES TO MOUTH	MILES TO PORTLAND
Mouth of Willamette River		...	12
Portland		12	...
Milwaukie		19	7
Oregon City	10	26	14
Canemah	50	28	16
Champoeg		46	34
Mouth of Yamhill River	60	55	43
Dayton (Yamhill River)			48
McMinnville (Yamhill River)			61
Wheatland		73	61
Salem	110	85	73
Independence	132	96	84
Mouth of Santiam River		108	
Albany	175	120	108
Corvallis	195	132	120
Harrisburg	290	165	153
Eugene	400	185	173
Springfield		188	176
Junction of Coast and Middle Forks of Willamette River		190	

3. *Snake River*

	ELEVATION	MILES TO MOUTH	MILES TO PORTLAND
Columbia River	312	...	237
Palouse		54	291
Riparia (Texas Rapids)	500	66	303
Penewawa		93	330
Almota		105	342
Lewiston	700	141	378
Asotin		147	384
Grande Ronde Rapids		171	408
Wild Goose Rapids		175	412
Imnaha	925	193	430
Johnson's Bar	1250	232	469
Hell's Canyon, foot		235	472
Granite Creek		242	479
Hell's Canyon, head		259	496
Ballard's Landing		265	502
Whiskey Bottom		325	562
Huntington	2100	329	566
Old's Ferry		334	571
Mouth of Boise River		391	628
Swan Falls	2300	456	693
American Falls	4300	714	
Headwaters	6500	1038	

SELECTED BIBLIOGRAPHY

Bancroft, Hubert Howe. *History of Oregon.* 2 v. San Francisco, 1888.
——— *History of Washington, Idaho and Montana.* San Francisco, 1890.
Clark, Robert Carlton. *History of the Willamette Valley Oregon.* Chicago, 1927.
Fitzsimmons, James, "Columbia River Chronicles," *British Columbia Historical Quarterly,* I (1937).
Gaston, Joseph. *Portland, Oregon; its History and Builders* . . . Chicago and Portland, 1911.
Gill, Frank B. *An Unfinished History of Transportation in Oregon and Washington.* Portland, 1914–1920.
Johansen, Dorothy O. "Oregon Steam Navigation Company: An Example of Capitalism on the Frontier," *Pacific Historical Review,* X (June, 1941).
Kemble, John Haskell. *The Panama Route, 1848–1869.* Berkeley and Los Angeles, 1943.
Lamb, W. Kaye. "The Advent of the *Beaver,*" *British Columbia Historical Quarterly,* II (July, 1938).
Lockley, Fred. *History of the Columbia River from The Dalles to the Sea.* Chicago, 1928.
Lyman, William D. *Columbia River; its History, its Myths, its Scenery, its Commerce.* New York, 1909.
MacMullen, Jerry. *Paddle-Wheel Days in California.* Stanford University, 1944.
Merchant Vessels of the United States. Washington, D.C., 1868–1945.
Mills, Randall V. "A History of Transportation in the Pacific Northwest," *Oregon Historical Quarterly,* XLVIII (September, 1946).
Open Rivers Number, *Oregon Historical Quarterly,* XVI (June, 1915).
Poppleton, Irene Lincoln. "Oregon's First Monopoly: The Oregon Steam Navigation Company," *Oregon Historical Quarterly,* IX (December, 1908).
Scott, Harvey W. *History of the Oregon Country.* 6 v. Cambridge, Mass., 1924.
"Shallow Draft Boats in Pacific Northwest," *International Marine Engineering,* XV (1910).
Smith, Frank J. *Marine Record of Oregon, 1850–1917.* Portland, 1917.
Symons, Lt. Thomas W. *Report of an Examination of the Upper Columbia River.* Senate Ex. Doc. No. 186. 47th Cong., 1st Sess. Washington, D.C., 1882.
U. S. War Department. Corps of Engineers. *Columbia and Lower Willamette Rivers, between Portland, Ore., and the Sea.* House Doc. No. 195. 70th Cong., 1st Sess. Washington, D.C., 1928.
——— *Columbia River and Minor Tributaries.* 2 v. House Doc. No. 103. 73d Cong., 1st Sess. Washington, D.C., 1933.
——— *Snake River and Tributaries.* House Doc. No. 190. 73d Cong., 2d Sess. Washington, D.C., 1933.
——— *Willamette River, Oreg.* House Doc. No. 263. 72d Cong., 1st Sess. Washington, D.C., 1932.
Victor, Francis Fuller. *All Over Oregon and Washington.* San Francisco, 1872.
——— *Atlantis Arisen; or, Talks of a Tourist about Oregon and Washington.* Philadelphia, 1891.
——— *The Early Indian Wars of Oregon.* Salem, 1894.
Wilson, Fred W. "Lure of the River," *Oregon Historical Quarterly,* XXXIV (March, June, 1933).
Wright, E. W. *Lewis and Dryden's Marine History of the Pacific Northwest.* Portland, 1895.

INDEX